Homemade Hollywood

Homemade Hollywood

Fans Behind the Camera

Clive Young

continuum

NEW YORK • LONDON

2008

The Continuum International Publishing Group Inc
80 Maiden Lane, New York, NY 10038

The Continuum International Publishing Group Ltd
The Tower Building, 11 York Road, London SE1 7NX

www.continuumbooks.com
www.cliveyoung.com

Printed in the United States of America on 50% postconsumer waste recycled paper

Library of Congress Cataloging-in-Publication Data
Young, Clive.
Homemade Hollywood : fans behind the camera / Clive Young.
p. cm.
Includes bibliographical references and index.
ISBN-13: 978-0-8264-2922-3 (hardcover : alk. paper)
ISBN-10: 0-8264-2922-X (hardcover : alk. paper)
ISBN-13: 978-0-8264-2923-0 (pbk. : alk. paper)
ISBN-10: 0-8264-2923-8 (pbk. : alk. paper) 1. Fan films--History and criticism. I. Title.

PN1995.9.F35Y68 2008
791.43'3--dc22

2008024007

Contents

This book is dedicated to Ava,
who wasn't around for the first one.

Acknowledgments

I'd like to thank the vast number people who helped make this book possible; I'll probably leave someone out but here it goes:

Chris Gore was extremely generous with his time and talent, writing the perfect foreword to kick off the book.

Many people let me interview them about fan films at various points between 1998 and 2008; among those sharing their knowledge were Myles "Moles" Abbott; Jeff Allen; Bryant Arnett; Dr. Robbins Barstow Jr.; Stuart Basinger; Art Binninger; Kevin "Zaph" Burfitt; Joe Busam; Bruce Cardozo; James Cawley; Sandy Collora; Dawn Cowings; Troy Durrett; Warren Duxbury; Shane Felux; Ernie Fosselius; Louis Fox; Daryl Frazetti; Charlotte Fullerton; Dan Galiardi; Lincoln Gasking; Don Glut; Fred Howard; John Hudgens; Dr. Henry Jenkins; Louis Katz; Marc Kimball; Albert Lamont; Paul Levitz; Jason Long; Cris Macht; Curt Markham; Evan Mather; David Noble; Chris Notarile; Joe Nussbaum; Valerie Perez; Dan Poole; Erin Pyne; Kurt Ramm; Tommy Ramone; Andrea Richards; Lance Robson; Eli Roth; Kevin Rubio; Aaron Schoenke; Anthony Shafer; Kevin Smith; Trey Stokes; Dan Streible; Chris Strompolos; Fred Tepper; Matthew Ward; James Watson; Bob West; Michael Wiese; Marv Wolfman; Timothy Zahn; and Eric Zala.

Hand in hand with that, a number of folks provided me with great photos and other materials; they include Greg Dohler, Jeff Hayes, Ken Lee, Glenn Reid, and Benjamin Singleton of the University of South Carolina Newsfilm Library.

A passel of people gave me hot tips, hooked me up with sources, helped me find information, or had access to rare materials that I never could have obtained on my own; accordingly, I'm indebted to Raymond Benson, Amanda Ford, Chris Mason, Steve McClean, Mike Scott, and Justin Young (no relation). Special thanks, too, to the Oceanside, New York, Public Library, which can interloan pretty much anything from anywhere.

Unfortunately, there were a number of people who gave me great interviews, photos, or other materials that I couldn't jam in here, no matter how hard I tried. I'm grateful for their help, so I'd be remiss not to mention Hank Braxtan, David Guivant, Josh Hawkes, Jonathan Lawrence, Cortney Macht, Tim Richardson, Daniel Riser, David Rogers, and Jason Wishnow.

When I was frustrated with the weak subtitle that I originally gave the book, Bryan Patrick Stoyle came up with "Fans Behind the Camera," which was ideal.

New York Comic Con 2008 played an important role in this book, and helping out on that score were Adam Bertocci of TheForce.Net fan film forum, Fanboy Will of FanboyTheatre.Com, and Jay Williams of Reed Expo.

Virtually everyone I know put up with me talking about fan films incessantly while I wrote this book. Those who endured more than most included Steve "Broccoli" Cohn; Keith and Karyn Cousin; the members of Docking Bay 516; Glenn and Ginny Greenberg; Mike Leib; Stacy and Elliott Levine; Rob Piecuch; Dave and Paroo Streich; and Tony Traguardo. Thanks, too, to the staff of NewBay Media for their encouragement, particularly Janice Brown, Fred Goodman, Steve Palm, Chris Walsh, and Frank Wells.

I couldn't have asked for a better publishing team than the folks at Continuum; thanks to John Mark Boling, Emma Cook, Claire Heitlinger, Gabriella Page-Fort, and particularly Dr. David Barker, for seeing the value of a book about fan films.

Thanks to my parents, Douglas and Judy Young, for encouraging me to write since I was tiny, and to my brother Keith and in-laws Steve and Annette Mansella for their unending support.

My glorious three-year-old daughter, Ava, dragged me away from the keyboard on a daily basis; thank you, little one.

Finally, it would take mountains of words to express my love and gratitude for my wife, Michelle; if I tried to write them all, I'd fill ten more books and still run out of room.

Chris Gore is a filmmaker, an author, the founder of *Film Threat*, and a huge nerdlebrity.

FOREWORD
Where No Fan Has Gone Before
by Chris Gore

The first time I remember seeing what might be termed a "fan film" was viewing the spoof comedy *Hardware Wars*. Like many who saw the original *Star Wars* back in 1977, I sought out anything to do with the movie, including that awful disco album. But the most unusual piece of *Star Wars*–inspired kitsch has to be the low-budget indie, *Hardware Wars*. The short was a reverent send-up, written and directed by Ernie Fosselius and produced by Michael Wiese. It was bad. Cheaply made. And the humor was lowbrow. I loved it.

While Fosselius and Wiese may have been fans at heart, they were actually experienced independent filmmakers, and *Hardware Wars* was, in spite of its cheesy, low-budget ways, professionally made. While *Star Wars* inspired a new generation of filmmakers, *Hardware Wars* helped to inspire fans and non-pros to pick up a camera and pay tribute to their favorite movies.

At their core, the best fan films are not about making something that could possibly equal the original; it's about taking that passion for the story and characters to a whole new level. They are made with no expectation of box office success or return on a financial investment, only with the intention purely to entertain. Which is why these admittedly flawed films not only deserve love from audiences, but respect—because they are honest.

Some fan films come in the form of direct re-creations of favorite movie scenes, or even whole films, as in the case of *Raiders of the Lost Ark: The Adaptation* by Eric Zala, Jayson Lamb, and Chris Strompolos. Other fan films may explore an area of that universe left untouched by the original creators, such as Shane Felux's ambitious 47-minute *Star Wars: Revelations,* which tells a tale between the two trilogies. There may be only 13 hours and 23 minutes of official time spent in the *Star Wars* galaxy as told by creator George Lucas, but there are literally hundreds of hours of fan films.

Perhaps the most influential modern fan film, the one that touched off the insane popularity of these shorts on the Web, has to be Kevin Rubio's comedy *Troops*. The 10-minute short is a brilliantly satirical look at a day in the life of stormtroopers from *Star Wars,* presented like an episode of the TV series *Cops*. These stormtroopers just happen to be around during key moments from the original movie, offering us a glimpse into their investigation of stolen droids and even a domestic dispute between Aunt Beru and Uncle Owen in which the pair are promptly fried.

I was actually at fan film's ground zero: the day when *Troops* unspooled to a packed room of about 500 people at the San Diego Comic Con in 1997. I recall the eruption of applause during the first screening and the chant, "Show It Again!" Never before had fans seen something so professionally made on every level, with costumes, sets, sound, and even special effects that were as good as the original. And all of it came from a fan, Kevin Rubio, who has since gone pro. That film was a lightning rod that inspired a new generation of fans, proving that they could use modern filmmaking tools to pay tribute to the movies they loved. In fact, armed with off-the-shelf software and affordable cameras, this new group of fans could make movies that surpassed the quality of the originals, at least in the area of special effects.

I find it humorous when I look back at the stack of shorts I made as a kid. I had nearly forgotten that I put considerable effort into a fan film of my own. As a single-digit-aged kid with a Super 8 camera and a few rolls of Kodak's legendary Kodachrome 40 film stock, I embarked on creating my own version of the space fantasy epic *Flash Gordon*. In the six-minute saga, I actually played a weak-looking and gangly Flash, with colorful pajamas as my uniform.

The kids from my neighborhood—Bill, Kurt, and Colleen—played Dale Arden, Dr. Zarkov, and Prince Barin. My basement was the setting for Flash's spaceship interior, a star field was created using Christmas lights, and the local park became the planet Mongo. Well, that is, if Ming's home world had monkey bars and a swing set. What the film lacked in special effects, decent acting, and production value was more than made up for when taking into account the love for the source material. I was so moved and inspired by both the original Buster Crabbe *Flash Gordon* serials from the 1930s and the camp 1980 feature that I wanted to explore that universe and create my own adventure. I'll be honest; my version of *Flash* was bad. Cheaply made. And the humor was lowbrow. I think only my mom loved it. But it was a first step—or misstep perhaps—toward making my own movies.

Regardless of the less-than-spectacular results of my Super 8 *Flash Gordon,* I was willing to dedicate my time and effort to a mountain of tasks, from making props, to building sets, to assembling makeshift models, to creating costumes, to organizing talent and even sacrificing lunch money for film and processing, because I'm the type of person truly in love with movies. I know that love well because it's that kind of devotion that connects every accomplished moviemaker I've ever met. Deep down, I think every professional filmmaker is a fan at heart. Considering the number of influences from fantasy and science fiction contained in the original *Star Wars,* from *Flash Gordon* to Buck Rogers to Westerns and war movies, didn't George just make one big-budget fan film?

1
Amateur Auteurs

Before we get started, let's get two things out of the way.

First, the average fan film stinks. The acting is lousy, the story is slow, the comedy isn't funny, and yet the drama is hysterical. Any true-blue cineaste who loves motion pictures to his dying breath should never watch a fan film, for fear of being blinded—or blindsided—by the incredible lack of quality, craftsmanship, or even basic understanding of how to make a moderately coherent movie.

Of course, he'd be missing out, because it's all those "faults" that make fan films exciting. If a big-budget, Hollywood feature is like a Celine Dion power ballad about everlasting love, then a fan film is a punk song about ditching school, written by the snot-nosed kid next door who only knows three chords. It's that kind of aesthetic—which is to say, no aesthetic. A fan film is real, it's raw, it's a blatant power grab in the name of the little guy; and most of all, it's fun.

Second, the fans who make these movies aren't psychos. They may love a certain franchise and know jaw-dropping amounts of trivia, but fan filmmakers actually tend to be well-rounded, social people who inhabit the real world and have other interests—like filmmaking, for instance. If modern suburbia is the measuring stick for what's "normal" in today's culture, then making an amateur blockbuster is about as average as it gets; fan filmers are "a demographic that is predominantly white, middle-class, technologically literate, and educated to degree level or above," according to Sara Gwenllian Jones in *Underground U.S.A.: Filmmaking Beyond the Hollywood Canon*. Frankly, you can add "male" and "between fifteen and thirty-five" to that list, too.

Do these fans spend thousands of dollars on movies from which they can never profit? Some do. Are they liable to dress up in *Star Trek* uniforms and enjoy playing Captain Kirk a little too much? Sure, there are plenty of people who've done that. Are those stupid things to do? Not at all; some academics even suggest that throwing on a costume and acting out pop culture can be a good thing, such as *Fan Cultures* author Matthew Hills, who wrote about impersonators, noting "it is only by passing through moments of self-absence that our sense of self can be re-narrated and expanded." If that's true, then every fan film is an opportunity for its cast members to become better people—not a bad deal at all.

Ever since fan films exploded into the mainstream in the late nineties, more and more people have started making their own flicks, from *Star Wars* shorts to *Harry Potter* epics, thanks to a perfect storm of factors—mature consumer technologies, fandom, and the Internet—which all converged at the same time. The result has been millions of amateur auteurs, all turning their basements into makeshift studios as they've spent their money on two things: technology to make movies, and pizza to get friends to be in the movies.

These films are about the journey, about regular people trying to get a little closer to understanding what inspired their favorite franchise by making it themselves. Using someone else's creation to explore their own creative impulses, fan filmmakers find new ways to express their ideas, and share that process with others, both on the set and online. So while most fan films—let's say 80 percent—never get completed, that's fine. It just means finishing wasn't necessary; whatever the cast and crew needed to gain from the experience turned up before they got to the final cut.

The 20 percent of flicks that reach the finish line, however, are radically changing the way Big Media interacts with the public. Only a few years ago, a fan film would be seen by the filmmaker's family and friends, and that was it; today, a homemade superhero movie can be seen around the world instantly, thanks to the Internet. That has the media companies that own major characters jumpy—you would be, too, if amateurs with nothing to lose were messing around with your billion-dollar franchise. Back when fan films were only seen by a few people, corporations regularly threatened to sue the filmmakers into oblivion; ironically, now that these movies can be seen by millions online, many companies are willingly turning a blind eye.

Mimicking Hollywood movies for a fraction of the cost, fan filmers often come up with ingenious solutions when it comes to getting the actors, effects, locations, costumes, and looks they need. Ever in search of perfection, some of these filmmakers are willing to risk it all—relationships, careers, homes, even their lives—for their microblockbusters.

Hundreds of fan films come into the world every year, but only a handful have any lasting impact—just like Hollywood movies. For that reason, productions featured in this book have been included because of historical significance or because they're typical of the flicks made during a given era, and the behind-the-scenes stories of these movies are just as compelling as the tales on the screen. However, before we discover how these amateurs made their films—and the ways that these little homemade movies are changing the future of media and fandom—we have to start with one basic question.

What the heck is a fan film? It's a good question. Naturally, the answer is pretty vague. In fact, it's so unclear that we'll give it two definitions—a classic one and a modern one.

The classic definition is that a fan film is a fictional movie created by fans imitating their heroes from pop culture. Fans have made movie tributes to their favorite characters since practically the dawn of film, so a basic definition like that just makes sense, but it's also pretty broad, making fan films sound like "real" movies. Many of the best known ones come close—*Star Wars: Revelations* and *Batman: Dead End*, for example—but there are thousands that are the cinematic equivalent of a two-year-old drawing on a wall with a crayon: sure, it's a creative expression, but the only person enjoying it is the "artist." Plus, many more modern efforts simply don't fit into that classic definition.

Today, in addition to the traditional fictional fan film, there are documentaries, musicals, comic book adaptations, remakes of entire feature films, and more. And just to complicate things, many of the most popular fan flicks have been made by aspiring professionals, using their films as signal flares to the movie industry—"Help, I'm over here! Hire me!" Movies like these can blur the line between "amateur" and "professional" beyond recognition.

So, to take another stab at it, a modern definition of a fan film might be "An unauthorized amateur or semi-pro film, based on pop culture characters or situations, created for noncommercial viewing."

In truth, however, the definition comes down to gut instinct, much like the cliché about porn: you know a fan film when you see one, and despite the fact that they may lack a budget, talented actors, plot or a tripod, fan films have one thing that many Hollywood movies lack: passion.

Since no one is getting paid, all fan films are true labors of love—and they're especially infused with that giddy sensation because they're filled with the excitement of fandom. These homemade epics express their adoration in many different ways, and are made for just as many reasons; sometimes, it's just a guy in a Batman suit who wants to see what he'd look like kicking ass. Other times, the films are made by fans who want to relive favorite movies by making their own versions. And still other times, they're critical attacks—tough love, if you will—born out of frustration at how the pros often crank out empty, vacuous garbage starring treasured characters when they could be making great movies if their enthusiasm wasn't directly proportionate to their paychecks.

Say what you like about moviemaking skill, ability, and, God forbid, talent, but passion is perhaps the greatest divide between fan filmmakers and the pros. While there are plenty of writers and directors in Hollywood who sincerely love the superheroes and outer space villains they get to play with, no doubt their fervor would be tempered if they were paying to make a movie instead of getting paid. That's fair—after all, everyone needs to keep a roof over his head—but inevitably, some level of passion seeps out of a project once it becomes a gig. Thanks to the long arm of the law, however, fan filmmakers never face that problem.

While many amateurs create fan films in hopes of getting attention and, ideally, a job in Hollywood, they are still bogged down by the fact that they're breaking the law just by making their backyard productions. They can't sell copies of their movies, nor can they charge admission to see the flicks. They can't even trade a homemade DVD of a fan film for a six-pack at the local deli (and admittedly, many fan films are better once you've had that six-pack).

The reason for the economic abstinence is simple: if fan filmmakers make any profit or gain from their movie, they can get buried in a snowstorm of legal filings. Nothing raises a copyright holder's ire like money going into someone else's pocket. Sure, the filmmaker may have spent thousands of dollars producing a good flick and hours promoting it, thus garnering tons of free publicity for someone else's franchise, but let a penny fall into his pocket in return for all that hard work and it's time to call in some muscle. Cry "havoc" and let loose the lawyers.

Of course, whether it's worth it to go after fan filmmakers with squadrons of legal eagles is another story, but it's fair to say that right after passion, profit is the next biggest aspect separating the amateurs from the pros—and filmmaking has always been about profit, since long before fan films came into existence.

◆ ◆ ◆

The history of filmmaking is well documented in countless books, but generally, it didn't kick in until the 1890s, as part of the Second Industrial Revolution. A number of people around the world claimed to have created the first motion picture camera, but regardless of who got there first, movies were an idea that took root quickly.

For decades, there were a number of sizes for film stock, and many companies created their own cameras and projectors (and sometimes machines that were both) that used proprietary film stocks, or, in one odd case, glass disks. It wasn't long, however, before 35mm film became the standard size for filmmakers, and the equipment that used it was only available to professionals, thanks to the Motion Picture Patents Company (MPPC), a monopolizing trust formed by the major camera manufacturers in 1908.

If you wanted film equipment, or wanted to go into the movie theater business, you had to deal with the MPPC because they owned the 16 patents on which virtually all film gear in the United States was based. As Patricia Zimmerman points out in her book *Reel Families: A Social History of Amateur Film,* "Unless consumers could afford the licensing fees on equipment or could amass enough financial backing to operate outside the holds of the MPPC, standardized equipment was not available."

Actually, there were obscure inventors who created their own jury-rigged cameras, and various "How to make your own movie camera"–type articles popped up in magazines like *Scientific American* as early as 1910, but amateur filmmaking was pretty much only written about in academic and technical journals, so the idea of making a home movie just wasn't reaching the average guy.

On top of all that, amateurs who somehow did get into moviemaking had to treat early film just as a professional would: carefully, because the stuff was dangerous! In the early 1900s, film stock was made with an incredibly flammable nitrate base; eventually a cellulose base was developed, creating "safety" film around 1912, but despite the obvious benefit of it not randomly catching fire in your camera, it wasn't widely available at first.

Not only did the early aspiring auteur have to be something of a daredevil to use film, he had to be rich. Initially, moviemaking was so expensive that it was only a pursuit for those with too much money and time on their hands. Take, for instance, one of the earliest fan films, based on the legendary 1927 silent horror mystery *London after Midnight*. Made sometime in the late twenties or early thirties, the two-minute short, shot outside a shoreline vacation cottage, features well-to-do flappers and their beaus laughingly "terrorized" by a friend dressed as Lon Chaney's vampire from the original movie. Ironically, the last known print of the real *London after Midnight* was destroyed by a fire at one of MGM's film vaults in 1965; as a result, this slight fan film has added significance today, providing an idea of what Chaney's performance might have been like in the original movie—not bad for a brief interlude that essentially shows how a handful of the idle rich spent their summer vacation.

As the 20th century progressed, modern industry took hold

and, for the first time, average people began to have ample leisure time. Rising to fill that void were entertainment and hobbies and, inevitably, the two mixed in many ways, including amateur filmmaking—better known as home movies.

The earliest professional cameras were expensive, complicated, handcranked monsters, but manufacturers realized that if they could simplify their products, there might be a massive market for personal movie equipment. Initially, the public was only interested in viewing movies at home; in a world without TV, watching a three-minute short on your own sofa was pretty exciting, so while home movies might have been prohibitively expensive to make, many families had their own projectors, and would buy professional flicks or obtain them from film libraries.

It was only a matter of time, however, before the cost of owning a camera came down and the public's interest in home movies went up, all of which led to a very profitable market for companies like Eastman Kodak and Bell & Howell. In 1921, 16mm became the standard gauge format for amateurs—not because Joe Average wasn't "pro" enough for 35mm, but because the companies were worried he'd try to save money by splitting the big 35mm film into two strips of 17.5 mm stock—which was another popular film size at the time. Locking things in at 16mm ensured that the little guy would have to keep paying big bucks for film—so profit really did separate the amateurs from the pros right from the early days of moviemaking.

The Great Depression hit and cemented the fact that only the wealthy could afford filmmaking as a hobby, but even so, the 1930s saw home movie technology take off. Another amateur film gauge, 8mm, caught on in 1932 and cameras began to get innovations like built-in light meters, electric drives (no more handcranking!), and film cassettes that simply loaded into the camera. Color and sound were also introduced for home movies but with moderate initial success, and any momentum that amateur moviemaking picked up was stopped by the outbreak of World War II in 1939.

During those early days of home movies, however, it was inevitable that fan filmmaking would develop. Whether anyone knew about those early efforts—or can find them today—is another story.

Surely thousands of people made their own backyard epics throughout the decades, but the vast majority of them came and went without ever reaching the public eye. And why would they? Until the advent of the Internet and public-access cable TV channels, most amateur filmmakers had no means of distribution—indeed most amateur films before the advent of video were single copies; if the film got ruined, the movie was lost for good. There was also little in the way of publicity about them; after all, how—and why—would an amateur filmmaker tell the world about his great homemade movie that few people could see anyway?

While there undoubtedly were many fan films produced around the world in the early days of amateur movies, those tiny productions are now virtually impossible to find. Perhaps they're hidden in garages and basements around the world; more likely than not, however, they've been forgotten, were thrown out during a spring cleaning or have disintegrated with poor storage and the passing of time. Another, more hopeful possibility is that in recent times, historic film preservation societies have begun amassing home and amateur movies, purchasing large collections of families' ancient reels, so it's possible that a few fan flicks are in good hands, just waiting to be rediscovered.

Because of all these factors—lack of distribution, publicity, and detection—it's impossible to know what the first fan film was, much less view it. Ironically, most people tend to point to the well-known 1977 *Star Wars* parody *Hardware Wars* as the first fan film. It achieved great popularity, but that short is hardly the first cinematic enthusiast effort. No, the earliest-known fan film predates *Hardware Wars* by more than 50 years.

2
From Con Men to the Apeman
The Birth of Fan Films

Fan films have always had a criminal scent to them—creative people doing what they're not supposed to, breaking the law freely as they use other people's copyrighted characters and the like. It's only appropriate, then, that the earliest fan films were essentially created by cinematic con men. They weren't hard-boiled grifters in a film noir thriller, however; more like harmless Professor Harold Hill in *The Music Man*.

In the famous musical, you may recall, Hill is a traveling salesman who seduces entire towns into purchasing marching band instruments for their kids, promising he'll turn the tykes into the greatest musicians ever. Naturally, as soon as the instruments arrive, Hill hits the highway, abandoning the band as he goes off to find another town of suckers.

Take that kind of trickery, drop it into the deep south of the roaring twenties, throw in a handcranked movie camera, and you have the unlikely start of fan production in the form of the earliest known fan film, *Anderson* "Our Gang."

Sometime around September 15, 1926, a pair of itinerant filmmakers-turned-con artists ambled into Anderson, South Carolina, and set up shop for a week. Their game? Making an amateur *Our Gang* movie, based on the long-running Hal Roach Studios series that brought the world Buckwheat, Spanky, Alfalfa, Darla, and the rest. While those characters came along during the sound era, the Our Gang series (better known these days as the Little Rascals) started out in the days of silent film; debuting in 1922, a total of 88 20-minute silent movies were made before the series transitioned to sound in 1928. As a result, even though few people today have seen the series' silent movies, they were very popular in 1926, and Anderson, like the rest of America, was very familiar with Our Gang.

The first order of business for the filmmakers, then, was finding a local movie house that would work with them; after all, if they were going to make a movie, they needed a place to show it. Their brand-new best friend, it turned out, was Percy C. Osteen, proprietor of the Egyptian Theatre.

Anderson might have been a small town, but it was great place to live if you liked movies, with four theaters to choose from. That made life complicated for Osteen, however; two of the four cinemas in Anderson were owned by a major company, Paramount-Publix, and the third mainly presented live acts, so the Egyptian had to fight for every customer that walked through its doors. Osteen had to try harder, charge less, and do more to win business—as did all independent theater owners (many would argue it's still like that today). That made him the perfect "partner" for the filmmakers. Hooking up with him would put a local face on their production, giving them instant credibility within the community—plus, they'd have a place to show their final product. So when the con men showed up and said they were making a movie for Hal Roach Studios—and, say, would you want to sponsor it and have it debut in your theater next week?—it was a no-brainer. Osteen agreed, gave them money, and the filmmakers were in business.

Quick as a flash, the local media blitz began; Osteen hung banners promoting auditions for the film outside his theater, and the local paper was contacted to write how Hollywood had come to Anderson in the form of a director and cameraman. A little publicity for their shady deal was fine with the filmmakers; in an age long before information flowed around the globe in an instant, it made perfect sense to get the local newspaper involved. Talking to the paper wasn't going to tip off Hal Roach that they were making a fake Our Gang comedy; heck, even if a copy of the article were to

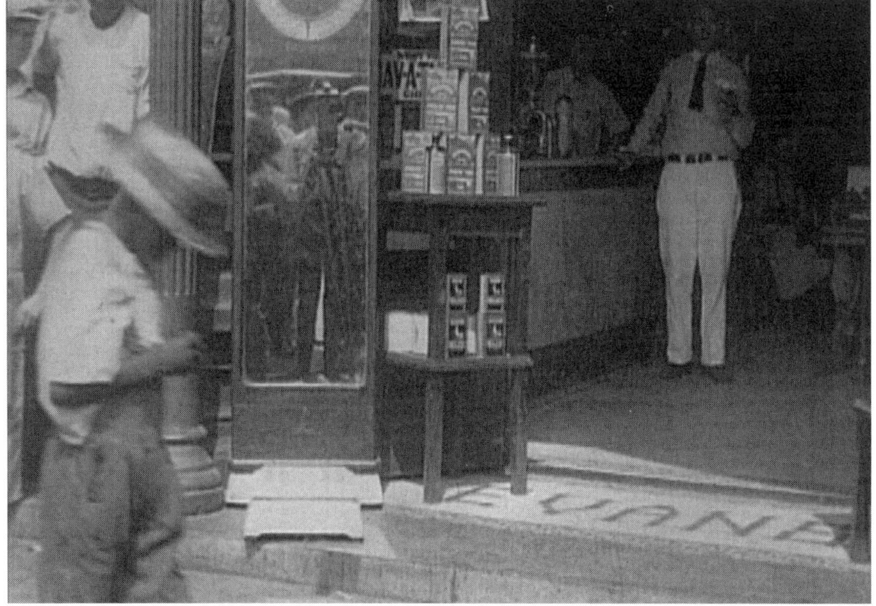

The filmmakers behind the earliest known fan film, *Anderson "Our Gang,"* managed to sneak themselves into the movie; when Farina goes to buy ice cream, the camera can be spotted in a mirror by the store's entrance.
(Courtesy of University of South Carolina Newsfilm Library)

miraculously land on Roach's desk, it would take weeks to respond, by which time the itinerant movie men would be long gone.

And who were these mysterious practitioners of the cinematic arts? No one really knows. As an associate professor in the NYU Department of Cinema Studies and director of its MA program in moving image archiving and preservation, Dan Streible has studied every aspect of *Anderson "Our Gang."* "As best I can tell," he comments, "they introduced themselves as being from Hollywood, and there might have been some way to justify that because one of them, the cameraman, probably worked as a stringer for a newsreel service connected to or distributed by one of the major studios, so maybe that was where he could say he had Hollywood credentials."

It's hard to know if anything the pair said was true, however, because they used false names the entire time they were in Anderson. The film's credits claim it was directed by Sammy Fox and shot by cinematographer R. R. Beatty, and the local paper, the *Anderson Daily Mail,* referred to them simply as Director Fox and "R. R. Beaty [*sic*], chief cameraman of Hollywood, Cal. and representatives of Pathé News." That certainly sounds credible, since the Hal Roach comedies were distributed by Pathé at the time; however, with some detective work, Streible learned there was no director or cameraman with those names working for Pathé at the time, that Pathé was never involved in the movie, and as the kicker, that Sam Fox was the name of a top publisher of music for silent films. In other words, they were covering their tracks, just in case. In an essay he wrote for the journal *Film History*, Streible guesses "they might have been bamboozlers, small-time producers trying to outfox small-town exhibitors by claiming Hollywood credentials. Certainly there were both actual and legendary cases of movie people scamming naïfs in the hinterland."

Regardless, the filmmakers kicked into high gear, sifting through 200 kids at the auditions; in fact, they shot footage of the wannabe movie stars waiting outside the theater and used it, making them all part of the picture. As Streible points out, "If you could get a lot of kids in your movie, then more parents would turn out, and you'd sell a lot more tickets than if you just cast a few of the best local talents. If you get 100 kids from the town in your movie, then you're guaranteeing that when the film's shown, it'll sell out because everyone will want to see them." The eventual cast filled out the characters, all of who had names either similar to, or taken directly from, the Hal Roach movies: Jackie, Fat, Mary, Freckles, Toughy, and Farina.

The flimsy plot of the film is really a series of vignettes, some of them surprising today in their casual racism. Farina—described as "the dark cloud of the gang"—misdirects traffic, causing a snarl; does a little soft-shoe to beg money from a pair of white newlyweds ("Shake those dogs, boy," the man orders in one title card); buys bananas only to have all but the smallest stolen away by his friends ("By bamama shrunk!" he exclaims); and the same thing with some ice cream he purchases. Meanwhile, the rest of the kids get into fights; harass, and then throw a pie at an old man on crutches; ride in a car; and watch a circus parade roll through town.

Only the first 11-minute reel survives today; apparently the second reel had the gang sneak into the circus and get caught by the

Anderson "Our Gang" contains numerous moments that are offensive today, from a casually racist tone in some segments, to the harassment of Old Man Crank, a disabled man on crutches who eventually gets a hit in the face by a pie, shown here just before launch.
(Courtesy of University of South Carolina Newsfilm Library)

cops, only to be allowed to stay by the circus owner, who treated them all to ice cream. If that sounds a bit like a legitimate Our Gang movie, it was—in fact, it was two of them, as the plot was a mishmash stolen from the real movies *One Wild Ride* and *Circus Fever*, both also from 1926.

If the locals thought it was a real Hal Roach production at the start, it appears that they soon figured out the ruse—and went along with it anyway, just to see themselves on screen. The *Anderson Daily Mail* reported conflicting information, calling the movie both "a home made production" and a "real *Our Gang* comedy," noting that director Fox had "successfully filmed home town movies in other cities," yet also boasting about his claimed Pathé connections: "Everyone almost has seen one or more *Our Gang* Comedies, produced by Pathé News." If anyone wondered whether the filmmakers were on the level, then eyebrows must have risen when

Osteen's sons, Marion and Harry, were cast as "Jackie" and "Freckles," respectively, and the plumb role of "Fat" went to Joe Hillard, the son of a local cop. While the pseudo–studio men were adept at making movies, they instinctually followed the same advice as found in Sun-tzu's *The Art of War*: "Keep your friends close, and your enemies closer." Putting Hillard in the film virtually guaranteed that the deal would play out fine, providing the film actually got made. Sweetening the con, the film started with a special credit page, thanking the police for their help making the short.

Filming began on the weekend, commencing the same day as the auditions and finishing up after school on Monday afternoon when the circus parade took place. The filmmakers were working fast—perhaps to get out of town that much quicker—because the film was shown the following Saturday, at the bottom of the Egyptian Theatre's bill. Ads for the cinema that week barely even mentioned the movie—all it got was the description of being shown as an extra: "Local, *Our Gang* Comedy. See your child in the movies. See the mischief these little rascals get into. You will be surprised how they can act."

The movie only played there for three days: Saturday, Monday, and Tuesday (the theater was closed Sundays). Saturdays were usually reserved for kiddie shows—perfect for the movie—while Mondays and Tuesdays always featured fare aimed at well-to-do housewives, who presumably would go to see their kids on screen. The film was filled with kids from wealthy families acting as barefoot scruffs—a fact that had a sad irony to it. Tthe town had a sizable poor community (most of whom worked at a nearby mill) that had a hard time affording luxuries like going to the movies; children who were actually living hardscrabble lives weren't a part of the film.

Once the short run was over, that was it. The film was never theatrically shown again, but somehow ended up in the Anderson County Library, which cataloged it simply as *Our Gang* Comedy, with the alternate title *Why Mothers Go Grey* taken from a silent film title card in the movie: "The Gang—why mothers get grey-headed." Unfortunately, the library no longer has the film, so the only known print is owned by the University of South Carolina Newsfilm Library, which lists it as *Anderson "Our Gang."* While it figures that a con of a film would go under aliases, one must note that in its coverage of the movie's production, the *Anderson Daily Mail* reported that the film had an entirely different title: *A Free Ride*.

That might have been an in-joke, as *A Free Ride* just happens to be the same name as the oldest American "stag" movie still in existence, according to Dave Thompson's history of the form, *Black and White and Blue*. Estimated to have been produced in 1915 or 1923 (according to the Kinsey Institute and historian Kevin Brownlow, respectively), the blue movie was scandalous to those in the know. Few readers of the *Anderson Daily Mail* would've gotten the joke, however, as all such "smokers" were extremely hush-hush affairs; even owning a stag reel—much less producing or screening one—could get you sent to jail back then. With a rather basic hitchhiking plot, the ten-minute silent film might seem quaint in this day and age, particularly when its participants drive an early automobile and are dressed (however briefly) in period fashions, but the fact remains that, even today, you still wouldn't want to watch it with your mother in the room.

It's entirely possible, then, that the two itinerant filmmakers would have known of the stag film, and since we're conjecturing, heck, there's even the slim chance they might've shot it. At the least, it's easy to picture the local reporter asking for the name of their kiddie movie, only to have one answer with a snicker that the working title was *A Free Ride*. Alternately, mentioning the stag film's title in the newspaper might have been a tip-off to informed members of the local male population that the filmmakers had some stag reels to show. Traveling from town to town, screening early porn flicks for the locals would've been a good way to score a few extra bucks, but it's impossible to know if the duo were doing so, owned stags, or were even aware of the illicit movie with the same name. It is almost certainly a fluke—Streible firmly believes it's an amusing coincidence—but then again, one could argue that *A Free Ride*'s influence can be seen in the pseudonymous credits on *Anderson "Our Gang,"* since the stag movie's director was listed as "A. Wise Guy," while its photographer was "Will B. Hard."

Under any title, however, *Anderson "Our Gang"* aka *Why Mothers Go Grey* aka *A Free Ride*, is a fan film, and it fits the definitions' criteria well. That the filmmakers were early porn gourmands is unlikely, but they clearly were fans of the *Our Gang* series, if only for the fact they knew the plots of two different shorts to cudgel together. Added to that is the distinct possibility that everyone involved was well aware that this was an amateur production and just went along with it for the fun of it—a perfect example of a fan film.

"Other people have started to turn up similar films that are just coming to light," notes Streible. "More than one crew was going around the country, doing that kind of thing from the twenties through at least the forties; apparently it was extremely common." Most of those productions weren't fan films, though, because while similar, they didn't expressly say they were Our Gang movies using the series' characters. Streible has learned of a similar effort in Atlanta (a 1928 amateur Our Gang film that has never been found), and researchers Dwight Swanson and Caroline Frick have traced the 1930s work of Melton Barker, a itinerant filmmaker who traveled around Texas and North Carolina, making at least eighty productions of the same movie, *The Kidnappers' Foil,* an original story done in the Our Gang style. If the filmmakers who walked into Anderson were amateurs at making quickie kiddie movies, Barker was the consummate pro: "He was actually asking parents for money to have their kids appear in the film," marvels Streible. "He was working it at both ends!"

Someday, someone will inevitably discover an even earlier fan production, but for now, *Anderson "Our Gang,"* the product of two con men and a town of people who probably knew they were being duped, is the earliest fan film.

* * *

Home moviemaking was still a rarity 10 years later when one of the earliest-known fan productions to fit the classic definition ("an amateur, fictional movie created by fans emulating heroes from pop culture") was made as three brothers filmed and created their own tribute to one of the era's most popular characters in *Tarzan and the Rocky Gorge*. A 12-minute black and white picture filmed in 1936, the mini-epic was the work of a family enthralled by moviemaking, particularly the eldest of three sons, Robbins Barstow. Just 16 at the time, Barstow found his film was the start of a lifetime passion with documenting virtually everything around him on celluloid and, later, video.

Robbins, along with his brothers, Paul (10) and John (14), was born to a Congregational minister, Robbins Barstow, Sr., who was president of the Hartford Seminary. The boys' early years saw plenty of uprooting as their father's work sent them to parishes around the United States, until the Barstows settled in Hartford, Connecticut, in 1930. Throughout all those travels, however, Robbins Jr. could count on the movies for a reassuring thrill.

"I have been a life-long movie fan and my earliest hero was Doug Fairbanks Sr. and his swashbuckling films—*Robin Hood, Thief of Baghdad, The Three Musketeers, Zorro,*" he recalled. The three brothers not only loved going to the movies, they were also full of energy, often play-acting Fairbanks' heroics. When Tarzan came along, however, he took everything to a new level.

The public was crazy for the yodeling hero created by Edgar Rice Burroughs in 1912. The noble jungle man raised by apes first appeared in *Tarzan of the Apes,* a novel Burroughs originally published in an adventure magazine. The character caught on, and over the years, Burroughs appeased his audience with more than 25 novels starring the vine-swinging protagonist. It wasn't long, of course, before Tarzan took to the silver screen, first in silent films and then most famously in six films where he was embodied by former Olympic swimming champion Johnny Weissmuller—all of which captured the imagination of kids across America, including the Barstows.

"Boy, those films, I just loved them," recalls Barstow. "Rudy Belmer, the film commentator, said that every boy in America was running around trying to emulate Tarzan's yell, climbing trees and so on—and I was one of those kids."

The difference was that while the Barstows and friends were playing Tarzan in Elizabeth Park across the street from his home, Robbins Jr. was also developing a keen interest in home movies. It was 1932 when he got his hands on a small Kodascope 16mm projector and began collecting reels of silent comedies and cartoons like *Felix the Cat* and *Mickey Mouse*. Before long, he turned

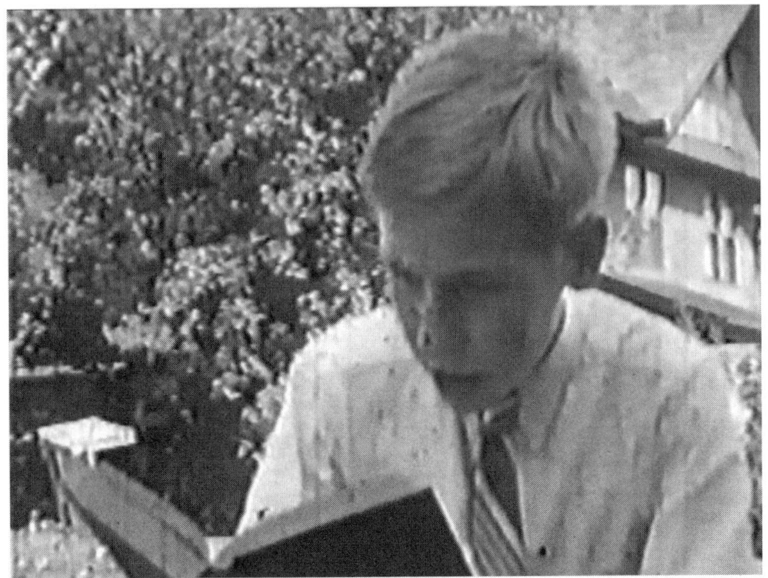

10-year-old Paul Barstow is inspired by a *Tarzan* novel to go to Africa in the 1936 fan film, *Tarzan and the Rocky Gorge*.
(Courtesy of Dr. Robbins Barstow)

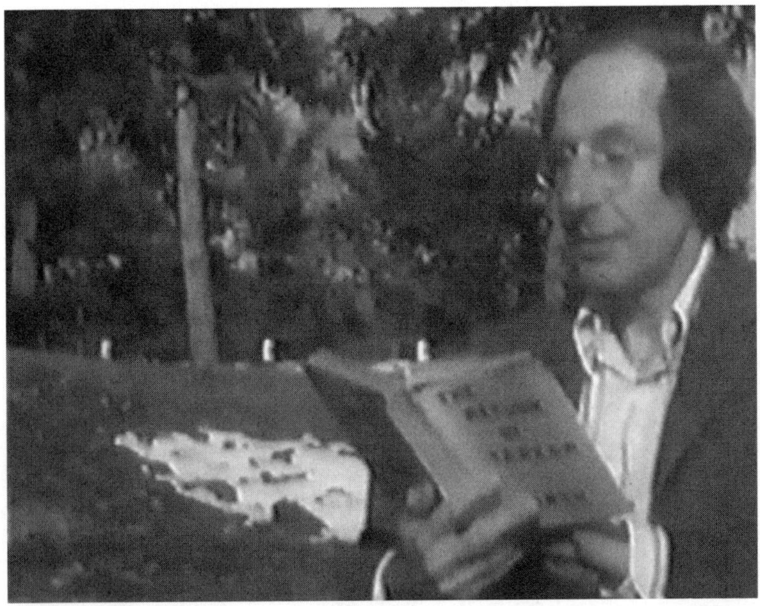

48-year-old Paul Barstow is inspired all over again in the 1974 remake/sequel, *Tarzan and the Lost, Last Whale*.
(Courtesy of Dr. Robbins Barstow)

the family's basement into a makeshift theater, charging local kids a nickel to see the short films on a hanging bed sheet, emanating from the hand-cranked projector.

It was only a matter of months until he purchased an Eastman movie camera. "It was somewhat unusual for a teenager to have a camera," he recalls. "I became a member of the Amateur Cinema League when I was 14, and I must have been one of their youngest members."

Enthralled by his new acquisition, Barstow began filming all kinds of things, but like most home movies, they were typical family events and scenes. Nonetheless, he usually gave them a twist—while raking leaves in the fall, he'd film himself dumping leaves onto the ground and later reverse it so that each leaf magically jumped up into his basket. All of his films were little vignettes, however, until one fateful family picnic in 1936.

"My father had a friend who lived in the rural part of Granby, Connecticut, northwest of Hartford," he comments. "We went up there to visit and have a picnic, and discovered they had this wonderful deep gorge that was millions of years old. The stream at the bottom ran through great big rocky sides, and we looked at that and said, 'Wow! Wouldn't that be a great setting for a movie?' So we combined that setting with the idea of Tarzan and developed this script." The three brothers created a tongue-in-cheek story, bought a few hundred-foot reels of 16mm film, and invited along three girls from the neighborhood for a day of filming and swimming in what turned out to be known as Huggins Gorge.

The film's plot is simple: young Paulus Rufus Barstinio (aka Paul Rogers Barstow) is reading a Tarzan novel in his front yard when he decides to go to Africa to meet the real Tarzan. Bringing along the three girls, Paulus meets evil Mahahatmi Slinkaround (middle brother John) along the way, who for no particular reason tries to stop the party from finding its quarry. After being shot and drowned by the villain, Paulus is instantly revived by the kisses of his safari mates. Eventually, they stumble across Tarzan (Robbins Jr., proudly showing off his cut physique), who joins them in jumping off rocks into pools of water until the explorers head home, shown the way by their newly reformed pal, Slinkaround.

The filming itself went smoothly. Robbins handled the vast

majority of the camera work, only handing it off to others only when he appeared on-screen. All the various hiking, fights, and so on were shot at one time, with the swimming relegated to the end of the day. Much like a real expedition into the unknown, they had a general idea of what they wanted to do, but there was a lot of improvisation, using whatever settings they came across in the forest and gorge.

When it came time to edit, the eldest brother again took the reigns, cutting film with a Eastman splicing block and gluing the edits together with film cement applied by brush. Whether it was teenage hijinks or just being unable to bear the thought of expensive film going to waste, Barstow used nearly every inch of film that he shot that day, working even unrelated shots—one of the girls lying atop a boulder in her swimsuit, for instance—into the story.

The end result was the 12-minute *Tarzan and the Rocky Gorge*. Since the film didn't have recorded sound, it had to be narrated live at every showing and, over time, a basic script of jokes developed. "We had a big party to show it to all the people in the neighborhood," recalls Barstow; the film was a hit with friends and family alike. "Our parents were very supportive; they thought it was great. They loved to talk to their friends and all our relatives about it—'Bobby's made a movie.'"

So while the project started out as a fun way to spend a summer afternoon swimming and hiking, over time it blossomed into a true family heirloom. Year after year, the film was pulled out at family gatherings and holidays, and occasionally even projected outdoors for friends and relatives. In an age long before home video first made reliving memories as simple as popping a tape into a VCR, the home movie and all the folderol around it—setting up screens, loading the projector, narrating the film live, and the rest—was a welcome ritual for the family. "It became a big part of our lives," says Robbins. "It got so I was invited to show it at different places—church groups and schools—because it was so much fun."

In fact, the film became so cherished among the Robbins clan that 38 years later, in 1974, the brothers reconvened in Wellesley, Massachusetts, where they spent a winter afternoon filming the eight-minute remake/sequel, *Tarzan and the Lost, Last Whale*.

As might be expected, much had changed since then. The intrepid 10-year-old explorer Paulus was now pushing 50, and his brothers had already passed the half-century mark. In real life, Paul, perhaps originally inspired by his first starring role, had grown up to become an actor, hitting a career highpoint appearing in the 1970 film *Tell Me That You Love Me, Junie Moon* starring Liza Minnelli before settling into a position as professor of drama and director of theater at Wellesley College. Meanwhile, John had become an evangelical missionary, working in Haiti, Puerto Rico, Panama, and the Caribbean; and Robbins had earned a PhD in education, eventually serving for 35 years as director of professional development for the Connecticut Education Association. They'd each married, so the expedition party in the sequel included wives and fully grown offspring; Tarzan, too, had the aptly named Son of Tarzan (twenty-three-year-old Daniel Barstow) following him around. Much as the brothers had progressed, so had the filmmaking technology they used, trading up from 16mm black and white stock to 16mm color film.

The eight-minute movie follows the same ground as the original, with better-framed shots capturing exaggerated reenactments of scenes first played out a lifetime earlier. Moments that pass without a second glance in the original film—such as Paulus counting on his fingers that his entire safari party is still with him—are performed with a gusto that suggests they'd become favorite moments during family viewings. While the Barstows had filmed the original with the intent of sharing it with anyone they could get to see it, the sequel is definitely a family affair, ending with the expedition uncovering a wooden placard of a whale—an in-joke that perhaps one needs to be a Barstow to fully appreciate. Despite the less accessible ending, the film has fun sight gags, making it just as enjoyable to outsiders (rather than shoot the hero like last time, Slinkaround pegs him with an orange, for instance).

The success of the original film, coupled with the ongoing recording of life around the Barstow house, imbued Robbins with the amateur filmmaking bug. Through the years, he continued to make small films and documentaries of his life and the world around him. The only major change was that he eventually switched to video in the late 1980s.

Barstow's Tarzan movies were finally transferred to VHS tape in 1993. As a result, he was finally able to add titles and credits to the movies but, far more important, at last he was able to record a definitive version of the narration for both films. Now, for the first time since *Tarzan and the Rocky Gorge* was shot 57 years earlier, he could simply sit back and enjoy the film with the rest of the audience.

Middle brother John passed on in the mid-1980s, as did Paul in 2005; brightening the sad occasions, the Tarzan films and what they had meant to the family were mentioned in eulogies at both funerals. With their passings, however, Robbins became increasingly interested in ensuring that his collected life work—the reels and reels of movies depicting everyday life at home and abroad through the decades—would find a safe haven once he passed on. In all, he estimates that his 16mm footage alone runs around 10,000 feet, resulting in nearly nine hours of home movies from the 1930s to the 1990s. After assembling, editing, and transcribing narrations for all his footage—14 reels of film, 12 videotapes, and a slew of DVD-Rs—Barstow donated the collection to the Library of Congress, where they became part of the archives at the Library's National Audio-Visual Conservation Center in Culpeper, Virginia.

The crown jewel of his creations, the 1936 Tarzan movie, has since reached an even wider audience; more than 70 years after it was created, the film was released as part of the compilation DVD, *Living Room Cinema: Films from Home Movie Day*, produced by the Center for Home Movies.

Given his academic background, maybe it's no surprise that at the age of 85, Barstow traveled to Bucksport, Maine, to present his Tarzan home movies at a film symposium on amateur fictional film, hosted by Northeast Historic Film, a moving image preservation society. Along with presenting his groundbreaking fan films, Barstow gave the society a DVD-R of the flicks and a new nine-minute documentary on their creation. Walking up to the podium, Barstow introduced the films in his naturally booming voice, breaking out into Tarzan's trademark yodel just to set the mood. Inviting the audience into his world, he spoke about the movies, what they'd meant to his family through the decades, and how they'd inspired a lifetime of documentary filmmaking.

Naturally, he videotaped the entire speech, preserving it for future generations.

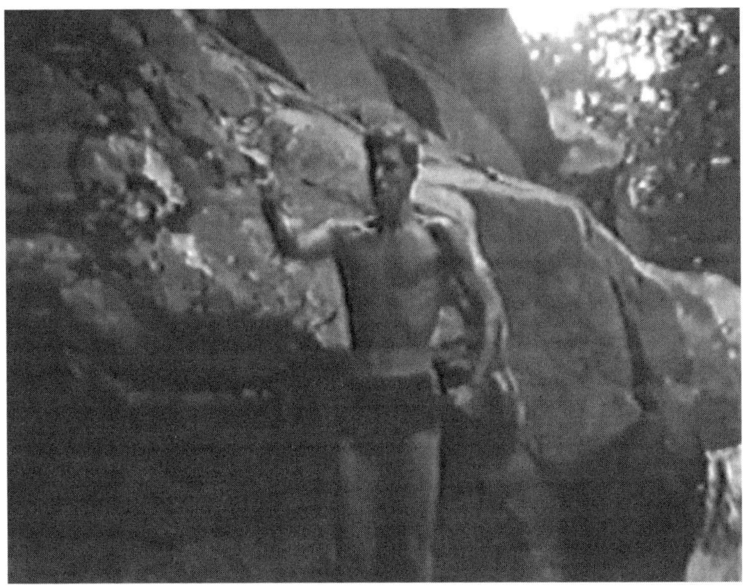

Writer/director/cameraman Robbins Barstow made himself the title character in *Tarzan and the Rocky Gorge*.
(Courtesy of Dr. Robbins Barstow)

3
Monster Kid Mania (1937–1969)

People have been fans since the beginning of time, back when some caveman's slap on the back convinced Urgh to keep drawing animals on the wall of his cave. Fast-forward thousands of years, and you will see that little has changed—some people like to create and others like to enjoy the fruits of that effort. If, as Charles Caleb Colton opined, imitation is the sincerest form of flattery, then fan films take that enjoyment to a whole new level, as people use their own creativity to pay tribute to someone else's creative act.

While the earliest known fan films might have been about movie characters like the Our Gang kids and Tarzan, throughout the years, the biggest driving force behind fan films has always been science fiction fandom, which got its start in the twenties and thirties when the sci-fi community first began to coalesce. That's not to say that science fiction was unpopular before then; after all, H. G. Wells and Jules Verne didn't die penniless after writing their classic books, and Parisian magician George Meliés is legendary for making the first sci-fi movie, *Le Voyage Dans la Lune (A Trip to the Moon)* in 1902—one of 498 fantasy-based flicks he made between 1896 and 1912.

Rather, although the works of these and other early science fiction creators were popular, most fans simply didn't know about each other, and in a time when mass media was still in its infancy and travel was difficult, individuals who liked sci-fi (or anything else, for that matter) would rarely know about fellow aficionados elsewhere.

Into that gap jumped Hugo Gernsback, who edited the first science fiction magazine, *Amazing Stories*, which he founded in 1926, the same year that the con men behind *Anderson "Our Gang"* made their pioneering fan film. Gernsback had something in common with them, as he was a bit of a hustler himself; after emigrating from Luxembourg to New York in 1905 at the age of 21, he went on to start a slew of magazines, businesses, organizations, and a radio station during his lifetime, in addition to writing his own robot novel, *Ralph 124C 41+*, first published in 1911. Today, he's considered one of the fathers of science fiction (thus the awards handed out at each Worldcon convention are called Hugos), and that high regard mainly has to do with his first sci-fi magazine.

While the fiction in *Amazing Stories* proved popular, its letters department was a draw, too; fans would write in and Gernsback would print the letters, complete with addresses. Suddenly, fans weren't anonymous anymore; they could find each other in the pages of the pulp magazine, write to each other, and even meet to discuss their favorite stories. It seems basic today, but the nexus that the *Amazing Stories* letters department became was nothing short of a revelation for the fans of the fledgling genre. Soon other sci-fi pulp magazines popped up and followed Gernsback's example, with sizable letter columns of their own, adding to fans' networking opportunities.

As fans continued to become aware of each other, naturally they wanted to meet up in person, so the first science fiction convention took place, right around the same time that Robbins Barstow was editing *Tarzan and the Rocky Gorge*. That first event only had 15 to 20 people, as a group of fans from New York City, including future sci-fi great Frederick Pohl, went to Philadelphia to meet a similar-sized group of enthusiasts. Despite the small attendance, that first step helped pave the way for fan films in the coming decades, as sci-fi (and later, comic book and pop culture) conventions eventually became some of the few—if only—places to see the occasional fan film until the advent of public access cable television and, later, the World Wide Web.

While science fiction grew in popularity over the coming decades, so did home moviemaking; perhaps it was inevitable that the two hobbies would become intertwined. As far back as far as 1937, one of the earliest sci-fi fan clubs, the New York chapter of the International Science Association, would show home movies of its model rocketry experiments at meetings, usually followed by a discussion of making its own "amateur scientifilm"—a fantasy effort that was never produced. Just two years later, the first World Science Fiction Convention, held over the July Fourth weekend in New York City, presented Fritz Lang's 1926 classic, *Metropolis,* as part of its events; the screening set a precedent for films to be used in convention programming—a revolutionary move at a time when sci-fi fandom was centered almost entirely around the written word. Fan films would eventually make the leap to convention programming fodder in the decades to come.

In the meantime, home movie equipment continued to gain popularity while it also became easier to use, making cameras and projectors more accessible to average folks—like Hugh Hefner, for instance. Years before he became America's most famous publisher, he was just another teenager making movies in his basement (no, not *those* kinds of movies). Turns out Hef was a prototypical "Monster Kid," fascinated by the films of Bela Lugosi, Boris Karloff, and Peter Lorre, predating the monster craze of the fifties and sixties that kicked off around the time he put Marilyn Monroe on *Playboy*'s first cover. Hefner's interest peaked at age 16 with the creation of his 1942 silent 16mm epic, *Return from the Dead*—a concoction of reanimation themes from Frankenstein, mixed with the bloodsucking ways of Dracula. The 15-minute flick, set in the lab of a mad doctor in Transylvania, featured classmates, typed dialogue cards, and a corpse who kicked things off by pointing to the movie's title, painted on a dangling bedsheet.

The film itself is a precamp hoot: "Gene, what are you doing?" asks a shocked girl, to which a poorly mustached young Hef grimaces in response, "I'm going to bring Steve back to life!" Following time-honored tradition, nothing good comes of the experiment and the film culminates with the future bon vivant expiring on the floor as he writes "The End" in his own blood. Hefner's obsession with monsters subsided later that year by his own recollection, replaced by other, well-known passions, but he did return to filmmaking in the seventies as the executive producer of numerous films, including *Monty Python's And Now for Something Completely Different.*

The future media mogul wasn't alone in making fan films, as sales of home movie cameras were starting to take off across the United States. The arrival of World War II put a dent in that however, as might be expected, and even when American troops came home, the hobby took a while to stage a comeback. Part of that, according to Zimmerman's *Reel Families,* was because of a 25 percent excise tax on all photographic equipment, which was started during wartime. Once the war ended, photographic sales dropped precipitously—as much as 40 percent between 1948 and 1949 for the entire US photographic industry—until the tax was reduced to 10 percent in 1949.

As GIs came home, settled down, and started families, they wanted to preserve their memories on film. As a result, by 1952, according to a Bell & Howell annual report, 6 percent of US families owned home movie cameras—and that number exploded in the years to come. As film historian Leonard Maltin notes in the documentary *The Sci-Fi Boys,* "When I talk about 8mm to some people younger than I am, it sounds as if I'm talking about the Cro-Magnon era of communication, but for many, many years, there was barely a middle-class household in America that didn't have an 8mm movie projector and a camera to shoot home movies."

They'd finally broken through, and it's not hard to see why. Even though the technology was intended for recording birthdays and holidays, on some level, consumers realized that these gadgets were tools for the democratization of visual communication; the silver screen was no longer the sole province of Hollywood. They gave regular people a new way to indulge creative musings, pushing back at the ordinariness of postwar, often suburban, life by making films. The growing ubiquity of consumer movie gear meant that anyone could have his 15 minutes of fame—even if he was only famous in his own house.

Ironically, the progenitor of the "15 minutes" concept wasn't much interested in suburbia, but Andy Warhol, that cosmopolitan soul, was still quite taken by amateur filmmaking. The artist who revolutionized the postwar era by finding art in the same ordinary consumer society that people were trying to escape got his hands on a Bolex camera in the summer of 1963, and he, too, started making movies—including fan films.

Obsessed with Hollywood stars since he was a child, it was perhaps inevitable that Warhol would be drawn to filmmaking, trying his hand at the medium that created the imagery and personas from which he had drawn so much inspiration. At the same time that he was becoming the toast of the art world in the early sixties, an underground film scene was springing up in New York City; now that average suburban families were buying their own home movie gear, prices had dropped low enough that even starving artists could afford a camera. Sizing up the scene, Warhol was stirred; using consumer-grade visual media to make transgressive cinema could be another way to explore the relationships among art, consumption, and the culture of the times.

Among his first efforts, shot on silent black and white 16mm film, were a pair of loosely narrative efforts, *Tarzan and Jane Regained . . . Sort Of* (1963) and the mysterious *Batman Dracula* (1964). They were fan films, but as might be expected, their visuals and content were filtered through Warhol's own unusual aesthetic. In keeping with his alternate view of seeing things, he usually shot at 24 frames per second, but insisted that his films be screened at two-thirds that speed, thus ever so imperceptibly slowing down the world he'd captured.

Tarzan and Jane was produced while he visited Los Angeles in the fall of 1963; filmed mostly in his suite at the Beverly Hills Hotel, the 80-minute experimental parody featured Dennis Hopper in a supporting role, while the main characters were played by underground film star Taylor Mead and Warhol's first "superstar," Naomi Levin, who spent a good part of the film naked.

Returning to New York, Warhol shot *Batman Dracula* in July 1964, and, to this day, little is known about the flick. The film is said to have never been completed, or was completed as a two-hour movie but never shown, or was shown but only at art exhibitions—take your pick. The homage was not authorized by DC Comics; reputedly playing up homoerotic undertones in the

Batman character and featuring various actors dressed in aluminum foil jockstraps, it's debatable whether it would get a thumbs-up even today. The film's Dracula was played by Jack Smith, an underground film director who pioneered the camp aesthetic, and Warhol's direction of the film—and numerous subsequent efforts—is said to have been heavily informed by his lead actor's viewpoint.

Two years later, the legendary *Batman* TV series hit the air, presenting Hollywood's camp take on the character, complete with a visual style influenced by Warhol's pop art, making the artist's unseen fan film all the more intriguing. Would it have anticipated the TV show in its content and portrayal of the Dark Knight? We'll likely never know; since the film was (maybe) never completed, many Warhol scholars presume it has been lost, although some unearthed footage did appear in the documentaries *Andy Warhol: A Documentary Film* (2005) and *Jack Smith and the Destruction of Atlantis* (2006).

In the art world, Warhol was virtually peerless at the time, but when it came to making incoherent, nearly plotless fan films he had plenty of competition in the form of the nation's teenagers. The mass influx of movie cameras into postwar life came right as the baby boomers were becoming preteens; as a result, millions of young kids wanted to put Mom and Dad's new toy to work, fashioning their own movies that were inevitably inspired by what they were seeing at the local movie theater every weekend: monsters, spaceships, aliens, superheroes, and more. Feeding that desire to make their own genre flicks was *Famous Monsters of Filmland,* a movie magazine edited by megafan Forrest J. Ackerman for an audience comprised almost exclusively of teenage boys obsessed with horror movies.

"It was a far more innocent time," explains Joe Busam, producer of *Monster Kid Home Movies,* a DVD compilation of not-so-scary fan films from the fifties and sixties. "Horror in films and literature was considered adult-oriented, and not healthy for kids and teenagers. As a result, this added to the intrigue for kids—the movies were scary and watching them became a right of passage, but because of parental and social disapproval, they became a sort of forbidden fruit."

For many of those young fans, *Famous Monsters* was the horrific snack to tide them over between helpings of fruit, and the magazine's editor served it up with glee. Ackerman had made his mark in fandom early on, writing his first published letter to a science fiction magazine in 1929 at age 14, going on to become a prolific correspondent to the pulp mags in the years to come. His encyclopedic knowledge of science fiction and horror movies led to his being hired in 1957 to write a one-shot magazine special about movie monsters; the resulting issue did so well that it became an ongoing publication that "Uncle Forry" wrote from "the Ackermansion" in Hollywood for nearly 200 issues.

While it could be argued that Ackerman's greatest contribution to science fiction was that he actually coined the term "sci-fi," his efforts to educate the young audience were equally impressive. At the time, most movie magazines focused solely on the stars, with gossip, fashion, and the like. Here, however, was a publication that marched defiantly to its own drummer, interviewing special-effects artists, makeup and wardrobe technicians, screenwriters, directors, and others. The magazine also sponsored amateur film contests from time to time, which seems appropriate, given that Ackerman appeared in one of the first fan-produced films, *The Genie*, with fellow mega-fans Bjo Trimble and Fritz Leiber, in the fifties.

His readers had plenty of choices when it came to home movie cameras. Both the 8mm and 16mm formats were still going strong, but had been around long enough that one could buy a secondhand camera cheaply, in part because Kodak introduced the Super 8 film format (also called Super 8) in 1965. The format was heralded for the film's high quality, because although it was 8mm wide, Super 8 had smaller sprocket holes, which allowed for an image area that was roughly 25 percent larger than regular 8mm film. Because of this and the cameras' inexpensive prices (they were usually made of cheap plastic), Super 8 was the last major innovation in amateur filmmaking before video cameras caught on in the early eighties. The format was ideal for Ackerman's acolytes, too, as it required a lot less technical expertise to get started (i.e., no need to ask Dad for help); users simply popped a standard 50-foot film cartridge into the camera and that was that.

For fans who wanted to make their own flicks, *Famous Mon-*

sters featured plenty of "how-to" articles that explained the ways stop-motion animation and other effects were created—information that wasn't available in books or taught in film schools at the time. As a result, many filmmakers today, including Peter Jackson (*The Lord of the Rings, King Kong*), John Landis (*Animal House, The Blues Brothers, An American Werewolf in London*), Joe Dante (*Gremlins, Matinee*), Dennis Murren (special effects for everything from *Star Wars* to *Jurassic Park*), and plenty of others, credit the magazine with igniting their passion for the movies and filmmaking.

While *Famous Monsters* turned makeup artists into heroes for thousands of teens, it also occasionally took one of its readers and introduced him to the masses. Kids would write in to Ackerman, bragging about their homemade efforts to animate crude clay figures or stage gangster shoot-outs with the kid next door, but one persistent teen from Chicago seemed to stand out from the pack, and wound up being featured in the magazine throughout the sixties. As Maltin puts it in *The Sci-Fi Boys,* "I was in awe of guys like Don Glut."

• • •

The name Donald F. Glut (pronounced "Gloot") is known to many film fans for a variety of reasons. Readers of *Famous Monsters* know him as the kid who kept sending in photos of his home movie epics that inevitably featured a dinosaur, Dracula, or perhaps Captain America. Fans of "classic" Saturday morning kids' TV might know the name from his screen credits, writing episodes of *Land of the Lost* and *Transformers,* while film buffs attracted to late-night cable TV fare may know his work directing B movies like *Dinosaur Valley Girls.* But most folks, if they know his name, recall Glut for having written one of the big best-sellers of the eighties—a book that's still in print and graces the shelves of sci-fi fans around the globe: the novelization of *The Empire Strikes Back.*

Long before he was writing about Darth Vader or inventing Castle Grayskull (yeah, that was him), Glut was a fan filmmaker, having started making movies in 1953, when his age was still in the single digits. By the time he ended his fan film career to go pro, some 16 years later, the amateur auteur had made 41 movies—all of which were commercially released in the two-DVD set *I Was a Teenage Movie Maker.*

Single-parent households weren't that common in the fifties, but that was his world. Living in a three-story apartment building in the north corner of Chicago's Lakeview district, Julia Glut did her best to raise her son, working as a typist to make ends meet while supporting his ideas and dreams as only a mother could. In fact, Don Glut credits her as a key reason why he eventually went into show business, opining that moms tend to let kids follow their interests, whereas dads push their sons to do traditional activities like sports. Baseball would have been an inevitable part of the young Glut's life, too, as the family lived within walking distance of Wrigley Field, home of the Chicago Cubs.

Frank C. Glut never had the chance to take his son to a game, however. A first lieutenant in the Air Force, he flew B-24 Bombers over Europe until he was killed in action over Benthe, Germany in February 1945. The 28-year-old left behind an infant son just shy of a year old, as well as, it turned out, an old Christmas present that would change the young boy's life forever. In 1940, when Frank and Julia were dating, she'd given him a 16mm film camera for Christmas; the gift provided a lasting chronicle of their years together, but eventually it became a crucial part of Don's life as well.

Like most kids in the fifties, the youngest Glut spent a lot of time at the movies. Today, the Music Box Theatre on North Southport Street is an 800-seat relic of the 1920s that hosts independent and foreign films, but back then it was the place where local kids spent their weekends catching the latest serials, Westerns, and rereleased Frankenstein flicks. Going to the movies wasn't an everyday treat though, so in an age long before regular people had home theaters, Glut dreamed of bringing the filmgoing experience home.

"At first, I didn't want to make movies as much as I wanted to show them," he explains. "We had a 16mm movie camera, splicer and screen in our home. And I loved movies about dinosaurs and monsters, but in those days, no one was selling such films to the public. I reasoned that the only way to show a movie with a monster on my own home movie screen was to make it myself."

Don Glut spent much of his teen years behind the camera; after making his first flick at age nine, he made 40 amateur movies over the next 16 years.
(Courtesy of Front Line Films)

It wasn't long before the impressionable kid was talking his mom into letting him use that old movie camera lying around their apartment. Julia always encouraged her son to follow his dreams, but nonetheless remained levelheaded about it; he may have wanted to become a cinematic prodigy, but the nine-year-old still wasn't allowed to play with the camera by himself.

As a result, his first films found the young director explaining to Cameraman Mom what he wanted to shoot, as he made his toys do battle with each other. A broken shutter smeared the images on the film, however, discouraging the budding cineaste enough that he didn't make another movie for three years. Once he did, however, he caught the filmmaking fever and soon couldn't stop producing homebrewed genre flicks and fan films.

Much as Robbins Barstow had done 20 years earlier, the preteen Glut set up a makeshift theater and charged admission to see films in his building's basement—a space that doubled as everything from a cave to a mad scientist's laboratory to a spaceship, depending on what movie he was shooting. Meanwhile, other parts of his neighborhood became his movie lot—alleys became hiding spaces for the Wolfman, his apartment building became a castle, and most exciting, a nearby Jewish cemetery on North Clark Street with graves from the early 1800s became the location for plenty of monster movies, since it contained numerous real gravestones inscribed FRANKENSTEIN.

Soon, Glut's mini-movies gained attention as the subject of multipage articles in pulp magazines like *Famous Monsters, Fantastic Monsters, Scary Monsters* (you may note a trend here), *Castle of Frankenstein, Screen Thrills,* and others. Photos from his films, featuring dinosaurs crossing grassy plains (nearby Schiller Woods Forest Preserve), superheroes soaring across the sky (dolls on fishing wire), and so on, thrilled amateur movie fans across the nation.

In fact, Glut made such a splash that years later John Carpenter—director of *Halloween* and *Escape from New York,* among others—told *Fangoria* magazine when recalling his youth, "There was one fellow who was really prolific; his name was Don Glut. He was making and starring in these incredible movies—Captain Marvel movies, various monster things—he was the king! At the time, what I wanted was to be like Don Glut. I never really did anything as good; I was never that technically proficient."

Of course, Carpenter and Glut were just two of the thousands making their own homemade horror shows. "Kids found it was a way to realize their creativity and imagination, a way to make their daydreams and urge to playact a reality," comments *Monster Kid Home Movies* producer Busam. "Additionally, I think it was a way of dealing with their fears. David Colton, an editor at *USA Today,* said in our DVD's introduction that 'by playing monsters, it kept the real monsters away.' In retrospect, I believe that to be true."

If the youth of America was using horror fan films to work out issues in a primitive *I'm OK, You're Frankenstein's Monster*–like fashion, Glut was using them to, as they would say today, build his personal brand. He began working in earnest to have the films seen by as many people as possible, donating copies to a local museum's circulating collection so that they would be loaned out to schools, and even getting one shown on a local late-night TV show.

Most unusually, the flicks were screened inside a former Chi-

Glut's 1964 fan film, *Captain America Battles the Red Skull*, was shown in "underground" theaters at the time; Glut went on to write adventures starring the hero for Marvel Comics. *(Courtesy of Front Line Films)*

cago Transit Authority bus that had been remodeled by beatnik D. Ray Craig into a rolling movie theater dubbed "The Great Mother Ship" (it was Craig who would first tell Glut about the University of Southern California film school, which they wound up attending together). The bus drove around all day, picking up groovy bohemians who wanted to watch underground movies, and the result was that not only were his films brought before a new audience but they were appreciated in a whole new way as well. While Glut may have been fairly serious when he made efforts like *Captain America Battles the Red Skull*, the movies were observed as tongue-in-cheek romps when viewed by hepcats informed by the recent arrival of Susan Sontag's groundbreaking *Notes on Camp* essay. Demurred Glut, "It was a very unusual, creative time."

That creativity was being expressed in a multitude of ways across the country, most famously through the music and fashions of the times, but the traditionally more bookish realm of science fiction was experiencing changes, too. One of the most notable arrivals was *The Man From U.N.C.L.E.*, a hit espionage series that developed the first modern fandom following. It wasn't alone, however; Hollywood spent much of the sixties producing comic book–, fantasy-, and science fiction–based TV series, ranging from *Batman* and *Lost in Space* to *The Addams Family* and *Voyage to the Bottom of the Sea,* to dross like *Captain Nice* and *My Favorite Martian*. While their quality varied, the shows heightened science fiction's profile considerably, and a corresponding rise in young, baby boomer fans began to alter the staid state of fandom in short order.

The realm of science fiction and fantasy was fairly tightly defined, and there just wasn't room in it for enthusiasm about, say, James Bond or the Green Hornet—although plenty of those characters' fans were also sci-fi aficionados. This led to the rise of "media fandom"—a catch-all label now used to describe rabid, geek-out fervor for anything from comic books to *The Dukes of Hazzard* to Neal Stephenson novels. While media fandom first flowered with *U.N.C.L.E.*, it went hog wild a few years later with *Star Trek,* as a letter-writing campaign staged by fans famously saved the series from cancellation after its second season. While the show was shut down for good in the spring of 1969, the Newark Public Library reportedly held the first convention, The *Star Trek* Conference, on March 1 of that year. Attended by about 55 people, it set the stage for the *Trek*-only events that exploded in popularity throughout the seventies.

Riding sci-fi's wave of popularity in the sixties, however, the annual Worldcon convention kept plowing along, held in a different major city every year, while smaller local sci-fi/fantasy, comic book, and horror conventions started popping up around the country. To fans who wanted to focus on specific genres, the "cons" were a necessity, but to young Don Glut, looking to reach as many viewers as possible, they were opportunities, and he began showing his movies at them whenever possible.

While many baby boomers lived in fear of being drafted and sent to Vietnam after high school, once again, fan films altered the course of Glut's life, as he was turned down to serve, having torn ligaments in both ankles years earlier when he jumped off his garage for a film stunt. Instead, Glut headed off to the University of Southern California in Los Angeles, where he was roommates with Randal Kleiser, who in turn went on to become George Lucas's roommate and, more important, direct the hit films *Grease* and *The Blue Lagoon*.

In Chicago, Glut had received nothing but recognition and encouragement for his films, but things changed once he landed in California. There, his efforts slowly went semipro, due to the Western and B-movie "stars" whom he convinced to appear in them, but the films received critical reactions—not from genre fans who loved them but from his professors at film school. While tales of the fantastic have kept Hollywood solvent since the dawn of moviemaking, they were considered far too immature to be taken seriously in the halls of academia.

"When I was at USC film school, I was not on good terms with the faculty," he recalls. "They looked down on you if you wanted to make commercial movies, because they wanted you to make Italian, avant-garde, New Wave types of films and documentaries and things. I almost got thrown out of USC because I wanted to make science fiction films and monster movies; this was long before Lucas donated all that money and they suddenly decided, 'Hey, commercial films are pretty good!'"

If he was unpopular with the faculty, Glut still made quite an impression on his fellow students; John Milius (who later cowrote *Apocalypse Now* with Lucas and directed his own genre flicks such as Arnold Schwarzenegger's *Conan the Barbarian*) went so far as to make a semifictional documentary simply titled *Glut!* Don agreed to be in it, but only with the provision that if it Milius ever remade it for a studio, he'd be cast in the title role. Milius balked, claiming Glut wasn't right for the part.

While USC's faculty may have disdained commercial films, such flicks were certainly on the students' minds, in part because of Glut. Aided by friends, he would secretly commandeer 16mm classroom film projectors to show the movie serials of his youth to fellow students. Glut explains, "When you read the interviews with Lucas and he talks about seeing serials at USC, well, I was the guy running them—at great risk to my own position there in the school. I used to go to parties and bring 16mm films that he and a lot of other people who became very prominent directors used to watch, and maybe that was the inspiration for Indiana Jones and Star Wars, somewhat in an indirect way."

After graduation, Glut closed out his fan film career in 1969 with *Spider-Man,* which found the webcrawler doing battle in a state park. The long string of amateur efforts had to end, however, as his time was tied up as he tried to launch music and acting careers before finally settling on writing, spending most of the coming decades writing comics (*Ghost Rider* and *Star Wars* among them), scripts for Saturday-morning kids' shows, and more than 30 books about dinosaurs.

Eventually the good karma engendered by potentially inspiring George Lucas paid off when he wound up writing the novelization of *The Empire Strikes Back,* but today, Glut has mixed feelings about the project:

> They told me that book had a million copies in advance sales before they asked me to write it, so had anybody else written it, maybe even if it had blank pages and just said *The Empire Strikes Back* on it, it probably still would have done very well. Then I got divorced right after that, and it's community property. The deal wasn't that great anyway—it wasn't like I got a fortune out of that, but I must say one thing: That book is a door opener, because it's still in print, it was a bestseller, and even though it was just a novelization—it wasn't my story—when you say that title, it's like magic and people think it's a much bigger deal than it is.

While the book did open doors, it never cracked the one that Glut wanted to unlock more than any other: the gateway to directing professional films. Tired of waiting, he wrote his own movie—a dinosaur genre epic, of course—and finally helmed his first feature film in 1997 at age 53—a full 44 years after producing his first home movie. The start of a new career directing low-budget, late-night cable fare, *Dinosaur Valley Girls* found the title characters wearing only slightly more clothes than the dinosaurs, but that was the least of Glut's concerns.

1969's *Spider-Man* was Glut's last amateur movie before turning pro; today, he is a prolific author and genre filmmaker. *(Courtesy of Front Line Films)*

"In mainstream Hollywood," he notes, "if you're not firmly entrenched in the business, there's a good chance you're not going to work after 40. Suddenly, my first opportunity came when I was over 50! When we got the go-ahead to do *Dinosaur Valley Girls,* I remember standing on a mountaintop looking down on the valley location, wondering, 'Am I even going to be able to survive this? I don't get any exercise or eat the right foods—what if I die on the set? What are my investors going to say?' And I really seriously thought about that."

What made the five-day shoot finish on time and on budget, it turned out, were the skills Glut had developed while making fan films:

> A lot of the time- and cost-cutting things I learned making amateur movies, I apply to my professional films because

> that's the only way to get them done. The sun is always going down too fast, the permit is about to expire, the actress is freaking out—all these weird things happen when you don't have the luxury of a big budget, so I do things fast. When they say, "We're not going to get done," I sit down and say, "Don't talk to me for five minutes." I picture the whole thing as a complete scene and go, "OK, now you have to trust me—we're going to do this without slating it maybe and we'll shoot this and this, but I guarantee you, it will cut together." And it always does.

• • •

Don Glut is, in many ways, a prototypical baby boomer, and his shorts are a fascinating distillation of the various media—movies, TV, print, and radio—that catered to the giant youth population of the era. His films can easily be seen as a prism of the influences around kids of the time, incorporating everything from monster movies and *Blackboard Jungle* in the fifties to the styles and look of the burgeoning flower power movement in the late sixties. It was a time rife with cultural warfare as his generation came of age, striving to make itself heard. Political and sociological expression was the name of the game, and in 1969, right around the time Glut was nearly done locking horns with the powers that be at USC, another young filmmaker in Los Angeles was having his own hard time at film school. The educational facility was the Art Center College of Design (which he later referred to as "the Nazi Training School of Art" in a 2006 radio interview), and the student was Marv Newland.

Born in Oakland, California, in 1947, Newland was like Glut in that he had grown up spending his Saturdays watching marathons at the movies, but while the former was enthralled by Dracula, the Wolfman, and the rest, Newland relished cartoons. The experience was indelible enough that when the Art Center began offering film courses, he dumped his design classes and switched to the world of celluloid. Initially, Newland gravitated toward live-action productions, but grew increasingly frustrated with the medium, the breaking point coming early one morning as he worked diligently on the thesis film that would allow him to graduate.

Newland was attempting to film the perfect sunrise for his picture, but clouds kept ruining the shot. Soon after, the film that he'd been working on for over a month got scrapped. With only two weeks left before the final assignment was due, Newland changed media, using line-drawn animation as he started from scratch on a new, soon to be legendary fan film: *Bambi Meets Godzilla.*

The British Film Institute's library synopsis of the short reads simply: "About wild animals of various proportions and the problem of survival." For those who haven't seen it, however, the blurry black and white film starts simply enough with a young deer gently noshing on grass in a field, while a murky recording of "Ranz Des Vaches" from Gioacchino Rossini's *William Tell* liltingly plays. The credits roll seemingly forever, and then, finally, Bambi does indeed meet Godzilla as the music changes to a concluding, lingering piano chord that cops the Beatles' "A Day in the Life." The end.

The "meeting" is undeniably similar to the opening credits of the TV show *Monty Python's Flying Circus,* in which Cupid's foot from Agnolo Bronzino's painting *An Allegory of Venus and Cupid* suddenly appears, but Newland wasn't influenced by it as is sometimes assumed. While both the film and the BCC *Python* series debuted in 1969, the show didn't begin airing in the United States until 1974. As a result, it's virtually impossible for Newland to have known about Terry Gilliam's animated *Python* intro while he spent two weeks working on the film in the room he lived in, rented from another animation legend—Adriana Caselotti, who had voiced the female lead in Disney's *Snow White and the Seven Dwarfs.*

Regardless of where the idea came from, the reaction to *Bambi Meets Godzilla* was instantaneous: people loved it. It's not hard to see why. With such a simplistic plot (and calling it "plot" is a stretch), the short is essentially an animated Rorschach blot: the metaphor one attributes to it likely says more about the viewer than the film itself.

Given the paucity of independent animation at the time, most took it as an in-your-face, protopunk-styled jab at Disney. Given the grim condition of the United States itself in those days, however, it's just as easy to perceive the darkly humored fan film as a political allegory, as the hippie movement that espoused peace and love ("Bambi") was crushed by Vietnam, a corrupt government, and escalating riots across America. The short may have been fueled by sick humor, but the knowing laughter that it evoked presaged the cynical, exhausted attitude that arrived with the 1970s. A few months later, the last remnants of the dream founded by 1967's "Summer of Love" would be burned at the stake by the Rolling Stones' violent Altamont Speedway concert, but a short like *Bambi Meets Godzilla* proves that the tides were already turning well before then.

For a tiny movie that only cost $300 to make, the film has had a lasting cultural impact. The short quickly became an underground sensation, shown with midnight movies around the globe, used as between-movie filler on cable TV throughout the 1980s, and appearing over the years in different video collections. Today, it continues to be a staple of animation festivals around the globe, and in the book, *The 50 Greatest Cartoons*, 1,000 animation pros polled on their all-time favorites chose it as number 38.

The fan film has its fans; no less than David Mamet called it "One of the great cinematic delights of the sixties" in his similarly entitled tome, *Bambi vs. Godzilla*, while William Tsutsui, in *Godzilla on My Mind: Fifty Years of the King of Monsters*, opined that it "may well be the greatest cinematic tribute to Godzilla ever." The film's ingratiation into modern culture is astounding for an underground short—numerous pastors have used *Bambi Meets Godzilla* to illustrate sermons concerning Hezekiah and the Assyrians, while academic papers on topics as varied as psychoanalysis and computer networking have referred to it. Steven Spielberg once proudly described his 1971 TV movie *Duel* to critics as *Bambi Meets Godzilla*, and the short was even noted as "brief—but hilariously effective" in the 2001 book *Jurassic Classics*, written by one Donald F. Glut.

Glut and Newland each tenaciously headed their film careers away from the mainstream and into the far more difficult waters of independent production. However, Glut has never wavered in his pursuit of working in the genres explored in his early fan films, while Newland has often aimed for more varied artistic expression. As a result, the animator has mixed feelings about his most popular work, having half-joked to the Canadian movie magazine

Take One, "That film ruined my career." Of course, it did nothing of the sort, instead proving to be a useful calling card and a perennial moneymaker (Animation legend Bill Plympton once claimed that *Bambi Meets Godzilla* grossed more than $100,000). After graduation, Newland went on to forge a career in Canadian independent animation; since moving to Vancouver in 1971, he's made dozens of films and commercials, won numerous awards, animated two TV specials based on Gary Larson's *The Far Side* cartoon strip, taught at the Vancouver Film School, and has become a legend and iconoclast in a field that has had few of either in recent times.

Despite all that, however, he remains best known for his first work, a short that he characterized on the KBOO radio show *Words & Pictures* as "a superficial, simple-minded, inept piece of filmmaking." The joke of *Bambi Meets Godzilla* is a timeless one, but the short's lasting popularity and influence have brought a new meaning to the cliché that in comedy, timing is everything, as he philosophically points out: "I think that if that film was made today, it . . . would have immediately been dumped onto the Internet, it would have been a joke for about two weeks, and then it would have gone away. So I'm lucky to have made it back in 1969—in the era of motion pictures on film."

4
Sci-Fi, Superheroes, and *Cinemagic* (1970–1977)

Marv Newland might be right that the fuss over *Bambi Meets Godzilla* would've "gone away" if his movie been made today and posted on You Tube, but that overlooks one key factor: In today's Internet age, things don't "go away." They may be forgotten, but whether it's a fan film, an illegal song file, or a photo of your dog naked, things posted on the Net tend to stick around, floating about in the digital ether forever. That experience had a precursor in the world of media fandom, however, as the rise of *Star Trek* conventions in the 1970s illustrated all too well, proving the old adage that absence makes the heart grow fonder.

It wasn't really "absence," of course—if anything, *Star Trek* refused to leave. Once Paramount stopped producing new episodes in the spring of 1969, the show entered syndication and it was then that the space saga truly became a phenomenon. Perhaps it was because of the show's morality tales, possibly it rode the wave of excitement over the first moonwalk in the summer of 1969, or maybe it was just that a key *Trek* demographic—grade-schoolers—no longer had to beg to stay up past bedtime to see it. Regardless, the show was "discovered" posthumously and quickly developed fans of all ages.

While the first *Trek* event had been held in 1969, the first true convention, featuring folks involved with the TV program, took place in 1972, attracting 3,000 fans—not bad for a show that, by then, had been off the air as long as it had been on. More than 6,000 people turned up for the 1973 meeting, and 15,000 came out for the 1974 gathering—while another 6,000 were turned away at the door. With explosive growth like that, *Star Trek*–only events left the sci-fi conventions choking on their space dust.

That separatist phenomenon was encouraged, however; for years, the show's fans had been sneered at by long-time sci-fi conventioneers who "dismissed *Star Trek* as science fiction for non-readers," according to Francesca Coppa in the academic essay "A Brief History of Media Fandom." That elitist attitude had been brewing for a while, fostered by the influx of sci-fi TV fans that had buoyed and built up the conventions during the sixties. Of course, as any hipster will tell you, something is only cool until *everyone* thinks it's cool—then it's hideously uncool. Resenting all the new kids moving in on their turf, longtime sci-fi fans pushed back and watched as those groups splintered off in the seventies to hold specialized conventions keyed to their interests in horror, comics, or even, God forbid, *Star Trek*.

It was at those early *Trek* conventions that the first inklings of "vidding," the only major form of fan cinema created by and for women, cropped up. In vidding, fans create music videos ("songvids") by editing TV series or movie footage together to explore character relationships or emotional content. The communities that participate in it generally keep a low profile, in part due to copyright concerns, but mostly because many songvid editors don't want to be widely identified with their creations, which sometimes delve into controversial areas such as slash (gay) fiction. Kandy Fong is generally seen as the inventor of the vidding form; as far back as 1975, she ran synchronized *Star Trek* slide shows at conventions, using multiple projectors to change images with a song's pace. As an example, one presentation featured shots of Spock, backed by Leonard Nimoy's creaky cover of Joni Mitchell's "Both Sides Now" from his 1968 LP, *The Way I Feel*. Together, the song and images explored the fact that the character is half Vulcan and half human; the end result was so clever that *Trek* creator Gene Roddenberry videotaped it so he could own a copy.

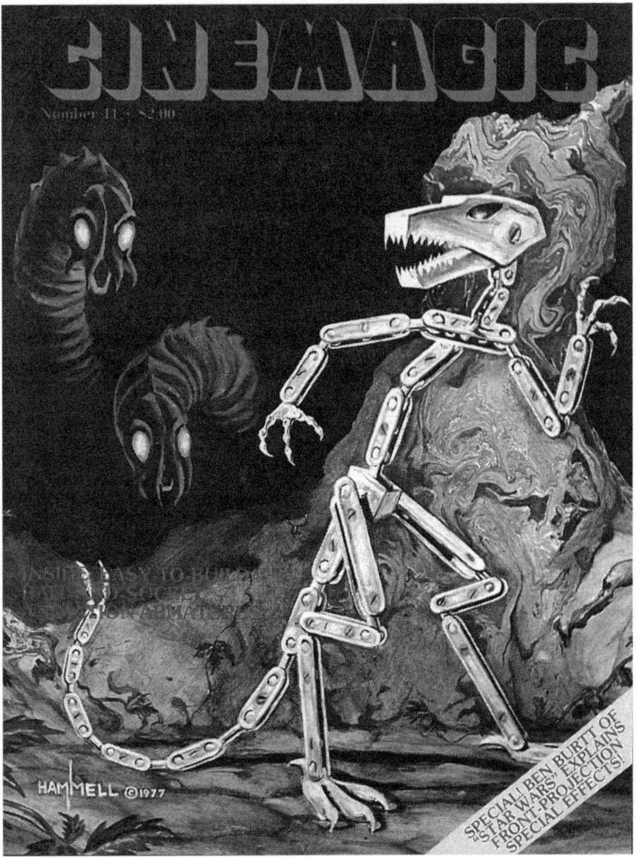

Cinemagic magazine taught amateur filmmakers how to create special effects for their Super 8 and 16mm flicks.
(Courtesy of Greg Dohler)

Women didn't have a monopoly on reinterpretive visual *Trek* media at conventions, however; fan films were present from the start. The late Ed Emshwiller, dean of the School of Film/Video at the California Institute of the Arts, started out illustrating science fiction magazine covers but began making movies in the fifties, eventually receiving a Ford Foundation grant in 1964. Films such as his short *Relativity*, a meditation about humankind's place in the universe, were often shown at sci-fi conventions, and it wasn't long before his son, Peter, started getting his own flicks screened at them as well. Working with his dad in 1969, 10-year-old Peter shot *Jr. Star Trek*, one of the first fan films about the famed series. The eight-minute, 16mm short eventually aired on PBS and became a staple of *Trek* conventions for years to come.

By that time, however, most sci-fi related conventions were screening amateur films and, invariably, stop-motion animation was part of the programming. Sensing a groundswell, Don Dohler, an amateur sci-fi/horror filmmaker in Baltimore, Maryland, created *Cinemagic,* a magazine dedicated strictly to stop-motion animation and homemade special effects; Dohler published 1,000 copies of his first issue in 1972.

Cinemagic provided aspiring genre filmmakers with much needed info on how to create flying rocket effects, build stop-motion armatures, or fake a bloody, disgusting chunk of scalp. While the magazine often sported articles by professional filmmakers and special-effects artists—among them *Star Wars* sound designer Ben Burtt and effects makeup great Rick Baker—most of it was written by Dohler, who had made amateur movies since he was 12. Ironically, he didn't become a professional filmmaker until after he'd been producing *Cinemagic* for a few years—and the move was due to a life-changing experience on January 27, 1976, his 30th birthday.

Dohler was working as the payroll manager of a local fast food chain when two men with sawed-off shotguns broke into his office, threw everyone to the floor and demanded that he open the safe. It was a bad situation—but it got even worse when, lying face-down with a gun barrel to his skull, he had to break the news: "You're gonna have to shoot me because we don't know the combination." Everyone in the room sweated it out for over an hour until the restaurant's manager returned, opened the safe, and let the robbers take off with heavy coin bags.

Having stared death in the face on a day about living, Dohler decided life was too short to be spent on a career he didn't love. Within months, he'd written, directed, and produced his first B movie, *The Alien Factor,* which became a basic cable mainstay for years. The cast and crew were made up of friends, associates, and even *Cinemagic* readers: fan filmmakers who worked on *Paragon's Paragon,* an ambitious, $1,900 *Star Trek* fan film featured on the cover of the spring 1976 issue, became professionals when they were pressed into service for Dohler's $4,000 production of *The*

Don Dohler, peering through his Bolex camera.
(Courtesy of videokitchen.tv LLC)

Alien Factor.

With each issue *Cinemagic* continued to grow, and much as the letters column in *Amazing Stories* had brought sci-fi fans together in one place decades earlier, *Cinemagic* became a nexus for amateur filmmakers by letting readers send in synopses of their movies. For amateurs making films that would be screened for dozens of people, the listings were a signal flare to the rest of the world about their movies that no one otherwise knew (or likely cared) about. Finding their films listed in print gave readers a burst of encouragement and proof that at least someone somewhere took them seriously.

Getting the rest of the world to treat amateur and semipro productions with respect—fan films or otherwise—has always been a problem, but for one fan in the early 1970s the situation was particularly frustrating: Marvel Comics loved his home-brewed Spider-Man movie so much that it promoted the flick to its entire readership. It was everything he'd dreamed of—but not quite enough.

• • •

Most comic book fans have never heard of Bruce Cardozo's 1974 epic *Spider-Man versus Kraven the Hunter*—a turn of events that's surprising when you consider that the story behind it involves people as varied as punk rock legend Tommy Ramone and Spider-Man's creator Stan Lee.

The reasons that the fan film vanished without a trace—even though at one point, it had been hyped by Marvel Comics itself—are both complicated and simple. One could say that Cardozo reached beyond his limits, got swept up in youthful enthusiasm, or simply refused to take no for an answer, but the rejection that ended the project turned what would have been a triumph for any fledgling filmmaker into a frustrating memory.

Growing up in the Bronx, Cardozo stood out among the local kids, making his mark filming home movies that aped the same serials that eventually inspired *Raiders of the Lost Ark*. While adults in the area might have dismissed his perpetual running around with a 16mm camera as childhood antics, Cardozo proved to be a lasting inspiration to his pals, including author Alan Kaufman, whose acclaimed 2000 memoir, *Jew Boy*, spends most of one chapter covering how Cardozo (renamed Bruce Weiss) tried to make his own superhero movie, *Voodoo Kid*. Cardozo's take on it? "It's mostly true—kind of about the hardships of making a film in the Bronx . . . or in any neighborhood besides Hollywood." (Keep in mind that when *Jew Boy*'s "Bruce Weiss" needs to film police racing to a crime scene and staging a manhunt, he simply throws a garbage can through a stranger's window and documents the ensuing chaos. As a wise man once suggested, "'Nuff said.")

Attending the High School of Art and Design in Manhattan, Cardozo furthered his efforts to learn filmmaking by taking classes in photography, where he became friends with Amy Heckerling, who would go on to direct *Fast Times at Ridgemont High* and *Clueless*. Eventually they both attended the Tisch School of the Arts at New York University (NYU) in Manhattan's Greenwich Village, where they wound up in film classes with future megaproducer Joel Silver (*The Matrix, Die Hard, Lethal Weapon*), who starred in one of Heckerling's student shorts, and fellow Bronx native, writer/director Martin Brest (*Beverly Hills Cop, Midnight Run, Gigli*), who eventually cameoed in *Fast Times at Ridgemont High*.

That Spider-Man was on Cardozo's mind while he attended the school isn't surprising—Spidey fought crime all over Manhattan; his alter ego, Peter Parker, attended Empire State University, which was clearly based on NYU; and the fictional hero lived in Queens, which Cardozo's family moved to during his college years.

Also, the young filmmaker became friends with a fellow comics fan who would eventually write for Spider-Man extensively: Marv Wolfman. A budding artist at the time, Wolfman, who attended the High School of Art and Design a few years before Cardozo, went on to become a comic book legend, helming Marvel Comics as editor in chief for two years and writing classic runs of *Amazing Spider-Man, Daredevil, Fantastic Four,* and *Tomb of Dracula* before moving to DC Comics to launch *The New Teen Titans* and scribe the landmark series *Crisis on Infinite Earths* in 1985.

Back when they became friends in the late sixties, according to Cardozo, Wolfman sold him—via Cardozo's father, a comic book dealer—a number of old comics, including an *Amazing Spider-Man #1* for $1.50. Perhaps unsurprisingly, Wolfman refutes the claim entirely: "I did not sell Bruce any books, especially not *Spidey #1*. Now, I did know him and I know about the [Spider-Man] movie . . . so I think this is just a faulty memory of his. Far as I know, I still have the book . . . somewhere." And as for the purported jewel of Cardozo's comic collection? "I sold it a few years later," he says, "for 20 to 30 bucks. Kinda too soon."

Today, near-mint copies of *Amazing Spider-Man #1* regularly go for over $7,000.

Comics weren't Cardozo's only reading material during the sixties, however; like many kids, he was an avid reader of *Famous Monsters of Filmland*, and loved learning the latest about the filmmaking adventures of—wait for it—Don Glut. "Don was the father of all this and I have the highest regard for him," says Cardozo. "He was as much a childhood inspiration as Stan Lee."

Unlike Glut, however, Cardozo didn't meet with much academic resistance to his dreams of comic-fueled cinema at NYU, so he decided to make a fan film for an assignment during his junior year in the fall of 1972. The class was experimental film, and the directive was to make a five-minute short; while most

Spider-Man versus Kraven the Hunter, a 1974 fan film shot in New York City, was made with the encouragement of Stan Lee and the Marvel Comics bullpen.
(Courtesy of Bruce Cardozo)

students took it as a license to conjure sub–*Un Chein Andalou* surrealism, Cardozo saw an opportunity to try difficult special effects and present a superhero in a dramatic light, unlike the then recent *Batman* TV show of the sixties. Intrigued, his professor Peter Glushanok gave the go-ahead, and the filmmaker teamed with classmates Richard Eberhardt and Art Schweitzer for the project.

Before the film was pitched to his prof, however, Cardozo asked for—and received—consent from Spider-Man's creator, Marvel Comics publisher Stan Lee. "That was one of the smart business moves, and I still have his letter today," recalls Cardozo. "They gave us noncommercial release on it to show it at film festivals, student things, and so on."

While it certainly wasn't the first fan film to be made for a class, it took about two seconds for the mere aspiration of an A to get thrown out the window; settling for a good grade wouldn't be enough for Cardozo and company. Instead, the three students decided to aim for a higher goal. They would make something so spectacular that Marvel Comics itself would want it to release as a professional movie. When the dust finally settled, their 5-minute assignment was a 20-minute epic, completed 18 months and $5,000 later (and that's in early 1970s dollars, when gas was 36 cents a gallon).

To start, they needed a story, a script, and storyboards—and of course, there were hundreds to choose from, because Marvel published them monthly. Finding the right issue to adapt was actually easier than might be expected, because it all came down to deciding which of Spidey's foes could be created successfully for the big screen. The Green Goblin would look ridiculous on film; Dr. Octopus was far too complicated with his many arms; the Lizard (a man-sized lizard in a lab coat) was both doable and laughable, but Kraven . . . now there was a villain they could pull off. The towering bad guy—an insane safari hunter with extraordinary strength and keen senses—was first introduced in *Amazing Spider-Man #15*, so that was the issue to adapt. Its plot, which knocked off the classic short story and film *The Most Dangerous Game* was simple enough: evil newspaper editor J. Jonah Jameson imports Kraven to New York to hunt down Spider-Man. It was perfect—the villain didn't require masks or gizmos, and they knew an actor who looked just like him, down to the bushy mustache.

In fact, the only casting problem was that their "Peter Parker," actor Joe Ellison, was less than enthused about getting in the superhero costume, so Eberhardt gamely suited up, playing the webcrawler throughout the flick in addition to his work editing and creating animation to simulate spider web shooting. Schweitzer contributed, too, as the fan film's director of photography. Soon, they had their assignment fulfilled, but that wasn't enough for what Cardozo had in mind: "We had a good five-minute piece in the first year, but it needed more than just the wild special effects—I had to get the story in there, the characters. I knew we needed more to carry it."

Realizing they were onto something, the team got NYU's permission to continue working on the project for film classes in their senior year. Then on August 1, 1973, they screened the short for Lee, editor-in-chief Roy Thomas, and others at Marvel, to show what they'd accomplished, and, more important, to try and convince Lee to let them make a feature-length Spider-Man movie for profit.

As Cardozo recalled, the publisher simply didn't go for it, citing that money was tight due to paper shortages. In response, the moviemakers found financial backers who offered to go into business with Marvel, but Lee reportedly still declined—and did so every time the trio stopped in to show the latest dailies of the movie over the coming year. He had his reasons for the denial, according to the filmmaker, but they weren't what you might expect.

"Stan thought we missed the boat entirely," says Cardozo. "[He felt] that a Spider-Man film shouldn't be true to the comic. He wanted to do a rock opera with Elton John and David Bowie. I'm serious; I'm not making that up. We had many meetings with him, and when he said that, I had to wonder if the guy ever read a comic book in his life. I know he's Stan Lee, but he was just in outer space when he said stuff like that. Everyone else at Marvel was very supportive and said, 'Hey let the kids do it.' [Our movie] was light years ahead of what the pros were doing at the time."

The suggestion that Lee didn't trust his own creation to carry an entire feature film is surprising, but to be fair, replacing it with a *Tommy*-esque rock opera was still a forward-thinking idea at the time, however bad it might have been. Running with it for a moment, one can *almost* see Sir Elton with his blocky glasses and bowl-cut wigs as the comics' vision of Dr. Octopus, but casting David Bowie, presumably as Peter Parker, seems pretty incongruous, other than it being a play on Ziggy Stardust and the Spiders from Mars. Where would such an idea have come from? Perhaps Lee would've been inspired by Marvel's 1972 concept album *The Amazing Spider-Man—A Rockomic: From Beyond the Grave*. Released on Buddah Records, the LP was full of bubblegum pop songs sung by Ron Dante—the voice of the Archies' "Sugar, Sugar"—that followed Spidey as he rescued his kidnapped Aunt May, matching a story drawn in the album's gatefold packaging.

Others at Marvel saw bits of the fan film and offered their views; famed artist John Romita Sr., yet another graduate of the High School of Art and Design, reportedly pointed out that Kraven was too short—that the evil hunter should tower over Spider-Man.

Realizing he was right, the filmmakers reshot numerous scenes, using different lenses and low angles to make the hunter appear utterly menacing. That, in turn, meant reshooting Kraven's arrival in America, decamping from a ship. When it was originally shot, hundreds of onlookers happened to be around the dock where they were filming, curious to see what was going on with that film crew and the guy dressed as Spider-Man. Taking advantage of the moment, Cardozo shot the scene to highlight the plentitude of "extras"; during the reshoot, however, only a few people were milling around, so the crowds wound up on the cutting-room floor for continuity's sake.

That they could get a ship and dock at all was indicative of the surprising power afforded student filmmakers in New York City at the time. "The mayor's office was trying to get filmmaking to come back to New York, so they'd do anything for you, all for free," Cardozo recalls. "We closed off a few blocks of Fifth Avenue; they'd give us permits, police protection, and they'd let us park in no-parking areas. We got ticketed a few times, but the city would kill them."

Not everything ran so smoothly; NYU's filmmaking gear was the pits at the time—the 16mm cameras were unreliable, while the heavily used editing equipment occasionally shredded film run through it. Fed up, Cardozo began using the Bolex 16mm camera he got when he was 15, and he also turned to punk rock legend Tamás Erdélyi for help. These days, Erdélyi is better known as Tommy Ramone, the last man standing among the founding members of the Ramones.

A rising sound engineer who had already worked on Jimi Hendrix's 1970 live album, *Band of Gypsys*, before he was 20, Ramone spent much of 1973 building a recording facility—Performance Studios, on East 20th Street in Manhattan—with future Ramones tour manager Monte Melnick. A trio of roughshod friends started practicing in the space, and before long, the former engineer wound up both managing and playing drums for the band the following year. Performance Studios became an incubator for the Ramones, and soon they began changing the face of rock.

During those few years between *Band of Gypsys* and the

Seen here circa 1972, the crew included future punk rock legend Tommy Ramone (left), Bruce Cardozo (center), and Art Schweitzer, who later became president of the 21st Century Entertainment studio in the eighties.
(Courtesy of Bruce Cardozo)

founding of Performance Studios, however, Ramone actually left the music business altogether, and that's when he and Cardozo became friends, working together at Focus, a film production house in midtown Manhattan.

"At that point, I'd worked previously at the Record Plant as an engineer, and I was getting into film, which is how I ended up at Focus," recalls Ramone. "They did a lot of stuff—commercials, educational films, animation—and I was working in the production department. I was also getting into film editing at the time, because to me, that was the creative part of it. Unfortunately, I never really got to pursue it because I got back into music soon after that, but that's why I was there. Also, it was a great place to work because it was right around the corner from the Museum of Modern Art, so I'd take really long lunch breaks and hang out, watching films at the museum. There was a messenger staff—a bunch of college kids—and I'd send them out, and keep them in line. Most of them were from NYU, and Bruce was one of them."

While Cardozo took the part-time job to help fund his fan film, he soon learned there were perks to befriending a film editor. Ramone explains, "We had great editing equipment. There was lots of stuff there and a lot of the time, it wasn't being used, so, you know . . . whatever."

Getting to use professional editing gear that didn't scratch and shred his film like NYU's equipment was a plus for Cardozo, but getting the second opinion of a professional like Ramone didn't hurt either. "I remember Bruce was very much into special effects and animation," says Ramone. "I would encourage him, give him comments and stuff like that."

Cardozo confirms, "Tommy had an eye for film, and he was very supportive when I was doing this." It figures that Ramone would have dug a Spidey fan flick; the Ramones were always comic book fans, and their cover of the 1960s *Spider-Man* cartoon theme was the very last song on their very last album, recorded years after Tommy had left the group. It's not too surprising, then, that when Cardozo had to create the biggest effect of the movie, Ramone was there to help break the rules and make it happen.

As Cardozo saw it, the flick had to feel anchored in reality, and the only way to sell that to the audience was to pull off an impossible effect: Spider-Man had to be introduced swinging through New York City. A few years earlier, Cardozo's hero, Don Glut, faced the same problem in his own Spider-Man movie and had to settle for dangling a lumpy action figure from a string in front of the camera. To call the result "awful" is generous, particularly in scenes where Spidey swings through the desert, where, you know, there's nothing to swing *from*. Still, options were limited for a fan filmmaker on a budget and it was a tall order to make web swinging look real, short of risking life and limb (and we'll get to that in a few chapters, too).

Instead, the filmmakers cobbled together a low-budget traveling matte, superimposing Spidey over a nighttime shot of Times Square in all its blinking-neon glory. To do it, they needed to film their hero swinging across a large, blank background, but unfortunately, NYU didn't have a studio, and the cost of renting a facility would be astronomical. Helping them out, Tommy Ramone snuck Cardozo and his crew into the big soundstage at Focus for some quick shots of Richard Eberhardt in the superhero costume, zipping by the camera in front of a large white cyclorama.

"The result looked very convincing," says Cardozo. "We had a few matte lines here and there, but it didn't look like an effect;

it looked very Steve Ditko, with him swinging through Times Square to this roof where there's a robbery going on."

Spidey fought a bloodthirsty lion through the same method; a traveling matte dropped the hero into footage shot at Jungle Habitat in West Milford, New Jersey. The Warner Brothers–owned theme park was a "drive-thru safari" where visitors tooled along in their cars while wild animals roamed freely around them. "That thing was not trained, so we had to shoot it from outside through a gate with a zoom lens," explains Cardozo. They convinced the park to open up and let them film (it was closed for the winter); in return, they gave the attraction leftover footage for use in advertisements. As a result, the student filmmakers not only got the lion fight they needed, but a résumé credit for having shot a TV ad as well. Not that the advertisements helped—Jungle Habitat closed due to poor attendance three years later, on Halloween 1976, and proceeded to top its already checkered past of mauled visitors and escaped beasts by letting the carcasses of 30 animals, including an elephant, a bison, a camel, and some zebras, rot in a pile until they were buried the following April.

Cardozo was lucky to get his matte shots when he did; Focus also went out of business in 1973. The company mostly produced cigarette ads for TV, but after Congress banned the adverts in 1971, Focus never recovered and went belly up. That sent the fan filmmakers back to the editing gear at NYU, but it also ended the fledgling film career of Cardozo's mentor: "Yeah, I went back into audio after that. And the Ramones . . . whatever."

So if Congress (the Man if there ever was one) hadn't banned cigarette ads, Tommy Ramone probably would have stayed in film forever, never building the studio that spawned the creation of punk rock—music that exists almost exclusively to antagonize the Man.

Now, the story arc for most early Spider-Man comics was usually the same: Spidey succeeded but Peter Parker ended the issue questioning the cost to his personal life—and that was similar to what happened to Cardozo and his crew when their fan film was finally complete. The trio introduced the short at a student film festival/grading session, where it was greeted with thunderous applause and an A. The screening that mattered most, however, was for a considerably smaller audience.

"When we finished it, we rented a screening room and had a premiere for Marvel; we brought Stan [Lee] there and maybe 20 people," Cardozo recalls. That viewing, too, got a loud reaction—but not the kind he expected: "When Spider-Man unmasked himself, Holly, one of Stan's secretaries, screamed, 'Oh my God!' Turned out she knew our Peter Parker—he was her ex-boyfriend."

When it was all over, however, it was all over. "We were real jazzed about it and so was everyone else—except Stan Lee," says Cardozo.

> Again, he felt the concept was wrong, but he was actually very generous. Stan said that he'd give us any other character for free, but he wanted Spider-Man for himself. He wanted to give us Daredevil and we certainly could have pulled it off, but because the sales weren't there, the financial people who were going to back us wanted the number-one creation. They said, "Yeah, he's giving you a loser character to try and revive the comic," so we never came to agreement. Looking back, I should have taken one of those characters! I was incredibly burnt out by then, and just wanted to move on and work for someone, not pour my own money into something. I should have persisted; that's probably why I didn't become a director.

When a Daredevil film was finally released theatrically in 2003, it grossed over $100 million.

Worn out, fed up, and facing life after graduation with a mountain of debt incurred by the fan film, Cardozo headed out west to Hollywood to make a name for himself in the special effects field, where he works to this day. Although the original permission letter from Lee allowed his movie to be shown at film festivals and the like, the short was rarely screened publicly, instead spending most of the next 30 years boxed up.

Today, Cardozo says the gap was because he knew in his heart that a Spider-Man movie would eventually be made, so why make someone's life easier by showing them how to do it? Even so, the decision to essentially take his ball and go home was surely influenced by his disappointment with how things turned out, particularly when, after Lee's insistence on the rock opera idea, Spider-Man became a legendarily bad live-action TV series in 1978.

By Cardozo's account, Lee had been up-front from the start that he wasn't interested in granting Spider-Man rights to them, and it's debatable how excited Marvel was about the movie. On one hand, the company asked Cardozo to pen an article for *Foom* #4, the winter 1973 issue of its fan club magazine, where he wrote that Marvel bullpen members who saw dailies "were very impressed and enthusiastic about the results and encouraged us to finish the project." In its Marvel-written introduction, however, there was no commentary as to the quality of the flick or whether the company liked it. At best, the intro acknowledged that the act of someone making a movie "represents yet another milestone in the madcap Marvel Age!"

Between that and Lee's reputed refusals, the writing was on the wall before the film was even completed, and yet the filmmakers persisted in hopes that they could change the comics icon's mind. Perhaps Lee really did want to make a rock opera, or maybe he was just trying to gently let down some well-meaning fans who were proud of their college project. Whatever his motivation—or lack thereof—it all led to the same answer: no. That the filmmakers had taken it as a challenge rather than an ultimatum, however, was a testament to their tenacity.

Whatever Cardozo's reasons for putting the film into hibernation might have been, it's clear that he was ready to move on. As it turned out, he couldn't forget about the film, but the rest of the world did. According to the filmmaker, the movie that meant so much to him made so little impact that when Schweitzer ran into Lee decades later in a dry-cleaners, the comic book legend had no recollection of the film or the team's meetings with him. Similarly, Roy Thomas, mentioned in the *Foom* article, doesn't recall it, nor does Romita. What had been audiences with kings for three college kids had been, perhaps understandably, just another day at the office for the Marvel bull pen.

Ironically, it was the 2002 success of *Spider-Man* in theaters (surprise—Cardozo liked it) that inspired the filmmaker—now a special effects pro with credits ranging from *Superman IV* to *Johnny Mnemonic* on his resume—to finally dust off his fan film and reintroduce it to the world, showing it at a handful of comic book conventions in Los Angeles and Las Vegas. To this day, screenings remain few and far between, as Cardozo, concerned about his epic winding up on the Internet, only shows it in person.

In a modern-day world where perfect computer-generated special effects are used even for car ads, convention audiences enjoyed watching the wall-crawler swing through the rancid, bankrupt New York City of the 1970s via old-fashioned traveling mattes. In fact, the response was encouraging enough that Cardozo was inspired to pick up the phone and try negotiating with Marvel one last time: "I called them 28 years later, trying to make a video deal, and I've been talking to them on and off ever since. They're about as difficult to deal with as they were back when I was in college."

Spider-Man versus Kraven the Hunter may never be seen by the masses, but the fact that its director is putting the fan film out in the public eye again is a success all by itself. With the passage of time, Cardozo was able put aside frustrations about what did and didn't happen with his production, and now enjoys the film for what it was. "I gave people a glimpse of the future in 1974, showing what could be done with Spider-Man," he comments. "People said the special effects were dazzling, but that wasn't really it; we had the audience rooting for him, like you root for a team."

Ironically, that kind of reaction—the excited, passionate viewer getting swept up in a fantasy—may have irked Cardozo most in the end. The early 1970s found Hollywood in one of its darkest periods, with films like *All the President's Men, The Godfather, Network, The French Connection, Taxi Driver,* and even a comedy like *M*A*S*H* reflecting the bleak seriousness of the time. To the fan filmmaker, it was obvious that a Spider-Man film would be a smash hit in cinemas, because all around him, audiences were desperate to have fun again at the movies.

"I'll never forget the feeling when I went to see *Star Wars*," recalled Cardozo. "I was in the second showing in LA, and it was like the entire audience was saying, 'Where was this thing?' It was just total hunger for that kind of movie; the audience was starved!"

5
Take It Easy, Kid—It's Only a Movie (*Hardware Wars*, 1977)

Ernie Fosselius and Michael Wiese are the Lennon and McCartney of fan films. Together, they created something meant for the kids that also won over their parents; they inspired a generation of creative souls who followed in their footsteps; and just like the Beatles singing away on the *Ed Sullivan Show*, they made their infectious brand of fun look invitingly easy.

But the analogy runs deeper than that, because while united in their art, the two songsmiths were always, distinctly, individuals. McCartney has traditionally been viewed as the one who provided focus, the artist/businessman ready to make the most of a given situation, good or bad. Lennon, on the other hand, was always too happy to point out the frayed threads at the edge of the canvas, and though that view informed his art to great effect, it also drove him to cut down targets with his acerbic wit, even when it was in his best interests to be quiet. Regardless of whatever they may have done apart, however, Lennon and McCartney remain best known for the work they created together—and such is the case, too, with Fosselius and Wiese, the braintrust behind *Hardware Wars*.

The short film is less well known to young *Star Wars* aficionados today, but in the late seventies, seeing the 12-minute satire was a true badge of honor among fans. You might have seen Lucas's original in the

Scott Mathews (standing) was recruited to play Fluke Starbucker; a musician and producer, he later worked with Barbara Streisand, David Bowie, Brian Wilson, John Lee Hooker, and Mick Jagger, among others.
(Courtesy of Michael Wiese Productions)

theater seven times, and sat in your living room, slack-jawed in disbelief at that stupid *Star Wars Holiday Special,* but if you hadn't found a way to see *Hardware Wars,* you simply weren't a hardcore true believer.

A wisecracking take on the original movie, *Hardware Wars* was purposefully as low-tech as possible, using hubcaps for space stations, eggbeaters for space ships, and an old flashlight for a lightsaber. As a fake trailer for a nonexistent movie—a very *long* trailer—it essentially retold the story of *Star Wars,* following the adventures of Fluke Starbucker, Ham Salad, Auggie "Ben" Doggie of the Red-Eye Knights, Princess Anne-Droid (complete with danishes on her head), and Darph Nader. Rounding out the cast were the robots 4Q2 (the Tin Man from *The Wizard of Oz*) and Artie Deco (a busted vacuum cleaner), plus there was Chuchilla the Wookie Monster, played by a brown puppet that bore a striking resemblance to a certain *Sesame Street* character.

Taking an *Airplane*-like approach, *Hardware Wars* still works today, lobbing jokes one after another to see what sticks. Filled with all-ages humor that nonetheless has a bit of bite, the movie has always been a hit with fans, and that includes George Lucas himself, who has said it's his favorite parody of *Star Wars*—a claim that, believe it or not, Fosselius disputes.

The flick is many things—a reverent spoof, a cult classic, and likely the most profitable short subject ever made. For all that, however, there's one simple thing it has never been: *Hardware Wars* is not a fan film.

That's right—the movie that thousands of *Star Wars* buffs, articles, and fan filmmakers point to as the great-granddaddy of all fan flicks is actually nothing of the sort. The short might look like it was made by a bunch of seventies stoner kids hanging out in their parents' basement, but in truth, it was a professional production from the start.

Wiese explains, "It's a great misconception that, one, we were students—we were already professionals; two, that we are fans—I don't own the *Star Wars* pajamas; and three, that we did it as a pathway to success—that's not the case at all. When we did the film, we had no idea *Star Wars* would become this phenomenon with multiple sequels. Also, I have to admit, it never really occurred to us that there'd be a market for *Hardware Wars*; we learned everything we knew about marketing after we shot it. We just made the movie for fun and as a send-up of Hollywood trailers."

However people perceive *Hardware Wars*, there are three things that can't disputed: the short film was a hit; it inspired thousands of amateurs to make their own fan films; and it changed the lives of its creators forever. It's a saga of Farrah Fawcett wigs, record producers, lawyers, more lawyers, Francis Ford Coppola, and plenty of household appliances—and a grown woman with danishes on her head.

• • •

Until its opening weekend on May 25, 1977, no one saw *Star Wars* coming; the studio that produced it, 20th Century Fox, was convinced the film would die on the vine, and even George Lucas didn't stick around, instead opting to head off to Hawaii, where he spent the days building sand castles on the beach with Steven Spielberg. Lucas himself was so dismayed about the film's prospects that the two directors entered a fatalistic bet: whichever movie did better—*Star Wars* or the upcoming *Close Encounters of the Third Kind*—its director had to give the other profit points on the picture.

Of course, Spielberg happily won the gamble, as that Memorial Day weekend marked the detonation of a cultural explosion. If no one had seen *Star Wars* coming, they sure knew about it in the years that followed, as the burgeoning franchise was all but unavoidable. People—not just traditional, die-hard, sci-fi fans, but average, everyday people—couldn't get enough of the space saga. Marketers sat up and took notice; in short order, fans and the general public were milked for every cent of interest they had—and they were very interested.

While kids were impressed, becoming a powerful fan base that only grew in the ensuing decades, adults were inspired by the epic as well—particularly folks in the film industry. Sure, most wanted to emulate Lucas's success, but there were others who had different designs altogether, such as two regular guys working on the fringes of the movie biz: Fosselius and Wiese.

"Everyone tried to talk me out of making *Hardware Wars*," Fosselius recalled. "They said, 'You'll never work in that town again,' and I said, 'Well, I haven't worked there yet, so that's OK.'"

It was easy for the two filmmakers to take pot shots at the motion picture establishment, as they both lived far from its grasp, with Fosselius in San Francisco and Wiese 20 miles north in San Anselmo. "I did about 20 films for *Sesame Street* as an assistant animator," notes Fosselius. "We did the first counting series, with spies who open their coats at the end, and the pinball series, which was 1 to 12. That was my first filmmaking experience." When he wasn't manning a light table with tracing paper to make animation cels, the filmmaker was playing in bands; a few years earlier, he'd helped found the troupe that became Oingo Boingo, the legendary New Wave act led by future film composer Danny Elfman (*The Simpsons, Batman*).

Meanwhile, Wiese was making documentaries in an office above San Anselmo's local art shop, just half a block from Lucas's audio company, Sprocket Systems (later renamed Skywalker Sound). "I was working on many projects around that time," Wiese recalled.

> There was *Radiance: The Experience of Light* with Dorothy Fadiman, about the lights that surround holy people in art—is it a metaphor for higher consciousness or do saints really glow? I was about to start *Dolphin* with Hardy Jones, which we eventually shot in the Bahamas and were the first to record human-dolphin interaction in the open seas—Cousteau, eat your heart out! Another project was a psychedelic mandala film, *Beauty*, that put the audience into a celestial trance, and I started shooting lots of stuff on global thinker Buckminster Fuller, who was a mentor and friend—we shared the same birthday.

With all that going on, it's no wonder that the two occasionally needed to let off a little steam. Whenever Wiese threw a party in his loft, he'd invite friends over and the evening's highlight would invariably be a shadow puppet play, where they'd hang a screen between two doorways, set up a lamp behind it, and the two friends would improv their way through film stories acted out with hands and makeshift props.

After a particularly crazed rendition of *Jaws*—complete with homemade shark puppets—left everyone rolling on the floor, the pair met up to get some Chinese food, and Fosselius started goofing around, pitching Wiese on making a film trailer for a movie that didn't actually exist. They could parody *Star Wars*, big-budget Hollywood movies, and over-the-top special effects in one swoop, he explained, acting out the film using salt shakers, chopsticks, and soy sauce bottles. Soon Wiese was snickering loudly in the middle of the restaurant, and *Hardware Wars* was born.

Fosselius would write and direct, while Wiese would produce and handle cinematography. While it wouldn't be a student film, they'd make sure it looked like one; *Hardware Wars* would be made on the cheap, as much for the deliberately cheesy look as for the economic necessity. More important, however, it would be made for the hell of it, and, who knew? If it was any good and they were lucky, maybe they'd get to meet George Lucas. After all, they'd seen him around San Anselmo; Wiese once spotted the director at a local street café and sent over a bottle of wine in hopes of starting a conversation. He got a polite wave from across the patio.

Fosselius, however, had a different agenda: "I know that other people involved wanted to impress George Lucas, but I wanted to get his attention in a different way. I'm a satirist; my idea is to go after things that I see that are pretentious—and make fun of them. A satire or parody can be irritating, and that was my goal. I knew when I made it that true fans of *Star Wars* would like it; whether or not George would like it, I didn't know. But that's the thing that I had to persuade people about in order to raise the money to make it—'People are going to like it, believe me!'"

Even as the pair made fun of Hollywood films, they still followed the first rule of the movie biz: Never spend your own money. Fosselius wrote the script in a way that didn't break copyright laws, so being allowed to show and profit from the flick wasn't a problem; instead, raising the $5,000 budget was tough, for the simple reason that there was nowhere to show the movie after they made it. Movie theaters hadn't shown short subjects since the 1960s, TV never aired them, and the Internet—home to millions of pint-sized movies today—was in its non-public infancy. Having no place to show *Hardware Wars* meant there was no way to recoup the cost; funding the satire would amount to charity.

"The whole thing was a miniature Hollywood deal where you had to sell the idea, raise the money to do it, and promise it would pay off for the investors," says Fosselius. "People said, 'I don't really think this is going to work, what security do we have?' just like any investment. I'd go, 'Well, here's a whole bunch of percentages,' and try not to give too many away, like the Mel Brooks movie *The Producers*, where they give away 200 percent of their play. I gave out most of what I would have gotten out of it just to get the money together, so for me, it wasn't really a financial stepping stone; it was a creative one."

Friend Laurel Polanick put up the $5,000 budget, and then joined the crew as the costume designer. Filling out those intergalactic threads, Fosselius cast most roles with people he knew, regardless of their acting experience. Case in point: producer/musician Scott Mathews may be known in the music world for having worked with and written songs for Barbara Streisand, David Bowie, Brian Wilson, John Lee Hooker, Mick Jagger, and plenty of others, but to Fosselius, he was the perfect person to don a blond wig and play Fluke. It was a good call; Mathews won a *New York Times* Critic Pick for his work in the movie.

While the flick was being cast, Wiese was busy calling in favors, borrowing a $2,500 5.7mm fisheye kinoptic lens for his 16mm camera so that they could swing a heavy steam iron just inches above it to replicate the real film's opening shot. Trying to get a take where the iron didn't wobble as it swung overhead, they risked the lens getting destroyed 98 times before getting the visual they wanted. Even making a purposefully imperfect movie, it turned out, required some level of perfection.

Shooting was held over the course of four days, with cardboard sets and special effects created in their temporary "studio"—a warehouse on 24th Street in San Francisco, though a few shots were grabbed on the sly in a boiler room beneath San Francisco City College. "It was all done guerilla-style," notes Fosselius. "I'm not sure if we even rented the warehouse. We told people it was student filmmaking, because they'd say, 'Oh, OK—you don't have any money? Go ahead.' Whereas if they found out we were a professional crew, they'd start charging for everything, because they'd figure, 'Oh, you're Hollywood people!'"

Following another Tinseltown tradition, the two filmmakers cameoed in their own movie, with Fosselius playing both the masked Darph Nader and the commander running the Death Star attack slideshow, while later, the back of Wiese's head appeared for a second during the dogfight. "What a performance," he comments. "I was sitting in for Ham Salad, who had already gone home."

Bob Knickerbocker, the rogue . . . er . . . rogue, wasn't the only missing actor during the film shoot. "The bar scene was shot on a Sunday morning at the Palms in San Francisco," says Wiese, "and no one showed up—everyone was still wasted from Saturday. A cop came by and asked us what we were doing as we unloaded lights; we said, 'Trying to shoot a movie, but our cast didn't arrive.' Ogling our donuts for the crew, he said, 'No problem' and started

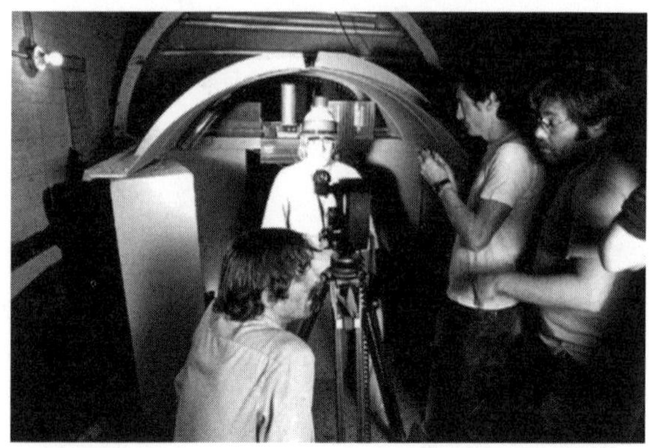

Ernie Fosselius squats by the camera while shooting the climactic dogfight scene in *Hardware Wars*.
(Courtesy of Michael Wiese Productions)

pulling people off the street to be in the movie. We gave all the women Farrah Fawcett wigs."

With shooting completed, they got to editing, working up a 26-minute rough cut. "It was a lot of fun for me creatively," says Fosselius. "I'm a pretty old-fashioned, analog person, so to me, all that 16mm editing is very mechanical and fun. You can't beat doing laser beams by scratching the film emulsion with a sewing needle rather than putting in some electronic effect."

The massive movie was eventually cut to 12 minutes after they showed it to friends. "Our first test screening was at a restaurant," Wiese recalls. "We set up the projector and turned out the lights while patrons tried to see their soup. There were a lot of laughs—and shouts to turn the lights back on—but we learned how to best space the comedy so the laughs wouldn't drown out the jokes that came next."

With all the gags lined up, they used selections from an obscure European recording of Richard Wagner's *Ride of the Valkyries* for the soundtrack, sticking to the ethos they'd had throughout to keep trademarked and copyrighted material out of the film, thus ensuring they could screen it for profit. The icing on the aural cake, however, came when they hired voiceover artist Paul Frees to narrate *Hardware Wars*—just he had the original advance teaser trailer for *Star Wars*.

• • •

By mid-fall of 1977, the movie was done, but they'd gone over-budget by $3,000. With the debt weighing on their minds, it was time to achieve the next two goals: to get *Hardware Wars* distributed so that they could at least break even, and to also put the film in front of George Lucas. As they saw it, achieving the latter would probably help with the former, but with no real way to contact the man himself, they were at a loss. At one point, there was even half-serious debate about putting the movie in a film canister attached to a parachute and then dangling the whole thing from a tree in front of the director's house, with a note attached reading, "From outer space." Luckily, they discovered that one of their friends, a carpenter, was doing some work at the house and was willing to pass it along.

Lucas eventually saw *Hardware Wars* on Thanksgiving Day that year, sitting down with dinner guests to watch it after their holiday meal. His review? It was "cute"—a review that left Fosselius beside himself . . . with anguish.

"I always wanted to be the court jester, not the king," he says, "but at least the court jester got to stand there and see the king's reaction. I never got that opportunity, so I never knew his true reaction. I'm told that he sort of took it OK; they said he thought it was 'cute'—which is a horrible word—but I never really knew what he thought of it, until much, much later, when I talked to Coppola."

While a low-key, one-word review like "cute" wasn't quite what they'd hoped for (perhaps the tryptophan in the turkey left him a tad subdued), Lucas still liked it enough to have his assistant Jane Bay arrange a meeting between Wiese and Alan Ladd Jr. ("Laddie"), the legendary head of 20th Century Fox, which had produced *Star Wars*.

While Fosselius and Wiese hadn't made *Hardware Wars* to break into mainstream cinema, clearly this was the Big Opportunity, so Wiese went to Los Angeles with the film under his arm and dreams in his head, ready to show it to the most powerful executive in Hollywood. Entering the Fox studio lot, his mind raced—maybe they'd distribute it and show it in theaters. Maybe they'd want Wiese to pitch ideas for films he and Fosselius could make at Fox. The sky was the limit, but when Wiese walked into the screening room, he found Ladd accompanied not by a clique of eager executives ready to shower him with contracts and money, but instead, a trio of stern-faced lawyers, all wearing the same three-piece suit. This was bad.

The attorneys, it turned out, were there to pass judgment on whether Fox could sue for copyright infringement. Wiese recalls, "They ran the show. No one laughed. Someone coughed and I counted it as a laugh—'They love it, they love it, they really do!'" Afterward, the lawyers conferred and gave their depressing analysis: Wiese and Fosselius hadn't broken any copyrights, plus, as a parody, the short was protected by the First Amendment, so in their professional estimation, there was no way to sue and make yet more money off of *Star Wars*.

With personal financial oblivion now taken off the docket, Wiese got back to the reason why he'd come there in the first place: he had a film to sell. "Laddie asked me what I wanted. I said, 'To have 20th Century Fox show it with *Star Wars*.' I'm still waiting for them to get back to me."

Eventually, Wiese visited Santa Monica–based Pyramid Films, a distributor specializing in health and education films, which had previously distributed *Radiance* and some of his other efforts. It turned out to be exactly the meeting he'd hoped to have at Fox: "Bob Kligensmith locked me in the office on a Friday night and wouldn't let me leave until we had a deal. That's why he was later president of Paramount Video and I'm not."

What's more, the company bought into the parody angle completely, going the extra mile to fit the irreverent film into the parameters of an educational film distributor. To help teachers lead classroom discussions, Fosselius was required to write a *Hardware Wars* study guide, which he promptly filled with questions like "What makes *Star Wars* such an easy target for satire?"

"I wrote it as a parody, but they accepted it as the real thing—that was pretty cool," he admits. "Then Pyramid got it out there; they distributed to everything that wasn't a theater—schools, churches, Rotary Club, whatever. Today, I get people who say, 'I saw it at the library' or at Sunday school—just the weirdest places."

While the massive popularity of *Star Wars* helped fuel interest in the short, Pyramid and Wiese were aggressive in getting the film in front of as many people as possible. It played film festivals, garnering nearly a dozen awards in short order; became a staple of between-movie filler on HBO and other cable channels; was booked into "midnight movie" shows and some screenings of *The Empire Strikes Back*; and even the LA school district bought dozens of prints—on the condition that a nude pinup was cut from the debriefing slide-show. "The Defense Department bought half a dozen prints, too," Wiese recalls. "Go figure—I think it was the title."

Before long, the little movie had become to the short-subject field exactly what the real flick was to feature films: the biggest hit ever. By the end of 1978, *Hardware Wars* had grossed more than $500,000, eventually leveling off around $800,000 by the end of the original *Star Wars* trilogy in 1983. Perhaps unsurprisingly, the two filmmakers eventually got an offer to produce a feature-length version of their space operetta, but turned it down with a sense of "been there, done that" finality.

Wiese explains, "We didn't think the joke would hold up for an entire feature film, but that didn't stop Mel Brooks from making *Spaceballs*, which we consider a blatant rip off of *Hardware Wars*. Of course, that's life feeding on life: Lucas ripped off Kurosawa's *Hidden Fortress*, we ripped off *Star Wars*, life goes on. We weren't the only ones to notice, though—Janet Maslin, a film critic for the *New York Times*, wrote in the first paragraph of her *Spaceballs* review what a wonderful film *Hardware Wars* was and then went on to trash *Spaceballs*. We wrote her a thank-you note."

Wiese went back to work on *Dolphin*, while Fosselius turned his satirical eye to Francis Ford Coppola's *Apocalypse Now*, filming the less successful *Porklips Now*. With the two films under his belt, Fosselius went into screenwriting, but while his scripts had trouble getting off the ground, ironically he brought things full circle when he wound up working on the opening sequence of *Return of the Jedi* with Lucasfilm sound designer Ben Burtt, providing the comic voice of a sobbing Rancor keeper, mourning the death of his pet monster beneath Jabba the Hutt's palace:

> Ben and I hit it off because he has a pretty good sense of

> humor and liked *Hardware Wars* a lot. I was walking down the hall at Fantasy Studios, visiting somebody for lunch, and they said, "Hey, come in and do a couple of lines for me, will ya?" I did some weird voice—turns out it shows up in the movie. Buy me a sandwich and I'll do a voice! They gave me a lot of work doing weird voices and screams during lunch hour, like the two Chinese pilots at the beginning of *Indiana Jones and the Temple of Doom* who bail out of a Ford Tri-Motor. Now I get *Star Wars* mail from people all over the world, not for *Hardware Wars*, but for *Jedi*. They'll send me a trading card that's some character that I did the voice for, and they want me to tell them how I did it and sign the card. It's really impresses me that they would know I did the voice, because I didn't get a screen credit. The funny thing is that I still get royalty checks for it; I have a classic one from 20th Century Fox for one penny, framed with a sign: BIG MONEY IN SHOW BUSINESS. That seems to be the theme of my career.

Meanwhile, *Hardware Wars* continued to have legs, excerpted in a 1980 *Star Wars* TV special, *SPFX: The Empire Strikes Back*. A year later, Warner Home Video released both of Fosselius's parodies on VHS as *Hardware Wars and Other Film Farces*, packaged with two other flicks distributed by Pyramid: *Closet Cases of the Nerd Kind* (Rick Harper's clever spoof of Steven Spielberg's *Close Encounters of the Third Kind*) and, lo and behold, Marv Newland's indefatigable *Bambi Meets Godzilla*. The VHS video was released with an extravagant $39 price tag and eventually sold about 6,000 copies to video stores and libraries.

Just two years later, *Return of the Jedi* was released, closing out the original trilogy, and then a funny thing happened: people realized they'd had enough *Star Wars* for a good, long time. Since 1977, the media had rammed the series down the public's throat; now, without new movies to look forward to, if people wanted a *Star Wars* fix, they would have to go looking for it—and they chose to do something else instead. The seemingly endless stream of toys, books, and other movie tie-ins slowly dried up, and by the late eighties, *Star Wars* was largely consigned to the backshelves of closets and minds everywhere. When the mania for all things *Star Wars* eventually ran its course, *Hardware Wars*, too, disappeared.

• • •

While *Hardware Wars* was a cult phenomenon seen by millions of people, it has a greater legacy than having merely amused audiences. In fact, the simple parody was wildly influential, because it became the first high-profile harbinger of today's fan film movement. While it may not have been a true fan film itself, plenty of viewers thought it was, and that, in turn, inspired countless kids to become backyard auteurs, making their own fan flicks.

The grand irony is that in reverse engineering a fan film, Fosselius and Wiese used household items for spaceships, when the number one unwritten rule of fan productions is that one must attempt to replicate "the real thing" as closely as possible. Instead, the steam irons looked like steam irons, the wigs were hopelessly fake, and the lip-synched dialogue rarely attempted to match the actors on screen. *Hardware Wars* positively reveled in its pseudo-amateurishness.

At the same time, though, the short also provided a sly commentary on how its own audience had swallowed Lucas's creation whole. Sure, a toaster firing burned bread was amusing as a visual non sequitur, but it also questioned the emotional worth of the *Star Wars* universe: *Why* was a TIE fighter blasting lasers everywhere so much cooler than a toaster and burnt crusts? The fact that spaceships were substituted with appliances was a reminder that within the *Star Wars* universe, there was nothing special about X-Wings or the Millennium Falcon; they were just tools, the same as a waffle iron. And when Frees narrated, he wasn't merely mocking the stuff on-screen; his lines poked a friendly jab at the fans, too: "You'll laugh, you'll cry, you'll kiss three bucks goodbye! Get in line now!"

So, whether intended or not, the pair of outcast filmmakers inadvertently became forerunners—and for two decades, standard bearers—of the fan film movement. Surveying their unexpected impact on amateur moviemaking, Wiese proved fairly philosophical about the turn of events: "We all emulate the things we love and that influence us. I'm pleased that fans make fan films; usually it is a labor of love and their first movie. They learn a lot and go onto other things—or they don't, and this is very sad. By the time Ernie and I made *Hardware Wars*, we were in our thirties and had made films before. This, too, is very sad."

• • •

With the exception of new novels and comic books that arrived in the early nineties, during the 14 years between 1983 and 1997, *Star Wars* was largely allowed to lie dormant. The franchise's core audience—Generation X—was now growing up, discovering more sophisticated entertainments and interests beyond lightsabers (like sex, for instance). By the midnineties, however, Lucasfilm decided it was time to remind the world about the franchise it had fallen in love with way back when. Following a carefully sculpted timeline of events, the public's interest would be revived through a theatrical rerelease of the original films, followed by a well-publicized, VHS box set (the latest in a very long line of such releases), videogames, and more, all leading up to the grand crescendo of May 19, 1999: the release date of *Star Wars: Episode 1—The Phantom Menace*, a film that proved as unwieldy as its title.

First came the theatrical rerelease; when Lucas announced he was going to reissue the trilogy in 1997 as Special Editions with up-to-date special effects, it was only natural that *Hardware Wars* would make a return, too. Warner's home video rights to the short had lapsed, so Wiese was toying with the idea of his own rerelease when he got a phone call from a Hollywood special effects pro.

Fred Tepper recalled, "When I first heard that they were doing a *Star Wars Special Edition* with new digital effects, I thought, 'Wouldn't it be really funny if they did that to *Hardware Wars?*' I told a couple of friends at Amblin Imaging, where we were working on *seaQuest*, *Star Trek: Voyager* and other TV stuff, and they thought it was a funny concept—so I searched for Michael Wiese on the Net, called him up out of the blue and told him the idea. He'd thought of rereleasing the film, but hadn't really thought of making any changes to it other than a nice new transfer and better sound. I told him my friends and I would do the CGI work for free just because, A, we were fans of the original, and B, it was just so damn silly."

Wiese warmed to the idea of new "special defects" for the re-release, but Fosselius, who had long since left the film business to forge an artistic career building ornate, mechanized wood carvings, had nothing to do with the effort.

"Ernie sometimes disappears for years at a time on creative projects and I don't hear from him," comments Wiese, "so I went ahead and did it. I met with these three nerdy guys—Fred Tepper and his pals; they were so nervous I could hardly hear them; they were treating me like Orson Welles! Their ideas for redoing some of the scenes were brilliant. Since we didn't have the brilliance of Ernie's contribution, I wanted to keep the integrity as much as I could with Ernie's original work, and we initially thought of using very low-res computer graphics, but that would just look cheap and probably wouldn't be funny, so we didn't go that route."

Tepper explains, "It was a question of where did you want the humor to come from? I thought the irony of quality effects depicting low-quality spaceships was more funny. After all, the idea doing a *Star Wars Special Edition* was to improve on the effects, so we agreed it should follow that concept, making waffle irons more believable, and everything would be a first take so it wouldn't get too refined."

The creation of the new effects went off without a hitch, accomplished by the team over one long weekend. Wiese and his company geared up to self-release the video. Everything was going smoothly—but there was a problem. "I sent Ernie the new version," remembers Wiese, "and he said he would have preferred a low-tech approach."

In fact, Fosselius was pretty ticked off. "It became the golden goose—everyone kept trying to squeeze more bucks out of it, but I was trying to move on to my next nonlucrative project," he reflects with a chuckle. "At that time, I was off in the woods doing wood carvings; I just wanted the movie to stand as a creative work, but they did it anyway and I had to get a lawyer to fight it the best I could. All I could do was get them to attach a sticker to the box to say that I didn't approve."

The sticker had some unintended consequences, however, as Wiese admits: "That started the rumor that there was a big rift between us—but there wasn't." Another unexpected result was that fans simply thought Fosselius was the director who cried wolf: "A lot of people took it as just another one of my weird jokes—that I had done it, and didn't approve of it," Fosselius explains, laughing. "At the time, I was pretty upset about that, but the fact is, that's the kind of thing I would do!"

With many of the flying irons and hand mixers now re-created using CGI, the revised *Hardware Wars: Special Edition* took on an odd patina, as the new facelift created an additional meta-joke by featuring new, high-tech, cheesy special effects re-creating old, low-tech, cheesy special effects imitating old, high-tech special effects. If that sentence doesn't make any sense, well, neither did the movie. A little too self-referential for its own good, Wiese's release of the *Special Edition* nonetheless went on to sell over 60,000 copies, this time priced under 10 bucks. With 20/20 hindsight, Wiese now has a different view of the remixed flick: "In the end, I agree with Ernie; the original is funnier and funkier." In fact, even Tepper agrees: "I still think the concept of a special edition is . . . funnier than the actual thing."

Later that year, *Hardware Wars* became even more like the real movie that inspired it when the short was licensed to become a three-issue comic book series from World Comics. Artist Justin Morenz spent four months creating the 18-page first issue, only to see the publisher go bankrupt when he handed it in. The comic was never printed and his $5,000 check for services rendered was instead rendered worthless. However, a panel at the nation's biggest comic book convention, the annual San Diego Comic Con, had been booked for the comic's release, so on a whim, Morenz showed up and found 500 people jammed into the room, all anxious to find out the latest adventures of Fluke and the gang. "We had all these people show up," he later ruefully told Colorado's *Pueblo Chieftain* newspaper, "and I just think of all the sales we could have had in that room."

The *Hardware Wars* saga didn't end on that low note, however. When he'd first seen the short in 1977, Lucas had labeled it "cute"—a gentle review that was positive but hardly the effusive

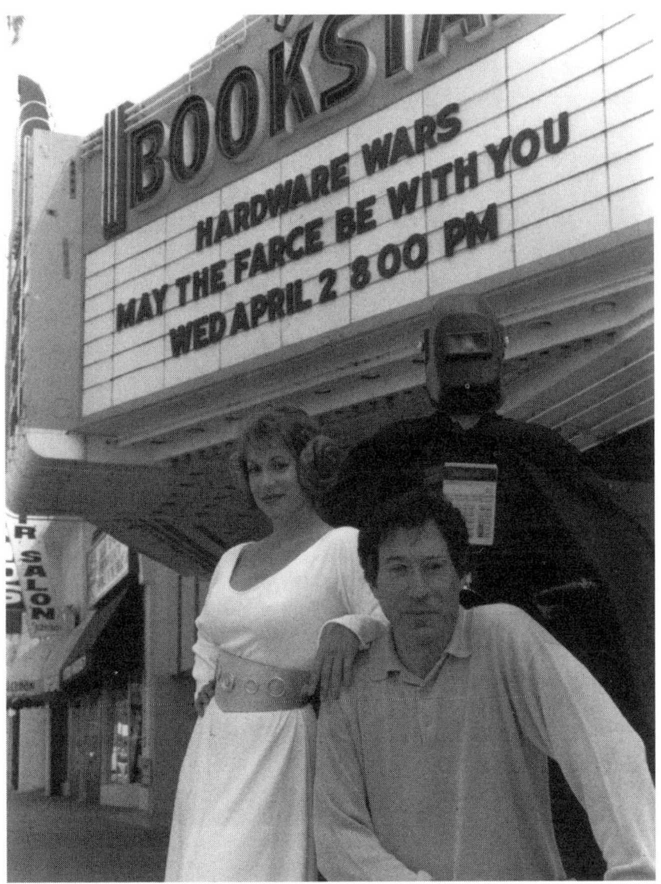

Commemorating the film's 20th anniversary in 1997 with the help of Darph Nader and original actress Cindy Freeling (Princess Anne-Droid), producer Michael Wiese rereleased the short with new "special defects" as *Hardware Wars: Special Edition*. *(Courtesy of Michael Wiese Productions)*

praise that Wiese and Fosselius had hoped to get. A full 22 years later, in August 1999, they finally got the ultimate accolade. By then, Wiese had moved to England, and happened to be watching the tube when Lucas appeared on UK talk show *The Big Breakfast* promoting *Star Wars: Episode 1—The Phantom Menace*. Asked about the hundreds of spoofs that had come up over the years, Lucas replied without hesitation, "*Hardware Wars* is my favorite *Star Wars* parody." Wiese had the review on his website in under ten minutes.

• • •

And here's where things go off the rails a bit, because if you'd think the seal of approval from Lucas himself would finally make Fosselius ecstatic, too, you'd be dead wrong. Maybe. In truth, even he isn't sure how he feels about it, but one suspects that much like the old *X-Files* slogan, he wants to believe.

You see, according to Fosselius, Lucas's declared love of *Hardware Wars* is nothing more than "revisionist history." The sentiment stems back to 1980, and the considerably smaller wake left by Fosselius's other satirical film, *Porklips Now*. Creating a parody of Francis Ford Coppola's Vietnam epic was an interesting choice, in part because of the longstanding relationship between the *Godfather* auteur and the younger *Star Wars* director. Coppola had mentored Lucas for years, producing his feature debut, *THX-1138*, and giving him his first directing gig, shooting *Filmmaker*, a documentary about Coppola filming *Finian's Rainbow*. A decade later, however, now the learner had become the master, creating the biggest film ever, while Coppola risked his career and mental health to make a masterwork that was met with mixed reviews and puzzlement. While *Hardware Wars* had ridden a wave of giddy, innocent excitement among moviegoers, *Porklips Now* went after an R-rated movie about a very sore topic that had left audiences polarized and confused—a reaction that Coppola may not have expected.

It was in this climate, then, that Fosselius sent a copy of his satire to Coppola, and while he may have been disappointed by the lukewarm reception he got from Lucas a few years earlier, he claims the reaction to *Porklips Now* was far colder (repeated requests for Coppola's side of the story remain unanswered).

Fosselius says weeks went by without a word from the Coppola camp, so he gave up expecting to hear anything—until Coppola called one night at 3 AM, recruiting him to join the campaign to get California governor Jerry Brown elected president. Soon the satirist found himself creating TV ads for the doomed crusade, but, he says, Coppola never once mentioned the short.

When Fosselius was invited to a party hosted by the auteur sometime later, he finally brought up the topic by bringing a

Porklips Now T-shirt as a present. As Fosselius tells it, Coppola wordlessly handed off the shirt to someone passing by and then blew his stack, making it clear in no uncertain terms that he did not like the film and felt it attacked him personally. This was capped off with, "I'll tell you one thing: I took mine a lot better than George took his!"

And that's the comment that haunts Fosselius to this day. "I went, 'Oh, OK. Well, sorry. . . .' I kinda backed away and left. But it's sort of an interesting thing—they talked about it! Like, as if they said, 'Well, what did you think of your parody?' 'Oh, I didn't like it.' So, after never really hearing how George felt, now this was the first word I had and maybe he didn't like his very much. I mean, if I were to believe Francis. So I don't know. I *still* don't know."

To be sure, there's plenty of reasons to think that Lucas *did* like *Hardware Wars*. After all, he would never have instructed his personal assistant to set up Wiese and Ladd for their ill-fated meeting otherwise, and as Fosselius himself notes, "*Hardware Wars* didn't hurt *Star Wars* at all; in fact, it helped because it enhanced the experience by reminding people of the original. Without it being there, the parody would mean nothing, so it was dependent on the film. In fact, that's why *Porklips* didn't make an impact, even though it's a much better-made film, I think, and maybe funnier—because less people saw *Apocalypse*."

Also, even if *Hardware Wars* did rub Lucas the wrong way initially, the man has been known to change his mind (Greedo shoots first; midichlorians; it's gonna be a dozen . . . wait, nine . . . oops, make that six movies), so if he eventually said it was his favorite parody, why not take that at face value?

Despite all this supporting evidence, however, Coppola's purported remark still plagues Fosselius enough that when Lucasfilm honored *Hardware Wars* with the Pioneer Award at the second *Star Wars* Fan Film Awards, held at the San Diego Comic Con in 2003, he was a no-show: "I didn't go pick it up because they were rewriting history to suit their needs." He'd spent two decades thinking that Lucas hated *Hardware Wars*, and even four years after it had received the papal blessing on UK television, the doubt was still impossible to shake off:

> It's hard; I can't really psychoanalyze myself about it, but I do think about it a lot: Why would I make these satires? Why am I so interested in that kind of thing? And why do I think that people are going to love me for it rather than be irritated—but in a way, I want them to be irritated! If they want everyone to love everything they do, that's a little bit unrealistic—and maybe I do love their movies. Maybe I like the movies enough that I want to spend a lot of time thinking of ways to make fun of them. Which is a strange thing to say, but if I didn't like them at all, I probably wouldn't even be interested in them.

"Maybe I'm trying to ingratiate myself into something by making the films; everyone has friends who tease them, and you know that they care about you, but they like to give you a hard time," Fosselius continues, laughing. "So maybe it's a desperate cry for acceptance on my part—by insulting people!"

• • •

Fosselius's dilemma with the directors may never be resolved, but the issues over *Hardware Wars: Special Edition* were worked out a few years later when he and Wiese reunited to produce the definitive version of the movie for a DVD release in 2002. Working together, they filled the disc with an hour's worth of extras, notably omitting the *Special Edition* in the process. Once again, the film was a hit, proving that even 25 years after they first hatched the idea over Chinese food, the farce was still with them.

Today, Wiese still markets the short, but spends most of his time producing documentaries and running a publishing company that concentrates on technical filmmaking books. Fosselius, meanwhile, no longer sees wood carving as something he took up after bailing out of a stalled film career; rather, both occupations are part of a broader vocation he began as a kid: satirist. Now he sell his own art; runs a traveling, hand-carved marionette show called *Cirque du So What*; and speaks at sci-fi conventions, billing himself as "Ernie Fosselius, Former Filmmaker and Celebrity Has-Been.'"

By treating his own appearances at conventions as metagags that fans can participate in, Fosselius proves that his satirical edge is as sharp as ever, holding nothing—particularly his own ego—sacred, but it's also indicative that the man has finally come to terms with his parodies, realizing in the process that his movies had a much larger audience than just two famous directors:

> *Hardware Wars* is the one thing I'll always be known for. It doesn't matter what great art I've done since then; I'll never be able to live it down. For a while, that bothered me—"Look what I've just done; forget about that old thing"—but I'm starting to enjoy the fact that people come up to me with a big old smile and say it was a happy memory for them, that they saw it in a school assembly and all the kids were cracking up. That's a wonderful thing; we affected them somehow with this strange little movie. So I'm trying to live up to that idea now, and accept it and welcome it—because what's wrong with making people happy as the best thing you did in your life?

6
Video Killed the Film Star (1977–1990)

While 20th Century Fox lawyers were watching *Hardware Wars* hoping that they could sue for copyright infringement, Hollywood's other popular space franchise, *Star Trek,* was liberally letting amateurs run rampant with its characters—provided that they stayed on paper. When a fan tried to bring his take on *Trek* to a TV screen, however, that laissez-faire attitude changed dramatically, marking one of the first times that a major studio tried to shut down a fan film.

Fan fiction had been popular among *Star Trek* fans since the show first hit the air in the 1960s, but it didn't truly kick in until the following decade. Without the Internet to aid in distribution, writers created their own "zines"—homemade, newsletter-type magazines—and self-published stories, using the inadequate photocopiers of the day or paying for small print runs at local offset printers. The zines were sold through the mail or at sci-fi conventions, usually at a price that just barely covered the cost of production; a top-selling issue might have a circulation of 500 copies, so it's safe to say that fanzine editors weren't getting rich on their efforts.

Paramount, which owns the *Star Trek* franchise, took no action against the amateur publishers throughout the period, even though money was changing hands (the big no-no when it comes to copyright violation). Legend has it that in the seventies, series creator Gene Roddenberry asked studio execs to let the fanzines go about their business, and eventually, it's said, a hands-off policy became the norm for the franchise.

While that's a romantic story, there are plenty of other reasons why Paramount might have turned a blind eye to fan fiction. First and foremost, it's entirely possible that the studio simply didn't know about the zines and fan fiction, or just as likely, knew but didn't care. Second, even if the company knew and had concerns about the fanzines, a studio is, above all, a business, and there would have been a disastrous financial return on investment to enact even one lawsuit against a zine, much less dozens or hundreds against homemade publications. Realistically, if Paramount won all monies generated by a zine, and was even awarded damages for an amateur publication having illegally represented *Star Trek* to a few hundred people at best, the amount gained would be insignificant next to the costs required for the studio to mount the lawsuit.

Additionally, it was likely beneficial to let fan fiction run on unabated, as the new stories were keeping the hardcore faithful interested in what was otherwise a dead TV show. The sets had been struck, the actors and crew had moved on to other projects, and the same 79 episodes were now endlessly recycling in syndication, but fan fiction helped keep the series fresh for its most ardent followers—people who, not coincidentally, banged the drum loudest for the series within the world of fandom. Keeping those überfans happy by letting them write stories about their heroes would have been a small price to pay to keep general interest in the show up, because that in turn kept the show's ratings high enough that stations would renew their syndication contracts. Prosecuting their biggest supporters—and moreover, ones who would clearly know how to reach hundreds or thousands of other fans with their ensuing tale of woe—would be a publicity disaster.

Regardless of the reason, the fan fiction element of *Trek* fandom was allowed to grow, and that eventually proved to be a worthwhile (i.e., moneymaking) decision for Paramount: Bantam

Books, which published licensed *Star Trek* paperbacks at the time, released two anthologies called *Star Trek: The New Voyages*, both consisting almost entirely of fan fiction originally published in zines.

However, Marshall McLuhan's observation that "the medium is the message" was very applicable here. If Paramount even knew about fan fiction, it likely realized that the medium of a poorly mimeographed zine was no threat to its golden goose—the TV series. Similarly, the handful of *Trek* fan films shown at conventions in the seventies were hardly a liability; if you were such a big fan that you'd go to a gathering, you knew full well that a herky-jerky, Super 8 film of kids pretending to be Kirk and the gang wasn't the same as a show on television.

If a *Star Trek* fan film was taken out of the convention context, however, and dropped onto TV, that was suddenly a very different story. Once the medium was no longer a portable movie screen in a hotel ballroom, but instead the smooth veneer of a cathode ray tube in someone's living room, now *that* was a threat. Just ask Art Binninger.

The fan filmmaker had started creating his own clay-animated *Star Trix* parody in 1974, when he was a motion picture laboratory specialist for the Air Force, stationed at Vandenberg AFB in Santa Barbara County, California. Romping around on intricate cardboard sets that were only a few inches tall, his clay "stars" included Captain Klurk, a vision-impaired Mr. Specks, drunk Mr. Scotch, and Klingons whose entire language consisted of belches. Though stop-motion animation was slow and time-consuming to shoot, Binninger found the results were amusing to watch, and making the flick with his Yashica LD-6 Super-8 camera was a great way to pass time on the base.

After being released from the Armed Forces in the midseventies, Binninger learned that *Star Trek: The Motion Picture* (1979) was being produced, and sent a copy of *Star Trix* to the feature's associate producer, Jon Povill, in the spring of 1978, hoping to land a production job. While there was no work to be had, Povill wrote back, remarking that he had "enjoyed viewing it"—certainly an encouraging word for a young, amateur filmmaker.

By 1987, Paramount and Binninger had each knocked out far

Set builder Grant Hiestand (left) and writer/director Art Binninger attack the clay cast of *Star Trix: The Flick*.
(Courtesy of Art Binninger)

more impressive sequels in their respective franchises, and the latter had gone so far as to create a 43-minute epic, *Star Trix: The Flick*. Proud of the fan film, which now sported rather fluid animation and advanced special effects like mattes, Binninger jumped at an opportunity to show it on a local public access channel in Santa Barbara, accompanied by a short "making of" documentary to create an overall one-hour program. Even though the show would only be seen by a handful of viewers, given Paramount's previous positive response, Binninger off-handedly decided to go "by the book" and contacted the studio once again, this time to get permission for the airing.

Instead, he received a stern letter stating, "It is a violation of the rights of Paramount under copyright, trademark and otherwise for you to have proceeded with such a production utilizing elements of Paramount's property. We therefore must insist that you not proceed further with your contemplated production." Binninger wrote back that he was flattered his clay figurines had become such a danger to the studio's bottom line.

His flippant retort provoked another letter—this time signed by a team of lawyers—that stated,

> Far more objectionable than the production of the film is the exhibition of it to other individuals or audiences, and the reproduction of it on videotape for or by others, whether or not a fee is charged therefor. Although Paramount . . . may not deem it advisable at this time to commence legal action and/or equitable proceedings against you for mere production of the film and your exclusively private use of it, any or all of us may elect to prosecute actions and/or proceedings against you for the exhibition of the film or videotape or the distribution thereof to third parties.

The legal team also demanded copies of the film, but Binninger instead fired off Povill's encouraging letter from 1978, adding that without fans like himself, the lawyers wouldn't have *Trek* around to keep them employed. He never heard from them again.

Decades later, however, Povill contacted him out of the blue, having heard about Binninger's travails years after the fact. Asking to see the letter, he remarked, "I find it extremely hard to believe that anything I wrote could have thwarted the pack mentality of the Paramount lawyers."

Luckily, it had. With the studio silent, Binninger handed *Star Trix* to the public access channel, where it aired four times. The grand payoff for going head-to-head with Paramount? He was recognized by a clerk at the local tire shop. However, Binninger likely wasn't the only fan filmmaker getting cease-and-desist letters from Paramount at the time; that may well have happened to another notable production—one that has never been shown anywhere.

Among *Star Trek* fans, few "lost" fan films are more legendary than the 1986 production *Yorktown II: A Time to Heal*. The reportedly 20-minute, Super 8 short, set between the end of the original series and the beginning of the first *Star Trek* feature film, featured series regular George Takei reprising his trademark role as Lt. Commander Sulu as he faces down a Klingon-supported terrorist group called Shark and finds his long-lost son in the process.

While little is known about the unseen movie, Takei shot all his portions of the film in one 18-hour day, reportedly cracking jokes with the amateur cast and crew, and rewriting his dialogue as necessary to better fit Sulu's style. Also involved in the fledgling production was another *Trek* pro, Andy Probert, who had designed the U.S.S. *Enterprise* spaceships for *Star Trek: The Motion Picture* and *Star Trek: The Next Generation*. For the fan film, Probert created the *Yorktown II*, implementing a cobbled-together look for the vessel.

Sulu's son was played by the film's writer/producer, Cal State business major Stan Woo, who got Takei involved based on a long-standing friendship with the actor. Woo claimed at the time that other Hollywood pros were involved, stating that Oscar-winning composer Bill Conti would create music for the short, that eighties TV action mogul Steven J. Cannell had given permission for the production to use sound effects from *The A-Team*, and that actor George Lazenby (James Bond in *Her Majesty's Secret Service*) had been briefly cast in the short until a scheduling conflict scuttled his participation.

Woo's dream was to show the movie at *Star Trek* conventions, but no one knows if *Yorktown II* was completed; word got out about the fan film, however, when it was the subject of a feature article in sci-fi newsstand mainstay, *Starlog*. It's entirely possible that the amateur production collapsed under the weight of its ambitious scope (Woo was looking into hiring a professional company to handle his special effects), but it's just as plausible that Paramount took note of the high-profile article and fired off a cease-and-desist letter like the ones aimed at Art Binninger. It's certainly not out of the question: The *Star Trix* animator received his first missive in June, 1987—the same month that the *Starlog* article hit print.

Despite his snarky letter war with Paramount, Binninger never experienced any legal repercussions; on the other hand, his enthusiasm had taken a hit, as he found himself having to juggle his fondness for the TV series with a bitter distaste for Paramount. "For years, I wouldn't buy the merchandise and would only see the films in the cheapest matinee possible," he recalls. "When they

Binninger tried a front projection effect on his Space Station K-Mart set, using the projector next to his camera to create a moving image in the background while he filmed new footage.
(Courtesy of Art Binninger)

flooded the market with products and series in the 1990s, I pretty much stepped back and began working on things of my own."

In the years since his fledgling fan films, homemade *Star Trek* productions have exploded in popularity. Benninger remarks, "I hope that someone in the studio front office has realized that the fans are the people who have sustained them during the lean times, and that attacking them is counterproductive."

As it turns out, they have, according to James Cawley, executive producer of the online fan film series, *Star Trek: New Voyages/ Phase II*. "There's a whole new group of people at CBS and Paramount who understand the value of the fans a hell of a lot more than they ever did," he says. "They see that there's no harm being done to their property—certainly a fan film that can generate interest to their trademark, so it's to their advantage to embrace it, let it go and let fans just have fun."

That change of heart, however, came too late for Binninger; his pop culture interests have changed, now skewing toward Popeye and *I Dream of Jeannie*—"I still have a soft spot for the original series and *Star Trek: The Next Generation*, but maintain a discreet distance from it now. Would that make me a recovering Trekker?"

• • •

Throughout the seventies and early eighties, the majority of amateur blockbusters—like *Star Trix*—were shot with 8mm and Super 8 film cameras. Home movie cameras were the only game in town, just as they had been for decades, and there was nothing to challenge them—until video came along.

Since the dawn of television, video cameras had lived in studios and nowhere else; even TV newscasts shot their stories on the street in 16mm, because video cameras were far too big and unwieldy to be used outside a broadcast facility. Film crews would race around, capture their stories for posterity, and head back to the studio to develop and edit the film in time for the 11 o'clock news.

As the seventies progressed, however, technology advanced enough that the pros began using video cameras. Tied by cables to portable (OK, luggable) recording units that were often 30 pounds or more, the cameras were comparatively minute next to their TV-studio counterparts. As is the case with any technological advancement, the professional cameras and recorders were eventually watered down into consumer products that anyone could buy—if they were rich enough.

The consumer cameras depended on a video-recording technology that had been available to consumers since the midsixties, but they used videotapes stored on awkward reels and usually recorded in black and white, so they never caught on outside of educational and medical markets. All that changed when Sony released the first Betamax video cassette recorder (VCR) in November, 1975; RCA's competing format, VHS, came out in September the following year. The two incompatible formats were rivals for a while, but by the early 1980s, VHS—cheaper and able to hold more content on a videotape—had clearly won the war, even though Betamax had better picture quality.

One area where Betamax initially seemed to be more popular, however, was in the burgeoning market for home video cameras.

Even simplified for consumers, the cameras were still extremely complicated and expensive, and much like the professional versions, the user would balance a heavy camera on the right shoulder, while hauling around the 30- to 40-pound "PortaPak" recording unit in a satchel on the left shoulder. All this was powered by rechargeable batteries that only held a brief charge, yet often weighed anywhere up to five pounds, adding to the already backbreaking weight of the PortaPak. In short, making home videos in the late seventies and early eighties was an expensive, exhausting, frustrating, and generally miserable hobby. And people loved it.

The advantages of home videos over home movies were as plain as day. Users didn't have to wait weeks for film to be developed, and they could fit hours of footage on a single videocassette as opposed to three minutes per film reel—plus, they could reuse the videocassette if they wanted. Additionally, video cameras recorded in color with sound (plenty of families were still using silent home movie cameras), and watching the day's footage meant sitting around the TV instead of having to set up a projector and movie screen.

To adults who had grown up watching grainy, out-of-focus home movies of Grandma's 90-billionth birthday, the video camera systems were miraculous; to the young kids of Generation X just coming of age, however, they were tools that could be used to construct fantastic home movies—many of them fan films—in ways that Super 8 never could achieve.

Film users sure were trying, however. *Cinemagic*, the amateur filmmaking magazine that explained how to create low-budget special effects, was doing exceptionally well, having grown to a circulation of 5,000 readers per issue. By 1979, it had built such a dedicated following that editor Don Dohler, who had squeezed out only 11 issues since founding it in 1972, sold the publication to the publishers of *Starlog*. Meanwhile, Dohler moved on to dual careers, juggling newspaper journalism in suburban Baltimore with B-movie production, creating late-night fare like *Fiend*, *Nightbeast*, and *Galaxy Invader*. His unusual life proved so fascinating that he became the focus of a feature documentary, *Blood, Boobs & Beast*, completed just before his untimely passing in 2006 due to cancer.

In the meantime, once *Starlog* bought *Cinemagic*, the publication got a slick, glossy makeover, issues came out on a quarterly schedule, and it landed on mainstream newsstands for the first time, reaching more amateur filmmakers than ever before. To its new owners, the magazine was headed for a strong future. Video was far from a threat when the first issues of the "new" *Cinemagic* were released, so the publication's narrow focus on stop-motion animation and other uses for movie cameras remained.

By the early 1980s, however, the battle between consumer video and movie cameras was in full swing, and the dream that glinted in each video manufacturer's eye was to be the first to market with a home video camera that wasn't a two-piece behemoth. That fantasy became a reality with the introduction of the one-piece camera/recorder—aka the camcorder—in 1982, when Sony debuted the Betamovie, a one-piece camera that could record directly onto a Beta videotape.

In 1984, Kodak, watching its Super 8 and 8mm film profits spiraling down the tubes, debuted the KodaVision2000, a durable, compact camcorder that used a new, different video format called 8mm—a name that initially created some confusion for consumers who thought it was an 8mm film camera. Instead, the compact videotapes became a standard across the industry, as Sony released its own 8mm video camera, the Video 8, the following year.

For 8mm and Super 8 film cameras, it was all but over. Kodak tried to keep home movie film alive by selling a home-developing kit so that users wouldn't have to wait weeks to see their footage, but it was a stopgap measure at best. Manufacturers tried to respond to the losing battle by offering newer, cheaper models with advanced features like autofocus lenses, boom microphones, single-frame exposures for stop-motion animation, and more. A decade earlier, consumers with a filmmaking fixation would have foamed at the mouth for such features, but by the late eighties, no one cared; video was the name of the game.

Home movie film would stumble along for the next two decades, going through brief periods of minor resurgence as artists exploited the grainy, shaky look of Super 8, or when commercials and music videos used 8mm cameras to create pseudo-vintage footage. Minor resurgences don't pay the bills, however, and in 2005, Kodak, struggling with the natural decline of film sales, stopped producing Super 8 Kodachrome, the format's premium film stock; a year later, Kodak shut down its last Kodachrome processing facility in Lausanne, Switzerland. Home movies had reached the final reel.

Underlining the home movie camera's fall from grace was the slow, inevitable death of *Cinemagic*. The publication, which had covered so many homemade Monster Kid flicks and fan films, was shuttered in 1987 after 15 years and 48 issues. *Cinemagic* had always encouraged amateurs to dream about the possibilities for their films, but with the world's move to video cameras, the magazine's own possibilities were grounded for good by grim economic realities.

"I remember this one article in *Cinemagic*," reminisces reader Stuart Basinger, "where the guy who wrote it wanted to film himself getting shot, so he taped a piece of leather to his chest, taped a cherry bomb over that and then put on his jacket. When the firework went off, he had to go to the emergency room and he wound up with a six-inch, permanent scar. I thought, 'Pal, didn't anyone ever tell you not to play with fireworks?' Of course, I had some scary moments, too, making my James Bond movie—like when the police showed up."

Basinger and his friend, Trey Stokes, were prototypical *Cinemagic* readers—just the sort of amateur filmmakers who would spend months shooting a 007 fan film. Having just graduated high school in their town outside Washington, D.C., the pair spent the summer of 1978 adapting the only Bond book that, at the time, had yet to be turned into a feature film; the result was *Moonraker '78*.

While they worked on the movie for a year, most of the shooting was accomplished that summer, whenever Basinger, who played Bond, and Stokes, the director, got together with friends. One weekend trip in Ocean City, Maryland, found them filming on the boardwalk, when they were inspired to shoot an on-the-beach fight sequence to open the movie. However, they realized something crucial was missing.

"Our friend Ray just went down on the beach and picked up this girl," Stokes says, laughing. "She said she'd be in it—but she had to ask her parents first. So there's us three teenage guys

James Bond movies always feature a sleek sports car and exotic locales; Stuart Basinger substituted his usual ride (missing its hubcaps) and a beach house for his fan film, *Moonraker '78*. *(Courtesy of Stuart Basinger)*

standing there with this little Super 8 camera, saying, 'Duh, hi, we wanna put your daughter in a movie.' They checked us out, made sure we weren't crazy, and watched behind the camera while we ran around. Then afterwards, one of her parents said, 'So, when's this gonna be on?' Which was a shock to us—that was the general lack of awareness of how movies were made. There was no E! channel, no DVD 'making of' featurettes back then; these people really thought three guys on a beach were making a TV show."

Although things went swimmingly while shooting on the beach, the results from their Canon Super 8 camera rarely matched what they envisioned, such as a special-effect shot that they scrapped because it looked exactly like what it was: a toy submarine with an Alka Seltzer bubbling out the end of it. Adding to the frustration was the high cost of production—a single roll of film cost $3 and development was another $2.50 (for a quickie comparison, a movie ticket was $3 at the time). As a result, although the pair had cut together large portions of the movie and shelled out over $1,000 during production, the fan film was eventually shelved. Still, they had fun along the way, gaining stories—and wisdom—in hindsight.

"We did whatever the hell we wanted," says Stokes. "We blew stuff up, drove cars really fast, jumped off cliffs—all the incredibly stupid stuff that everyone does as teenagers, 'cause that's just how we thin the herd. If you can survive your teen years when you're dumb and don't know anything, OK, you can go breed. We just happened to do it on film." Case in point: the moment Basinger alluded to before, which could have gotten them arrested.

Stokes had a summer job at the University of Maryland, working next door to a heating plant for classrooms and dorms. Sticking his head inside the huge building, he'd marveled at the towering machinery, ladders, and catwalks. Instantly, he knew it would make a great setting for a chase scene, so he talked his pals into filming there; he just neglected to talk the university into it, too.

"We didn't get permission to do any of it," he says, laughing. "I was around there all the time, so I said, 'Let's just show up and walk in.' There weren't many people who worked there and they didn't give a damn anyway. We just went in and improvised this crazy chase—running around, leaping off stuff, pretending to throw people off the catwalks 50 feet above the ground—and they didn't care; they were fine with it. In retrospect, it boggles my mind that we had the audacity to do that, but the scene looks great; it really moves. To this day, I still go 'That may be the best action scene I've ever directed.'"

Ironically, it was the tail end of that scene that brought on the biggest drama—a moment that had to be left on the cutting room floor. Basinger-as-Bond had escaped the heating plant, and now had to steal a getaway car while shooting his way through a gaggle of guards. Because Stokes and Basinger had only three kids to represent an army of bad guys, they decided the guards were clones; that way, Bond could kill the same people over and over.

"Stuart ran into the shot," relates Stokes, "and just as he went past the camera, he heard me say, 'Oh shit!' I was looking through the viewfinder and saw a cop car roll into the background. 'Oh shit' kind of meant 'cut,' but I didn't actually say 'cut,' so he did what he was supposed to—bang a guy on the head, shoot two other guys dead and then run like hell. So in the outtake, you can see the police stop in the distance, Stuart blows everyone away—and then suddenly realizes the cops are watching. He completely freezes up and stands there, toy gun in hand, looking at them—and the punch line to the shot is, after all that, the cop car drives away! Of course, they did come back."

Basinger recalls, "Something like 20 police drove up and we said, 'Oh boy. . . .' The guy in the plant who let us go ahead had gone home for the day, and his replacement didn't want us there, so he'd called the cops." That, combined with the other police witnessing the "shootout" firsthand, made for a sticky situation. Comments Stokes, "Yeah, we had to explain ourselves—'It's a toy gun; uh, sorry.' But we were helped by the fact that he was pantomiming; there was no actual bang—and the dead guys stood up at the end of the shot."

Even though the fan film went unfinished, it had a profound impact on its creators: Basinger went on to become a video editor, eventually working for the Fox News Channel, while Stokes headed for California to become part of the movie business.

While it was shelved indefinitely, much like its hero, the Bond movie escaped death. It was during some downtime at one of his video jobs in the early nineties that Basinger transferred his old film footage to video on a whim and started tinkering with it. The result was a completed edit with the addition of submarine stock footage, material from a *Sports Illustrated* swimsuit video for his opening title sequence and a handful of special-effects shots from various Bond flicks.

> "Technology saved the movie in a lot of ways," says Basinger, because I was able to fix a lot of things. Back in the day, you'd splice the film and then use special tape to connect the shots together—and those taped frames were always jarring; they looked terrible. When I re-edited the film on a computer, I was able to remove them and that improved the look a lot. Also, back then, we made a huge model of our bad guy Dax's island hideout; we filmed it but it never looked right, so it wasn't in the movie. The model was too big to keep, so I used my Dad's Nikon to take some photos of it, figuring, "If I can't keep it physically, maybe someday I can use the photo." So years later, I pulled out the photo, scanned it into my computer and made a masked cutout of it—and I was able to place that over footage from *Our Man*

Moonraker '78 director Trey Stokes sets up an exploding helicopter effect.
(Courtesy of Stuart Basinger)

> *Flint,* so that a submarine from that movie heads towards my island. I called up Trey and told him our hard work paid off—sure, it took decades, but our model was finally in the movie!

Later, Basinger souped up the fan film even more, cleaning up spots on an Avid Media Composer system after hours at Fox News, making a DVD for friends and placing *Moonraker '78* on YouTube for a year, until MGM demanded that it be taken down. The final version features modern video editing, a dubbed-in soundtrack and plenty of sound effects—but still no dialogue. "In this case," joked the filmmaker, "actions really do speak louder than words."

• • •

Basinger and Stokes weren't the only ones who wanted to make their own James Bond movies back then. In 1977, when George Lucas and Steven Spielberg wound up making sand castles in Hawaii on the opening weekend of *Star Wars,* Spielberg mentioned he wanted to direct a Bond flick. Lucas replied that he had something even better, and told him the story that would become *Raiders of the Lost Ark*.

Four years later, that first Indiana Jones film spent the summer of 1981 tearing up the box office, but while it recalled the serials that had motivated them to become filmmakers, neither Lucas nor Spielberg could have foreseen it would in turn inspire a 100-minute fan film only a few years later, this time by teenagers using video cameras. The result—Raiders of the Lost Ark: The Adaptation—was astounding, and the story behind it was just as amazing and death-defying as the feature film itself.

7
Indiana Jones and the Lost Fan Film of Mississippi

It all sounds like something out of a Steven Spielberg picture: Misfit outsiders forge deep bonds with each other as they embark on an impossible quest, and after great hardship, they find maturity and confidence as they succeed against the odds, living happily ever after. You'll find this story line time and time again in flicks Spielberg has directed and produced, from *E.T.* and *Close Encounters of the Third Kind* to *Empire of the Sun* and *The Goonies*. However, it's also the plot to a real-life, Spielberg-induced story—and even more surprising, the part where fictional characters would call it a day and live happily ever after is just the halfway point.

Now, if this particular story was a Spielberg movie set in the early 1980s, Eric Zala, Chris Strompolos, and Jayson Lamb would be the heroes, and the camera would introduce them, one by one, as middle schoolers from single-parent homes, sitting bored in class, daydreaming—wishing, hoping, praying—for some excitement to liven things up in their quiet, southern town just outside Biloxi, Mississippi.

For Strompolos, that first whiff of adventure came in the summer of 1981, when he went to see *Raiders of the Lost Ark*. It looked to have a great pedigree—directed by Spielberg and produced by George Lucas—and the picture was sure to be exciting. Settling into his theater seat with his popcorn, Strompolos was instantly sucked into the classic thrill-ride movie where archeologist Indiana Jones risks life and limb in one amazing feat after another, all in pursuit of the Ark of the Covenant. Harrison Ford galvanized the screen as the iron-jawed hero who could teach a class, win a fight, outrun a boulder, beat the bad guys, get the girl, and never lose his hat.

Despite all its flash and bluster, though, the film had an emotional resonance for the 10-year-old Strompolos. An only child living with his mother, he found that Indiana Jones affected him differently than most kids, as the gentleman rogue became, if not a father figure, a bona-fide idol all the same. "He was the type of hero on the screen that felt very real," Strompolos reflects. "Very human, flawed, self-reliant, sharp, kinda macho, a man of few words and definitely a man of action. And I think for a boy growing up looking for a male role-model to emulate, he just blew me away. I wanted nothing more than to inhabit that world."

So, he did. By the summer of 1983, Strompolos was making his own *Raiders* fan film remake, running around as Indy, complete with vinyl "leather" jacket and charcoal smeared on his face for stubble. What started out as a way for three "tweens" to kill time, however, soon became an all-consuming, life-changing passion. "We figured we could knock it out in a summer," recalls Strompolos. "We had no idea it would take seven years."

• • •

Strompolos met his director on their daily, hourlong school bus ride when Zala (rhymes with "Layla") spotted his *Raiders* comic book and asked if he could borrow it. Soon after, the young Indy-wannabe saw a class film by Zala at a school assembly, and it wasn't long before he was on the phone, recruiting the 12-year-old to work on his idea for a grand remake.

Once Zala got over his initial disappointment at their first meeting ("I thought he was going to have sets and costumes and other kids involved, but all he had was a 'making of' book"), and they set to work on preproduction—a process that would take 18 months.

First, they drew costumes and made a list of as many shots as they could remember from the movie. Zala, who dreamed of

Director Eric Zala (left), star Chris Strompolos (center), and cameraman Jayson Lamb began making their shot-for-shot remake of *Raiders of the Lost Ark* in 1982 when they were pre-teens. They finished seven years later.
(Courtesy of Rolling Boulder Productions)

becoming a comic book artist, then drew 609 storyboards based on promotional photos, as the film hadn't been released on home video yet. *Raiders* was rereleased to theaters in May 1982, so the enterprising pair went to the movies to sneak in a tape recorder; if they recorded the film, they could capture dialogue, inflections, and reminders of different shots. Not nearly as smooth as his hero, a nervous Strompolos tried to get the recorder in, but was caught and thrown out by an usher, so Zala stuck it under his own shirt and emerged from the theater with a precious—if garbled—copy of the movie on audiocassette.

There were a million other hurdles in the way, of course: The boys needed explosions, gunshots, and someone else to run the camera in certain spots, since Zala was going to play Belloq, Indy's white-suited archrival whose head explodes at the end of the film.

Strompolos found the answer to all those problems in the form of Jayson Lamb, another kid from school, slightly older than Zala, who had plenty of ideas about how to make the project happen. An avid reader of magic books from the local library, Lamb knew how to make fake blood and set things on fire without burning them; clearly, this was a kid to have on their side.

Part of the reason why they didn't start taping until the summer of 1983 was that the trio had a serious camera problem: They didn't have one. If nothing else, however, they at least knew what kind they wanted. According to Zala, "We never actually had much of a discussion on which format to go with; it was always Betamax."

Strompolos's mom, an investigative reporter at a local TV station, twice rented a video camera for the kids and got a station employee to give them a five-minute tutorial on how to focus, white balance, and so on. Cutting-edge technology like that cost an exorbitant $50 per outing, however, so once it became clear that *Raiders* wasn't going to be built in a day—or even two—renting was out of the question. Faced with little choice, the threesome pooled their money, got considerable investment from their parents and purchased their own two-piece, Sony Betamax camera and PortaPak.

The hefty system was difficult for adults to manage, but it proved even more unwieldy when used by undersized preteens. Keeping one's balance while trying to tape something was no easy feat: "Poor, diminutive Jayson had to trudge along in the swamps with this monstrosity strapped to him," recalls Zala.

There were other issues, too. "They hadn't perfected the technology of silent tapeheads yet, so you always heard the heads rolling in the background—*nehhhhhhhhhh*," says Strompolos. "It was never made for the abuse we dished out. With the heat and humidity, mud, dust, mosquitoes and three boys trying to keep it clean, it was always getting repaired at Al's Audio in Biloxi for months on end; after a few years of that, it gave up and died on us." When that happened, Lamb worked all summer delivering pizzas until he could buy his own VHS camcorder—a one-piece camera that made life considerably easier for the young cameraman.

Back in 1983, however, once they finally had a way to capture their adventures, it was time to start having some. They needed a truck for Indiana Jones to be dragged beneath; a boulder for him to outrun; a submarine to hold onto for hundreds of miles; and a bar to set on fire during a massive fight with Nazi henchmen—but there was something they needed that was far scarier than any of those things: a girl to play Indy's love interest, Marion Ravenwood. "In retrospect, it's good that we chose *Raiders*," notes Zala, "because it only has two female parts, and we didn't know a lot of girls back then."

Initially, the role was taken by a seventh grader, Stephanie Ewing, who shot a few scenes that summer. Production halted with the start of school in September, and wouldn't resume until after classes ended the following year—a pattern they would follow for the rest of the decade—so it wasn't until the summer of 1984 that the filmmakers discovered they had a problem: "Marion" had moved to Alaska with her family.

All Ewing's scenes would have to be reshot—including the one that had nearly ended their production for good: the Nepalese bar.

In the original film, the bar is set on fire when Indy and Marion duke it out with the Nazi brainiac Toht and his evil cohorts. It's hair-raising to watch in the real flick as the burning building collapses around them, but when enacted by kids who've merrily engulfed Zala's basement in flames, it takes on an added urgency—one starts rooting for them to get out of the scene alive.

The reason they dared to set the place afire was because Lamb had a magic book that suggested mixing isopropyl alcohol with water to produce short-lived flames. Inspired, they bought dozens of bottles from K-Mart and drenched everything. "When you poured it on wood and lit it up, the wood didn't burn, just the fluid—we thought that was great," recalls Zala, aghast at the memory. "In the outtakes, I'm walking around with a Mason jar filled to the brim with alcohol, and a lit torch in the other hand. All I needed was one stray spark to make it explode like a Molotov Cocktail—and yet there we were, splashing it all over the set."

As a result, when they shot the scene, the bar was on fire, drapes were aflame, and worst of all, one henchman—played by Zala, since he didn't want anyone to get hurt—was also on fire.

"I thought I was playing it safe, because under my costume, I

For a fight scene inside a flame-filled bar, Zala was doused in gasoline and set on fire. "I thought I was playing it safe, because under my costume, I had a fire-retardant raincoat. How stupid we were."
(Courtesy of Rolling Boulder Productions)

had a fire-retardant raincoat," he recalls. In fact, Zala was so overconfident that when it came time for his friends to set him on fire, he passed on the water/alcohol mix and had them douse him in gasoline instead.

Carefully, they stood by with a fire extinguisher and a blanket to smother the flames, and struck a match. Once Zala was lit up, he ran around, screamed on cue and fell to the ground as planned. The friends rushed in with the blanket and covered him. Then they yanked it off to see if he was OK. He was still on fire, so they threw it back on. Then they pulled it off again. This happened repeatedly, so fast that instead of smothering the flames, the blanket actually fanned them. Scared witless, the kids fired the extinguisher at Zala—and miraculously, he was all right; only his hair was singed. Incredibly, young Zala was furious that they'd used the extinguisher, because refilling it would take money from the budget.

Letting bygones be bygones, however, the kids rushed to the TV station where Strompolos's mom worked; there, they could commandeer an editing station to view their footage. When an employee saw the shot of Zala flambé, though, it only took one concerned phone call for the production to be shot down in flames.

When the various parents discovered what their kids had been up to, they were—to put it mildly—upset. The movie was over, period. Looking back as a parent today, Zala can't really blame them: "How stupid we were, quite frankly. I'm aware that I'm going to have trouble holding the moral high ground when my kids are old enough to see the movie. They'll see the fire scene and I'll say, 'Don't set yourself on fire; do as I say, not as I did.'"

A year later, in the summer of 1984, the trio begged and pleaded with their folks to let them work on the fan film again, and with enough cajoling, the parents consented, providing there was adult supervision around for the more dangerous scenes. That was fine with the trio, as they had recruited Peter Kieffer, a laid-back tenant who rented one of the numerous cottages in Zala's backyard. He was more than happy to let the kids run wild—and they obliged. First on the agenda was a reshoot of the bar scene with the new Marion, Angela Rodriguez, whom Zala met at church. Everything went up in flames again—except the director, who wisely retained the footage of himself on fire from the previous year and cut it in when they finally edited the scene together. Miraculously, there were again no mishaps.

The "director on fire" moment was the only shot from the summer of 1983 to make it into the movie. "We scrapped most of the footage from the first few years, just because it was so horrible," remembers Strompolos. "We started with no concept of lighting, composition, or production value; we just thought if you put on a costume, got in front of the camera and said the lines, the magic would happen—and that simply wasn't the case. We shot for an entire summer, then sat down to watch our footage; we were so excited to see our little masterpiece, and then so discouraged because it was the most unbearably boring, awful footage. We shot the jungle scene over and over, the bar scene a few times, and other parts, until we finally got them right."

One of the scenes they redid a few times was Indy and Marion's passionate kiss, substituting Zala's bedroom for a ship's cabin. Preparing for the scene meant Strompolos had to stretch as an actor—after all, he'd never kissed a girl before. After the shoot, he was happy that the smooch looked good when they played it back, but even better, it had to be reshot because swamp frogs could be heard in the background. Perhaps unsurprisingly, all of this led to an on-again, off-again romance between the two stars, but if the kiss was a big success for Strompolos, there was a different bedroom situation that was a complete fiasco: the building of the boulder.

Raiders' signature moment occurs early on, when Indiana Jones is chased out of a cave by a massive boulder barreling down on him. Before they even had a camera, one of the first things Strompolos and Zala attempted was to build a boulder in the former's bedroom, using cardboard, bamboo, and duct tape. The 12-year-olds stayed up all night and the result looked great; unfortunately, it was too big to fit through the door. This proved to be the first of many attempts over the years to create the iconic rock.

Their second try was to get a three-foot-high cable spool and wrap cardboard around it; when they shot the scene, low camera angles were used in an attempt to make the boulder look bigger than Strompolos, but every playback told the truth: he was being chased by a short, cardboard cylinder. Figuring the third time was the charm, they tried using papier-mâché, plastered around a $30 weather balloon, but it deflated overnight before everything dried, creating a lumpy, caved-in blob instead. Next, they used chicken wire, and that seemed like it was going to work, even though, as Zala notes, "I sliced up my hands putting it together." That boulder was not to be, however; Hurricane Elena picked up the incomplete framework one day and tossed it deep into the Gulf of Mexico.

The project finally started rolling when Zala's mom recommended talking to a local boat builder, Mic Sajway. "We dug a big, carefully measured hole in his backyard, three feet wide and three feet deep, and that became a mold for fiberglass," recalls Zala. With the pair of bowl-shaped molds, some gray spray-paint, and some connective work, Sajway created a six-foot round boulder that weighed 100 pounds. Best of all, the fledgling filmmakers got it for $100, on the condition that Sajway could keep it when they were done to use as an example of his handiwork.

Unlike the previous boulders, which were never very durable, the fiberglass edition stood the test of time; 18 years later, the filmmakers needed the fake rock for a photo shoot (more on that later), visited Sajway, and found it tucked away in a dilapidated boat behind his house, covered in moss. Its creator, eyeing one less piece of debris in his yard, told them, "Yeah, you can keep it, actually." Since none of them lived in the area anymore, the boulder became an odd lawn ornament in Zala's mother's yard, until Hurricane Katrina whisked it away in 2005. Katrina may have leveled New Orleans and half-destroyed the Zala house (it was later repaired to its original state), but the boulder was discovered months later, 250 yards away in a swamp, none the worse for wear other than a few holes thanks to flying tree limbs.

Back in 1986, however, the team finally had its boulder, but needed "tracks" for it to roll down, so Zala paid a local logging company $40 to drop off two untreated telephone poles, each 40 feet long, in his yard. "You should have seen my mom's expression when this 18-wheeler showed up to drop them off," says Zala, "and then had to turn around in my driveway." It took five loggers to place them in the cave set—i.e. the Zala garage, remodeled with Spanish moss and Styrofoam stalactites. The end result? A great moment in the film where Strompolos honestly looks scared as he's chased by a big boulder that's about as heavy as he is.

While the first big set piece of the movie was now nailed down, there were still other key moments, like the action-packed sequence where Indy carjacks a truck carrying the ark, fends off an endless stream of Nazis onboard and winds up being dragged beneath the vehicle before finally taking it over. To shoot the scene, they'd need Nazis and deserted roads far from parental supervision—oh, and a truck they could beat to hell.

Finding the setting was simple; they used a network of rarely traveled dirt roads—now the site of a subdivision—behind Strompolos's house. Getting the truck was just as easy, it turned out: Another tenant who rented a cottage from the Zalas donated his ancient 1964 Ford pickup, the motor of which was dead. Zala got his younger brother, Kurt, to jury-rig some brakes (those were missing, too), strung a tent over the truck bed and voila: instant Nazi transport, albeit one that couldn't actually move. As a result, the entire scene had to be shot with the truck either being pushed or towed by a friend's VW Beetle at about 15–20 mph, all the while driven by "kids who hadn't quite gotten their permit yet," according to Zala. Filling the truck with evil bad guys was also easy—they simply talked friends into showing up in old Boy Scout uniforms with the patches ripped off.

When Nazis fell or were thrown off the vehicle, usually it was Kurt taking one for the team, but sometimes it was just as dangerous to be behind the camera, too. "There's a shot where the

Chris Strompolos as Indiana Jones, perched atop the Nazi transport as it rolled along swampland dirt roads. Because the truck was dead, it was pushed or towed for each shot by a Volkswagen Beetle. *(Courtesy of Rolling Boulder Productions)*

truck careens through a batch of Arab vendors' stands along the road," Zala recalls. "The tables are covered with big ceramic jugs of water; ours were spray-painted wine bottles, actually. Shooting it was all well and good . . . except one of the jugs flipped into the air, and smashed against the windshield, caving in a section about a foot around. Jayson shot the whole thing while in the truck's cab, with Chris at the wheel, and it nearly broke through the windshield at them! They were pretty rattled after that."

Things only got more stressful for Strompolos, who did all his own stunts, including the part when Indy hangs off the front bumper only to let go and be dragged behind the truck. "It was pretty harrowing," he admits. "I was dragging under the front of it, the grille started to come off, and I was getting crushed against the ground as the truck was moving, so I got a little scared. We definitely didn't show that part to our parents until the final premiere!"

The resulting scene may have taken two weeks to shoot, but it was as action-packed as the real thing, sporting the same wild, kinetic energy as Spielberg's version, and today, the trio proudly considers it to be the most fully realized part of the movie.

The submarine segment, which takes place in the movie soon after, required considerably more patience. Zala recalls,

> Chris drove down to Mobile, Alabama, to talk to one Captain Difley, who ran a tourist park that had a retired World War II submarine and battleship—and he was told, "No,

> you can't shoot here." The following summer, he put on a tie and jacket, strode into the office and asked again—and this time, Difley said no. Third summer, he went down there again, but now he brought our storyboards and shooting schedule, and presented us in the most organized, professional manner possible for 16-year-olds. Finally the captain said, "Fine, fine, shoot it—but we're not shutting the park down for you." So we actually shot that day around bemused tourists; I'm not quite sure what they thought of us. There was a big sign there that read DANGER—NO SWIMMING! ALLIGATORS!—but we needed Chris to swim to the submarine. As the director, I thought about it, and then I sat down with him and discussed our options; "Chris, you gotta swim really fast."

Another hard-to-get setting was the Sahara Desert; their set was a "dirt farm"—a few acres of scraped-up land used to supply red clay to construction sites. The trio were originally rebuffed by that location's owner, too, but after his wife saw the trio on a local TV morning show (yep, it was Strompolos's mom's station), she nagged him into letting them shoot there. In a case of "careful what you wish for," Zala and crew now had to figure out how to get 20 kids in Arab costumes to their set 60 miles away, organize them, feed them, and get them home. But they did it.

"I still remember sitting at my mom's house," says Zala, "watching the playback as we ate spaghetti, surrounded by those 20 kids, and I saw the shot of Indy and the others, digging at the Well of Souls in silhouette as the sun goes down behind them. I was so excited, and really felt it was coming together."

As the years progressed, the team slowly completed more and more of the movie; they replicated what they could—going so far as to find the same 1936 issue of *Life* that appeared as a prop in the original—and replaced what they couldn't, such as the spider monkey that Indy carried around in the middle of the movie. "For some reason, there weren't that many spider monkeys in southern Mississippi," notes Zala, "so we were going to use a cat when Chris said, 'Well, how about Snick?'" His dog, Snickers, took on the role with gusto, even re-creating the monkey's "sieg heil" salute with the help of a low-budget special effect: fishing wire around his paw. Snick wasn't the only nonhuman in the fan film, however; five live snakes, loaned from a pet shop, slithered around dozens of fakes from Toys 'R' Us and sliced garden hoses painted black for the famous snake pit scene.

In fact, there was only one major portion of the film that they left out: the "flying wing" segment, where Indy battles a massive, bald-headed, Nazi mechanic beneath an experimental plane. "We storyboarded it and had a little, single-engine plane on an airfield picked out," recalls Zala, "but here's the rub: The scene culminates with the plane exploding, and we couldn't do that. We had trashed the truck, but there was no way we were going to get to do that with a donated plane. That meant we'd have to blow up a miniature with a firecracker instead—and this may sound funny now, but we didn't want the movie to look cheesy."

Letting the scene slide, however, even for such a superfluous action beat, left the budding director unsettled; Zala had recurring dreams for a decade afterward that they were finally shooting the flying wing.

• • •

By 1988, all three filmmakers had moved on to college and were now juggling summer jobs with their crazy hobby. It had been six years since Zala, Strompolos, and Lamb had started in on the project, and they'd made it over every hurdle. Strompolos had managed to keep excited about his pet project even though he spent most of his teens at boarding school, returning to Mississippi only for summer vacations. "I spent most of the year in New York, but it wasn't like *Raiders* went away for me," he says. "We were actively staying in touch, writing letters back and forth about props we'd found, ideas we had, new production possibilities. I'd find a dagger and ship it back to Mississippi, and meanwhile, Eric and Jayson would be working on sets and things, and when I flew back, we'd pick up where we left off. It was never, 'I don't want to do it anymore, I want to go to a party;' it was always, 'When do we start *Raiders*?'"

Zala, too, managed to keep his enthusiasm going over the

years, despite breaking his arm on set (he fell out of a tree), singing his hair when he was on fire, and even Strompolos's short-lived attempt to steal his girlfriend—a move that all involved regretted. And then there was the time he had to go to the hospital to get his cast removed—from his face.

In the production's final scene, where the Nazis finally open the ark, Belloq's head explodes grotesquely. To pull off the special effect, Lamb wanted to make a plaster cast of Zala's noggin so that they could make a wax replica to destroy for the movie. Things took a turn for the worse, though, when they used the wrong kind of plaster—and discovered that industrial plaster heats up when it gets wet. Zala was trapped inside, unable to speak while he hyperventilated through drinking straws jammed up his nose. When they put a pen in his hand, he wrote only one word: Hospital. When doctors finally freed him, Zala lost all his eyelashes and half an eyebrow—but they had their cast, and the hair grew back.

A few nights later, the wax replica head was set up outside Strompolos's house. Lamb used a slide projector to place an image of Zala's face onto the dummy head, and the effect looked perfect; they were ready to shoot the head explosion—literally. With the video camera rolling, Strompolos pulled out a shotgun off-screen, took aim, and squeezed the trigger. He missed, but the loud shot rang through the quiet evening air. He tried again—and missed. In fact, it took a few attempts before he finally nailed the wax head—which ripped apart quite nicely—but by then, the police were on their way. "The cops got reports of gunfire, and gee, it's these 17-year-old kids in the middle of the night with a shotgun," remembers Strompolos. "Somehow I managed to talk our way out of it."

The movie's climax is the opening of the ark, and that turned out to be also the production's final scene, too. By all rights, it should have been a joyous occasion. "After six years, we were done shooting and we'd built it up in our heads that we'd be hugging each other with tears streaming down our faces," remembers Zala. "It wasn't like that at all. Chris and Angela's romance had waned, so it was awkward. The final shot was them strapped to the pole at the end, screaming, 'Ahh,' with the ghosts—which were baby powder poured into fans—going by behind them. I called, 'Cut—OK, that's a good one,' and that was it. It was completely anticlimactic. Chris walked up to me and said, 'We're finished—big deal. Now we have to edit this thing.'"

Editing was comparatively fast, however, done at the TV station where Strompolos's mom worked. As the final cut came together, sure, there were a few bizarre moments where Indiana Jones would leave a scene as a confident 17-year-old and enter the next one as a short, squeaky-voiced kid of 12, but they were surprised at how well it all fit together. Part of that was because over the years, they'd pre-edited sections together, so those segments were simply copied to their master tape—a move they now regret. Every time a videotape is copied to another videotape, the duplicate—called a "generation"—loses some picture and audio quality; a further copy of the duplicate is even more degraded. By the time they finished editing, the final version was six generations down, making for a fairly grainy viewing experience, despite their best efforts.

Some of those efforts were pretty clever, though. Being able to use a professional editing bay helped save a few scenes, including the opening of the ark, where unleashed spirits fly around the heroes and Nazis. The baby powder ghosts they'd created left something to be desired, so Lamb filled a fish tank with water, stuck chunks of cotton onto black sticks, and then dragged them around in the water as he videotaped with no illumination except a blacklight above the tank. The visuals of the blue, hazy cotton superimposed over footage of the actors was incredibly effective.

Throughout the summer of editing, Zala was thrilled about reaching the end of the road after seven years of hard work. "The TV station allowed us to edit after 10 at night," says Zala, "and I'd have to leave at 5 AM to go off to my summer job at Burger King; that was a real bummer. It's never lots of fun to work at a fast-food joint, but it's harder when you've stayed up all night because after almost six years, it's all starting to come together and you're seeing it unfold. That was immensely satisfying and exciting, so it was hell to tear myself away."

If Zala was thrilled, the others just wanted the project over and done; it'd been years of work, they'd grown up and had also started growing apart. Rifts were developing, but the strained friendships finally hit rock bottom one night when Zala couldn't make it to the station. Tired of the whole project, Lamb and Strompolos went there to work on the sound, but their answer was to slap John Williams's soundtrack over a few scenes and declare it done. When Zala confronted them on it, Strompolos made his position known with a simple "Go fuck yourself" and drove off into the night with Lamb in the passenger seat, leaving Zala standing in their dust.

That was that—until the following summer when 1989's *Indiana Jones and the Last Crusade* hit theaters. Zala gingerly invited Strompolos to go see it, and they had a good time—enough so that their friendship resparked and they agreed it was time to take another shot at finishing the movie properly. Soon they were back at the TV station, placing music cues from the soundtrack and fixing the audio as best they could. It was perfect timing—entering their sophomore year of college, the trio were now young men, and it was time to close the book on their childhood dream.

That summer, they finally had a world premiere, complete with limos, adoring crowds, and the rest. Zala recallS, "We rented out an auditorium in Gulfport because anything that takes seven years deserves a party. We had about 200 friends and family show up, and it was great!" It was also an eye-opening night for their parents, who saw all the death-defying stunts their sons had been up to for the first time. "They knew we were pretty crazy," says Strompolos, "but they didn't have much choice in the matter—we just kept going; we were unstoppable." That is, until that evening, when their epic film finally became a thing of the past. "It was a wonderful night." Zala recalls, "and as far as we knew, the *Raiders* chapter of our lives was finally closed."

• • •

That moment in time should have been the Spielbergesque happy ending—and yet for the filmmakers, things were just getting started. Strompolos largely kept the film a secret from his college pals, dismissing it as an overgrown childhood lark, but Zala occasionally showed *Raiders* in the TV lounge of his dorm at

New York University, where he was studying film. Zala explains, "At school and later in the corporate world, I'd dust it off maybe once a year and show people—and they liked it a lot—but when I pressed the 'eject' button on the VCR, it'd be back to the real world. That's all it was."

Eventually, Zala and Strompolos graduated their respective schools and wound up living together in Los Angeles. There, they worked at video game company Electronic Arts while they followed their dreams: Strompolos tried to break into acting, while Zala polished a script that would launch him into the Hollywood scene. None of it came to pass, however.

Instead, they started going their separate ways again; after a few years, Zala had shelved his script and moved up the corporate ladder, while Strompolos had become the lead singer of a band, indulging in un–Indiana Jones–like behavior. Soon he was neck-deep in the rock 'n' roll lifestyle—dating a stripper, getting snared by drugs, owing people money, and generally screwing up—while his friend was on the executive fast-track at the biggest company in the videogame industry. The disparate lifestyles took their toll, and soon it was obvious their friendship was over. Zala became director of quality control for Electronic Arts, moved to Florida and married Cassie Grace, a girl from high school that he'd re-met at their 10-year reunion. She'd never seen the *Raiders* remake and wouldn't for a while. By the time she did, however, everything had changed yet again.

• • •

Back in New York, Zala's college roommate, Frank Reynolds, had become a film editor at Troma Entertainment, the tiny studio behind gleefully Z-movie fare like *The Toxic Avenger*. Before they graduated, Reynolds had made himself a copy of *Raiders: The Adaptation* without mentioning it to Zala. Somehow the tape wound up at his job at Troma, but when Reynolds left the company, he accidentally left the tape behind. His replacement, Gabe Friedman, found it lying around the office, watched it, and promptly sent a copy to his friend, Eli Roth, another NYU film school grad. Within a few years, Roth had made his own mark, writing and directing the 2003 independent horror movie, *Cabin Fever,* which wound up grossing $30 million. That, in turn, paved the way for his next film, the ultraviolent hit *Hostel,* which grossed $80 million in 2006.

While that film was about agony as allegory, seven years earlier in 1999, Roth was awed by the far simpler, more innocent fare of the bootleg *Raiders* fan film. Watching it, he couldn't believe his eyes—but he recognized the impassioned teenage filmmaking that was unfolding on the screen. "I shared the same kindred spirit and had made similar films," comments Roth, "only mine were shot-for-shot remakes of *The Texas Chainsaw Massacre* and *Pieces.*" Holding onto the tape, over the years he showed it to a number of friends—and one of them was Harry Knowles.

Knowles is the founder, main writer and general bon vivant of Internet movie site aintitcoolnews.com, but on that particular day in December 2002, he was the host of Butt-Numb-a-Thon 4, an annual 24-hour movie marathon held in honor of his birthday at the Alamo Drafthouse theater/restaurant in Austin, Texas. As fate would have it, Roth, who'd come to Austin for the event, faced a quandary—what kind of birthday present do you give the cinephile who's seen everything?

"I wanted to give Harry something unique," says Roth, "especially since he was so instrumental in helping get *Cabin Fever* sold four months earlier at the 2002 Toronto Film Festival. I made a copy of the *Raiders* tape and gave it to him at the beginning of the night. The festival goes from noon to noon, and at about 8:00 the next morning, there was a break for breakfast."

Roth suggested they pop in the tape, then briefly introduced it to the crowd. Puzzled at first, the audience soon went berserk, having a great time watching the unscheduled, blurry home movie—a tenth-generation copy, for those keeping score at home. The video was nearly unwatchable, but it hardly mattered.

"The audience went wild," says Roth. "The tape stole the show, which both pleased Harry to no end, but also drove him a little crazy. We had a room full of geeks that actually booed when we had to shut off the video projector to watch a sneak preview of *The Lord of the Rings: The Two Towers.*"

Still, the audience's approval of the mysterious *Raiders* tape left

Ain't It Cool News founder Harry Knowles (center, with Strompolos, Lamb, and Zala) saw the film in late 2002, 13 years after it was completed, and immediately began championing it on his website. *(Courtesy of Rolling Boulder Productions)*

an impression on everyone that day—particularly Roth, who realized he might be able to get the fan film to the director who inspired it. Surely that must have been a dream of the kids who had made the flick. "I had been those guys growing up," says Roth. "I was that kid with the video camera making movies, thinking, 'What if one day Steven Spielberg saw this?'"

Of course, he was right on the money, according to Strompolos: "We'd sit around, going, 'Hey man, wouldn't it be cool if Spielberg and Lucas and Harrison Ford saw this?' But we knew that would never, ever happen. My dad lived in California at the time, so I had the 12-year-old mind-set that I was going to use my dad to track down Spielberg. I was talking out my rear end; I had no idea what I was saying."

Now, unbeknownst to any of the Raiders gang, it looked like it might happen. Since selling *Cabin Fever*, Roth had been taking meetings all over Hollywood and had one coming up in January with an executive at Spielberg's own studio, DreamWorks.

"The tape was so amazing that I knew even if this was my one and only meeting there, I had to try to get the tape to Spielberg. I gave it to Paul Lister at the end of my meeting, who called a few days later and said 'I love it, I'm giving it to Spielberg.' The next weekend, he called again and said, 'Steven wants to write these guys a letter—how can we get in touch with them?'"

Roth had no idea, but he was willing to find out. Tracking

down Reynolds via Friedman was a dead end—Zala and Reynolds had been out of touch for years. Eventually Roth did an Internet search on every name in the credits, until he found a phone number for Jayson Lamb in Oakland, and soon he was in contact with all three filmmakers.

"My conversation with Eric was amazing," Roth recounts. "He couldn't believe it. I told him to look up the comments on the message boards at Butt-Numb-a-Thon and he was just stunned that people were applauding his work all these years later." A few days later, Zala, Strompolos, and Lamb each found a letter in their respective mailboxes, sent by Steven Spielberg:

> Wanted to write and let you know how impressed I was with your very loving and detailed tribute to our *Raiders of the Lost Ark*. From the hugely imaginative substitution of a dog for a monkey that your Indy carries around on his shoulder to the smallest detail of Indiana's voice rising when he says, "It's a date . . . you eat 'em." (Which, by the way, is something I asked Harrison to do when he had to recreate the line in the ADR room.)
>
> But beyond all the mimicry of the original *Raiders*, I saw and appreciated the vast amounts of imagination and originality you put in your film. Again, congratulations. I'll be waiting to see your names someday on the big screen."

They were thrilled. Zala proudly framed it on his office wall at Electronic Arts, where it became quite the conversation piece, a fitting capstone for his personal *Raiders* saga. And once again, if life was a Spielberg movie, this, too, might be the point where everyone lives happily ever after—but the story *still* wasn't over.

Three months later, Zala, Strompolos, and Lamb flew into Austin for what was announced as the world premiere of *Raiders: The Adaptation* at the Alamo Drafthouse. Tucked away in Zala's bag was a pristine DVD of the film, which he'd had professionally transferred from videotape a few years earlier at the insistence of his wife.

"Cassie never saw it until we started dating after our high school reunion," notes Zala. "She'd heard about it at school when we were kids—'Eric's that guy who's been making this *Raiders* movie forever, and every summer, he says he's going to finish it but he never does.' So years later, when I asked, 'Hey, wanna see it?' she said afterwards that she'd been a little reluctant because, what if it really sucked?" She was left as awed as everyone else who'd seen the flick, however, and insisted that Zala get the aged, degrading master tape transferred to DVD (a process that cost $5,000 at the time) before it evaporated into a blizzard of static.

While the Alamo Drafthouse had previously screened a hazy VHS tape of the film, now it would be presented in the best quality possible—it still looked like aging 1980s videotape, but at least it was clearer and more audible. Other things became more clear and less hazy in Austin that weekend, too.

While speaking at the screenings and exploring the city was fun, the weekend reunited the trio for the first time in ages. Three years earlier, when Zala had moved to Florida and left Strompolos and his rock 'n' roll ways behind in Hollywood, there had been an air of finality. They'd grown too far apart and their friendship had reached the end of its natural life—but it turned out that Strompolos had changed his ways since then. He'd regained control of his life and gotten engaged, no less; as the weekend wore on, it was clear that the real Strompolos was back. Once again, the film that had brought them together as kids had reunited the team, even if it was only for a weekend of screenings that would surely play only to a handful of people.

The showings were a sold-out hit, it turned out. Zala recalls, "We had our little successes before, but when we got a standing ovation from 300 strangers, suddenly we realized for the first time what we really had here." It was a great moment, but once again, as it had been throughout the entire filmmaking process, the payoff was emotional, not financial. The trio didn't see any money from the screenings; as the people who'd broken copyright law years earlier by making the film, they still had to ensure that they weren't profiting from the movie.

Since then, the trio have shown the film at countless festivals and events, but only in cases where ticket sales will go to nonprofit organizations. Of course, there are exceptions, such as the time they were invited to show it at Skywalker Ranch to Lucasfilm employees, who asked afterward if it would ever be released. The trio looked at each other and told the crowd, "We don't know . . . ask your boss." Lucas was in Japan at the time, but the team still received a tour of the ranch, even checking out the Ark of the Covenant prop from the real *Raiders*.

Back at the Alamo Drafthouse in 2003, however, the audiences' wildly enthusiastic reception cemented in the mind of Harry Knowles that the fan film and its behind-the-scenes story were worthy of their own movie, so he corralled the filmmakers together and put in his two cents. "One thing he recommended," remembers Zala, "was to hold back and not just take every opportunity that was sent our way, or go slathering it all over the Internet. That was good advice; we've kept to it and been glad that we did. Copies have leaked out there on the Internet now, but honestly, people who see it that way miss out. When we do screenings, the audience makes it an event, a shared experience; you can't get an event out of a little postage stamp-sized screen on your laptop."

Knowles's advice worked: Today, *Raiders: The Adaptation* has become a legendary fan film not only because it's well done but also because most people haven't seen it. The trio from Rolling Boulder Productions—as they started calling themselves—kept things low-key and wouldn't give copies to anyone, even after Hollywood became interested.

Knowles introduced the trio to a few potential movie agents, and Zala and Strompolos started thinking about some other film ideas they'd had over the years, but the pair still hadn't generated enough industry buzz to really garner attention. That came soon enough when Jim Windolf of *Vanity Fair* interviewed the trio for a 10-page article on the movie, capped by the photo shoot in Mississippi that led to finding the boulder in Mic Sajway's boat. The story ran in early 2004 as part of the magazine's annual Hollywood issue, and soon *Raiders: The Adaptation* was being talked about all over Tinseltown—even though no one had seen it.

In late February that year, producer Scott Rudin swooped in and purchased life rights from the trio to produce a film based on their story, with Daniel Clowes, writer/creator of *Ghost World* and *Art School Confidential*, as the screenwriter on the project. While it was all good news, ironically, it's Strompolos, the dreamer of the group, who put the sale into perspective, noting with a laugh, "It's not as exciting or as glamorous as people think—a six-figure deal announced in the trades is not really a six-figure deal."

Nonetheless, the trio was proud of it, as was Roth: "People asked me why I never optioned their life story or got the rights before I showed the tape to anyone, but I never had any interest in that. This wasn't some project for me; it was bigger than that. It was far more important to see them get their dream of getting that tape to Spielberg, and of being appreciated for what they did. Plus, I've had so much good fortune in my career, I was happy to help. They're all back to doing what they originally set out to do, and I just feel that, karmically, it was my place to help them get back on track."

That track, it turned out, had Hollywood as its final destination. Their unexpected success emboldened Zala and Strompolos enough that they wanted the movie deal to be the beginning of their Hollywood adventures, not the end. A few months later, they teamed up to write a new action/adventure script, *What the River Takes*, quitting their jobs to focus on it full-time. "I don't think either of us would have pulled ourselves out of our safe, little lives alone to do this," says Strompolos. "Eric and Cassie had been married a few years and had a kid on the way, plus he had a good corporate job with Electronic Arts. Meanwhile, I was just married, and was director of business development for a DVD production company, running the facility. So we were doing OK, paying the bills, 401K plan—and when you rip yourself from that level of comfort, it's a shock to the system. You need an underlying level of conviction there."

They truly believed in themselves, and for those moments when their certainty might falter a bit, they knew that someone else with a bit of movie experience was rooting for them, too. Back in 2004, the *Vanity Fair* article and the ensuing deal had created something of media whirlwind around the trio, and soon they were booked on TV and news shows around the world to tell their story. Winding up in Los Angeles to appear on *The Late Late Show with Craig Kilborn*, the three were on their way to the set in a limo when they got a phone call. It was their agent, calling to say that Spielberg wanted to meet them around noon the next day at the DreamWorks offices.

Steven Spielberg met the trio in 2004; they all swapped behind-the-scenes stories of their respective *Raiders*.
(Courtesy of Rolling Boulder Productions)

"Getting a letter was a wonderful thing," recalls Zala, "but meeting him took it to a whole new level—I started feeling sick. But the next day, we walked up to the receptionist at Dream-Works and I said the most absurd thing I've ever said: 'Hi, we're here to see Mr. Spielberg.'"

The trio were ushered in for what Zala now suspects was supposed to be a quick, 10-minute meet-and-greet, but as they began trading stories with the director about their respective *Raiders*, the conversation took on a life of its own. Soon, their host was having an assistant put on blooper reels from the real *Raiders* and 1984's *Indiana Jones and the Temple of Doom* to share with them. When the trio finally left, the better part of an hour had gone by and they were all walking on air.

"To this day, we don't know what prompted the meeting," say-sZala. "Maybe Scott Rudin set it up, or maybe Mr. Spielberg saw the *Vanity Fair* story and wanted to meet us in person; we have no idea. It was great to meet our boyhood hero, though, and in a way, it was a vindication of all the hard work and dreaming we did. I mean, when Steven Spielberg says he enjoyed the fan film that you slaved over for seven years, that kind of blows your mind."

And apparently the feeling of being honored is mutual. Spielberg himself sees the labor of young film love as something akin to an Oscar, as he related in an interview with UK film magazine *Empire* in 2006, calling it simply "the best piece of flattery George and I have ever received."

8
Swing Time
(1990–1997)

The shift from home movies to home video was revolutionary, and while it didn't happen overnight, by the end of the eighties, Super 8 film was down for the count. One area where film still had the advantage, though, was in editing. Video users either had to plunk down thousands of dollars for a basic linear video editing system, or get their hands on a second VCR and edit things together piecemeal using the PAUSE button without mercy. Even then, it was a hit-or-miss way to build a home movie—inevitably, the resulting master tape would have badly timed edits, occasional wobbly images at the start of a new shot, bursts of static, or all three.

Luckily, problems like those didn't plague Kevin "Zaph" Burfitt and Myles "Moles" Abbott, two video game programmers in Melbourne, Australia, who pushed the technology of the day as far as it could go. In 1990, the duo created *StarLego,* the first fan film edited on a home computer, years before software to do such a thing was available to consumers. Adding to their feat, they did something else with video that was virtually impossible without a film camera: stop-motion animation. "I'd always wanted to do that, ever since seeing Ray Harryhausen's *Jason and the Argonauts,*" says Moles. "I would've done it years beforehand, if my father's Super 8 camera had the ability to do frame by frame—but it didn't, and the rest is history."

For eight months between 1990 and 1991, the pair of 24-year-olds spent their weekends animating a hysterical, shot-for-shot parody of the opening scenes of *Star Wars: A New Hope,* using the famous plastic toy bricks. Created long before Star Wars Lego sets were available, and soundtracked by the music and dialogue from the real film, the makeshift satire featured impressive tracking shots and laser effects, as well as plenty of sick humor: cute, little Lego soldiers would explode into showers of blood, while Princess Leia, hit by a laser pistol set to "stun," melted into a black cinder. The technological key to making the flick, however, was a Ferrarilike home computer, the bleeding edge of technology: "We were using a 286 computer with a Truevision Targa+ 2MB capture card," Zaph says, "and wrote all the software needed to make the movie ourselves."

While Moles estimated they spent about 300 hours shooting, Zaph spent an additional 100 hours writing the software that allowed them to use a video camera, attached to the capture card, to make still photos. "We would deconstruct the next five-second piece we were about to do," says Moles, "to work out which sounds that actions were occurring on. Each still was played for four frames of video, and we were able to store 32 frames on the 286, then play them back like a flipbook on the screen, using the software Zaph wrote—but first, I painted some lasers and things onto the appropriate frames."

In the software, Zaph created the ability to "onion cell" the last frame, making one frame semitransparent over the previous one to allow comparison—a feature that came in handy not only for animating but also for emergencies, when Lego people fell over and had to be put back exactly in place. "We'd never even heard of the term 'onion cell,'" comments Moles. "It was only later, watching a 'making of' show, that we saw it being done—and we said, 'Oh yeah, we did that.'"

While the homemade software was handy, it stretched the little computer to its limits; as a result, after every few seconds of footage, they had to take a leap of faith. Zaph explains, "Here's the scary part: We got out our master tape, which already had the *Star Wars* scene's sound on it, then pressed RECORD on the tape deck and PLAY on the computer. Then, in five seconds, we pressed STOP . . . and hoped that it worked. Then—and here's the second scary part—we deleted the frames off the computer, and began the next segment, with no way to go back! We did this three or four times every weekend for eight months, and we never managed to destroy the master in all that time."

Although *StarLego* was animated using a computer, none of the files were saved; the only permanent record of their hard work was the lone master videotape. "There was no going back to redo a scene, so there was no use for having the entire thing stored," remembers Zaph. "It's the kind of thing that a filmmaker would never dream of doing, but a programmer would—if you don't need the data anymore, why waste space keeping it? I realize it's a hard concept to get around, but each segment was around two megabytes and there just wasn't the space to be keeping that sort of data." It wasn't the last time Zaph would work hard coding in the name of Star Wars; a full 17 years later, he was part of team that created the 2008 video game *Star Wars: The Force Unleashed*.

Back in 1991, however, Zaph and Moles wound up unknowingly echoing the decommissioned Chicago Transit bus that used to show Don Glut's fan films in the early sixties. In order to give *StarLego* the launch they felt it deserved, the pair premiered it on a travel coach hired to take 48 drunken friends to a blowout party two hours away at a seaside vacation house.

"They loved it, but missed a lot with all the noise and partying," remembers Zaph. "After showing the movie, we partied all night long, which included a bathtub of green jelly, a body painting room, a live band, a room full of mattresses and much more. The party cost us over $1,000, which was all the money we had between us, but it was worth it. When the bus picked us up again the next morning, we auctioned off the entire *StarLego* cast to try to recoup costs—and got about $20 total. Our old bosses own the melted Princess Leia."

StarLego may have been created using then-cutting-edge computer technology and custom software, but the whole process still started with one piece of equipment that had become commonplace by the nineties: an 8mm camcorder. By the late eighties, Beta camcorders were a distant memory, and that switch was indicative of the times. With film and Beta both out of the picture, there was still something of a format war going on, except now it was merely a battle between one-piece camcorders: VHS versus 8mm. Ether way, consumers were getting smaller cameras that could run far longer on rechargeable batteries and had built-in effects, whether rudimentary (fade in/fade out), more advanced (awkward in-camera titles) or just plain esoteric (ghostly "inverse" settings).

One of the most peculiar in-camera effects of the day was a "half freeze-frame/half live splitscreen" feature found on the Panasonic PV-430. Why anyone would want such a feature is known only to Japanese camcorder designers, but there was at least one consumer who bought the camera just for that ability. Using the camera, $400 and virtually everything he had—except perhaps common sense—he created the most action-packed Spider-Man fan film ever: *The Green Goblin's Last Stand*.

• • •

Dan Poole graduated high school in 1986 with a dream to become a stuntman, but living in Baltimore, far from Hollywood, and with no formal stunt training outside of martial arts classes, he had to settle for something a little less dangerous: mail clerk at the National Aquarium.

Since his dream job remained only a fantasy, Poole made the most of his mailroom gig, getting to know everyone on staff, and that had its perks: coworkers would slip him free aquarium passes he could give to friends and family, but even better, the AV department let him borrow video gear on the sly virtually every weekend. Camera in tow, he'd gather some friends, press RECORD, and see what happened—and when he started hopping in front of the camera, dressed up in an old Spider-Man costume his mother Bea had made for him, no one batted an eye.

A Spidey fan all his life, Poole read in 1987 that the web crawler was going to reach the big screen soon, and while in truth the project had been stuck in development for at least five years at that point, all Poole knew was that this was his big chance. What would be a greater movie debut for an aspiring stuntman than to become his lifelong hero?

Seen here as Spider-Man's alter ego "Peter Parker," Dan Poole starred in, directed, and adapted *The Green Goblin's Last Stand* from issues 121 and 122 of *The Amazing Spider-Man*.
(Courtesy of Alpha Dog Productions)

Backed by his buddies, the borrowed camera and more than a few six-packs, Poole started out shooting video of himself in costume, climbing to ridiculous heights, decking thugs (friends) in a supermarket loading dock, and fighting the costumed supervillians that were Spidey's stock-in-trade. The whole process, however, proved harder than expected; costumes for the villains were hard to scrounge together and neither Poole nor his pals had much experience in composing a shot to get the right look. Although they tried as hard as they could, given their limited means and experience, Poole knew their results would never grab Hollywood's eye. Not that anyone in Tinseltown would've noticed at the time; multiple studios were battling over who owned the rights to make a Spider-Man feature, and not a single frame of film would be shot until it was worked out. Comic book fans around the world may have rolled their eyes at the news, but for Poole, it just meant he had more time to sharpen his visual résumé.

By the spring of 1991, though, he'd given up in disgust. He was no longer just some kid out of high school—he was 23, still working as the aquarium mail clerk, still making movies with his friends on weekends, and what did he have to show for it after four years of backbreaking work and equally body-destroying stunts? Nothing. They'd made a 20-minute fan film where he battled gangsters; a short piece where he fought Mysterio; and a 50-minute project, *The Quick and the Dead*, pitting the web slinger against Bullseye and Kingpin. Poole hated all of them. None of the shorts captured his stuntwork properly, and they looked exactly like what they were: the work of hopeless amateurs. The only good thing about them was his friend Eric Supensky's hammy turn as Peter Parker's boss, J. Jonah Jameson, and how would that help him get a stunt gig on a Spider-Man feature? And when were they going to make that movie anyway?

That September, however, Poole heard Stan Lee, Spidey's creator, announce big news on *Good Morning America*: the Spider-Man movie was back on—and James Cameron (*Terminators I* and *II*) was signed to direct.

"That was all it took for me to get excited all over again—and this time, I had the plan," remembers Poole. "We were gonna make a five-minute demo reel of the best Spidey action ever. No plot—just amazing stunts, battles with Doc Ock, Electro, everybody. I knew I could get the job if I could somehow get Cameron to watch it."

He'd cross that bridge when he got to it, but a more immediate concern was that the villain costumes were still impossible to put together, especially since he barely had a budget. Reading old Spidey comics to find the best slugfests to re-create, Poole read *The Amazing Spider-Man*'s landmark two-issue battle, *The Green Goblin's Last Stand* and *The Night Gwen Stacy Died* (issues 121–122), where the web slinger's greatest enemy dies—but not before murdering Peter Parker's girlfriend, Gwen Stacy. The tale, which was adapted for the first Spider-Man feature film 10 years later in 2001, was so exciting that Poole realized he didn't need to fight a truckload of villains—just one. The five-minute demo reel was off; they were gonna make a movie.

"I was struck by inspiration while we were bowling," he recalls. "I tore off the corner of a 12-pack of beer we had and wrote down the scene order. I wrote throughout September and we started to shoot in October. I had a real fire in me—total focus—and I made a big effort to mirror the comics; to me, it was like doing a scene from the Bible; you don't take liberties."

Recognizing his limitations as an actor, Poole was still going to play the main role of Spider-Man/Peter Parker, but wanted to fill out the cast with more experienced performers pulled from the local theater scene. Peter Parker's girlfriend, Gwen, turned up in the form of actress Allison Adams. Her qualifications? She was the first blond who agreed to play the part. Meanwhile, Poole spotted Jimi Kinstle in a production of *Scrooge*; Kinstle was perfect for the dual role of crazed millionaire Norman Osborn and the Green Goblin. The actor nailed the Goblin's insane laugh from the 1960s *Spider-Man* cartoon series, and soon had the archvillain's over-the-top style down pat.

Once Kinstle was cast, he needed a costume. Supensky had learned sculpting from his father, an art professor, so it didn't take long for various art supplies to be (ahem) "borrowed" from a certain college. Soon, they had a plaster cast of Kinstle's face for the Goblin mask, and clay molds for the batlike latex ears. "Eric had promised me that the mask would move with Jimi's mouth, and it didn't—I complained, and he just shrugged," Poole recalls. "I was pretty tough on everybody, and now I look back and think, 'My God—how dare I be demanding of these people who were working for free?' I was so focused on making it perfect that I didn't really see it at the time; I wanted everyone to put as much into it as I was."

Poole jokes now that the production was half financed by his job: When searching for props and costume items, he often traded passes to the National Aquarium for the things he needed. For instance, one trip to a fabric shop uncovered bizarre scaly, green fabric that became the Goblin's costume, and soon they had a supervillain.

That costume got a lot of exposure to the elements, as much of the fan film was shot outdoors, including an apartment building rooftop that became the site of a huge fight between hero and foe. In shot after shot, Poole would jump off a hidden mini-trampoline so that he could artfully dart through the air like Spider-Man, or he'd sprint along, leaping over parapets until he jumped through

The Panasonic PV-430 camcorder's strange "half freeze-frame/ half live splitscreen" feature was used to create walls for Spidey to climb. They'd carefully take a freeze-frame of the side of a building, then turn the camera sideways and shoot Poole crawling, so that he appeared to be climbing the wall.
(Courtesy of Alpha Dog Productions)

a decorative arch into thin air, plunging out of sight—onto a five-inch ledge above a seven-story drop.

He wasn't the only one doing stunts on the roof, however. One of the Green Goblin's trademarks was his Goblin Glider, a small, bat-shaped rocket with wings that he rode. To achieve the effect, Poole's pal Dave Hayward built a clever, rotating seesaw with the gilder on one end, and a crewmember—usually Poole's step-brother, Skip Justis, hanging off the other end as a counterweight, allowing the villain to zoom by on the glider in carefully angled shots. Kinstle only did some of his own stunts, so four other people played the Goblin at various points in the movie—including Poole. "Some days, I could only get one other person," he recalls, "so I'd ask them to hold the camera and I'd switch costumes to get the shots I needed. There's a few points where it's actually *me* fighting *me*!"

By this time, he'd bought his own camcorder using money saved from moving furniture part-time, so the Panasonic PV-430 was available whenever he needed it, as was its strange "half freeze-frame/half live splitscreen" feature, which was used to create buildings for Spidey to climb. They'd carefully take a freeze-frame shot of the side of a building, then turn the camera sideways and shoot Poole crawling along the edge of the roof. The result was a surprisingly effective bit of fake "climbing"—which was still dangerous because, again, if Poole slipped, he'd fall off the building. Unlike Spidey, he'd have no webbing to safely swing on.

Except for the time he *did* swing off a building. This time, it was an abandoned office structure on Water Street, a few blocks from the aquarium. "I tracked down the owner, met with him in my official aquarium polo shirt to try and impress him, and explained what I wanted to do," Poole recalls, laughing. "He said, 'No way! You stay the hell away from my building!' He couldn't believe that someone would present this idea to him. I really wanted that location, though, so we just ignored him."

Instead of staying the hell away, the aspiring Spidey clung to "webbing" and leapt off the third-floor fire escape, arcing out wide with no safety measures whatsoever. It was an insane risk to take, dangling from a rope gripped through slippery cotton gloves, but he felt no one would "believe" a Spider-Man that wasn't seen swinging between buildings.

"I went there on a Sunday morning," says Poole. "It was just me and my cousin, Ray Schueler, and I chose him to shoot it specifically because I knew he wouldn't stop me—he believed in me, gave me the obligatory 'Be careful,' and tried to keep me in frame. Actually, the only thing Ray was afraid of was police, but I told him, 'Dude, it's Sunday morning, the area is a ghost town on weekends; there won't be any cops.'

"So we got there, climbed onto the fire escape, were about to haul the dufflebag and rope up after us, when I looked down the alley, and saw a cop in the window of a deli across the street. Ray was ready to jump off the fire escape and just start running, but I said, 'Dude, relax.' I went over to the deli and he was the stereotypical cop, eating his donut and coffee. 'Officer, how are you? My name's Dan Poole; saw you looking across the way, figured you're wondering what the hell we're doing.' I lifted up my sweatshirt to show him the Spidey shirt, and I told him I was a college student, because if I said I was a struggling independent filmmaker trying

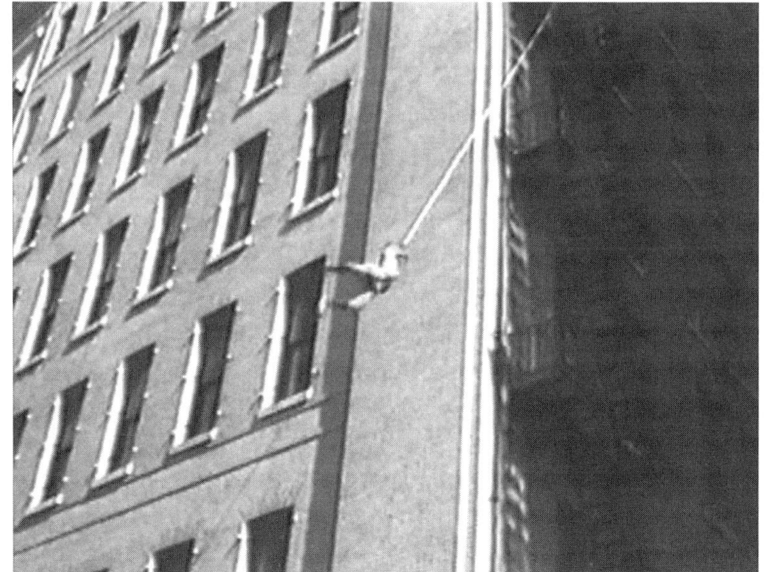

After nearly being caught by police, Poole swung multiple times from an abandoned building on Baltimore's Water Street, risking his life because he felt he needed the shot.
(Courtesy of Alpha Dog Productions)

to put together a demo reel to impress James Cameron so I could get a job, that would mean nothing to him. So it was 'It's a class project, we have permission from the building owner, so if you get any "suspicious people" calls, it's just us and we'll be up there for about an hour.' And he's staring at me and shrugs, 'OK, good luck, don't kill yourself.'"

The heart-stopping swings from the fire escape were shot quickly from different street corners; although it was a potentially deadly 30-foot drop to the solid concrete below, Poole claims he wasn't scared: "I knew what I had to do, and I knew what I was doing to some degree. It's the same thing a million kids have done forever, swinging out over a lake or a river—the only difference was, I knew I wasn't gonna let go." (As the author, I'd like to take this moment to say that if you, dear reader, are now thinking it'd be a great idea to swing off a building, *don't*. Thank you.)

Months later, when he screened the movie for his father, Spider-Man swung out into the great abyss and the elder Poole's eyes lit up. He turned around slowly, peered at his son a moment, and said, "Boy, you better get a job before you kill yourself."

Strangely enough, the jaw-dropping stunt does two things in the fan film. Primarily, it stops the movie cold, immediately taking the audience out of the story and filling the room with gasps of 'I can't believe he was crazy enough to do that!' At the same time, however, the extreme realism of a grown man swinging off buildings without a net truly illustrates what a terrifying moment it would be to spot the web slinger while walking down the street. The computerized special effects used throughout the Spider-Man feature films may make for some spectacular shots, but they never induce a wince of nervous fear that Spidey's about to become a red puddle on the sidewalk. In that creepy regard, Poole beat the pros, hands down.

Those skills were useful for plenty of other dangerous stunts, too, like Spidey crashing through barrels, and walls; artfully swinging one-handed beneath an overpass as vehicles zoom by below; riding atop a car taking corners at ridiculous speeds; and dangling—and dropping—from a warehouse girder, 35 feet above the ground. "Eric came in and saw me hanging from the ceiling with about 4 inches of trucker blankets below as a safety mat," says Poole. "He had a fit and wouldn't let anything happen until he found enough things to pile up and make it a little safer."

The hazards didn't stop there, however; one scene called for the Goblin to shoot rockets at the hero, so Schueler fired roman candles from off-screen so that his cousin could dodge them. Another Goblin trademark—exploding pumpkin bombs—were handled more safely. Whomever was in the villain's costume that day would throw softball-sized foam pumpkins directly at the camera; after a dozen or so throws, they'd dangle one from a wire in front of the lens and blow it up. Later, during the editing stage, they'd use the toss that best matched where the pumpkin was in the picture when it exploded—and the result was seamless. Blowing up a pumpkin in Poole's face was just as simple; they filled an orange balloon with talc, stuck a small pin out of Spidey's mask, the Goblin shoved the balloon in his face and pop—clouds of powder everywhere.

Another clever effect was Spidey's web shooting, which looked fabulous. A mix of milk and water was poured into a pressure sprayer connected to an 18-inch metal tube, which was then jammed into the Spider-Man costume at the elbow, so that the nozzle came out at the wrist. Angling the camera to carefully keep the sprayer out of the shot, Poole would make a web-firing motion with his fingers, and a friend would spray the mixture on cue—a simple, effective effect.

As shooting drew to a close, Poole found himself exhausted, bruised, and beaten by his project. At one point, production had stopped while he spent a month in a neck brace after crashing into a pile of metal shelving brackets, but nearly a year after he'd first heard about Cameron's Spider-Man movie, Poole finally called "cut" for the last time. Then he slept nonstop for the next 24 hours.

Editing was just as grueling; Poole would occasionally get to use the editing equipment at his job, but most of the fan film was pieced together at Towson State University. Years earlier, he'd met a film professor there—Barry Moore—when a friend had screened their early, 20-minute Spider-Man/Mysterio movie. Impressed that a nonstudent was working harder on a fan film than his pupils were on their graded productions, Moore encouraged him, saying, "If you ever need anything, call me." Poole took him up on it when it came time to edit *Green Goblin*, and soon was spending 11 hours at a stretch with the university's TV edit bays—simple A/B decks with an edit controller. It all went smoothly—until his master tape, with more than half the movie completed on it, was eaten by a VCR. Having to start over was hard, but the sound edit—as basic as it was with sound effects, music from movie soundtracks, and the dialogue recorded by his camera—was worse:

> The sound edit was especially difficult, because all the sound had been recorded through the camera's microphone; Jimi and I even did ADR [dialogue dubbing] into the mike on my camera under a blanket for soundproofing. I tried to do as much as I could, professionally—with semiprofessional equipment—but it was hard. I couldn't get the volume levels where I wanted them, the sound effects weren't working, and I had been trying to do the sound edit on the aquarium's equipment, but it wouldn't work. At that point, I just gave up.

> My spirit was crushed; I was destroyed. I left the aquarium on Pier 3 and walked to Pier 5 and stopped. I thought about how I should just give up, this thing is going to beat me down, it's never gonna get me where I want anyway, why am I even bothering, it's a nightmare and no one else cares. I stood there and thought about all the work that went into it, and then I decided just to push the sound effects louder, past where the AV guys said I could go, 'cause an effect's only for a second, and I got rejuvenated. But the edit on the whole was a depressing time.

The fan film was completed in November 1992, 14 months after it was started. Poole screened the movie for friends and family at a Christmas party, then spent the next few years trying to get it into Cameron's hands. He mailed it, went to California and tried to drop it off at the director's office, handed it off to one of the director's assistants, and even gave it to Cameron in person—twice—at public appearances. The movie always came back unopened; for legal reasons, Cameron, like everyone else in Hollywood, wouldn't accept unsolicited materials.

One person who did see the fan film, according to Poole, was Stan Lee, who wrote a letter congratulating him on the project while adding that he couldn't help with the quest to be a part of the real Spider-Man movie. Poole says he also heard from sources inside Marvel that Sam Raimi and Avi Arad, the respective director and executive producer of the Spider-Man feature films, watched *Green Goblin* while working on the series' first movie. In Poole's estimation, a graveyard scene in 2002's *Spider-Man,* where the Green Goblin blows off half of Spidey's mask with a pumpkin bomb to the face, was too similar to the balloon-full-of-talc scene to be a coincidence.

A decade passed between the making of the fan film and the debut of the Hollywood feature, and for most of that time, *The Green Goblin's Last Stand* was a relic of Poole's past. He left the aquarium to become a freelance producer/videographer, doing local TV ads and creating corporate and industrial videos for people whose suits didn't have a big spider on the chest.

On a whim, Poole sent a copy of his fan film to a comic book

Poole (with camcorder) prepares to shoot Jimi Kinstle as the villainous Green Goblin on his Glider—which was attached to an ingenious, off-screen seesaw to simulate flying.
(Courtesy of Alpha Dog Productions)

zine, *Hero Illustrated,* which wrote a brief story about it; someone there made a few copies for friends, and much like *Raiders: The Adaptation,* the tapes began circulating unbeknownst to Poole. While the earlier movie remained a well-kept secret for years, *The Green Goblin's Last Stand* was an instant underground hit. "Michael Dougherty, who cowrote *Superman Returns* and *X-Men 2,* said somebody in Texas sent it to him, and I couldn't believe my movie wound up there," claims Poole. "He said, 'Man, I don't think you own this thing anymore—it's got a life of its own now.' It was for sale at every comic convention and people were talking about it, so it was a grassroots thing, which was cool but also infuriating—I didn't risk my life just so someone else could make money."

Trying to stop the bootleggers, Poole put the entire movie online with a postage stamp–sized version in the fall of 1999; within months, more than 2 million people had downloaded his fan film, and it seemed as if each one sent him an e-mail with the same questions, asking how he did the stunts and effects. The best way to answer everyone, he decided, was to shoot a documentary on the making of his flick—and unlike the fan film, which he couldn't profit from due to copyright laws, he could make a few bucks this time. Realizing that Marvel might not be as enthusiastic as he was about the project, Poole wrote to the company's lawyers, asking if they had any objections; he never heard back and took their silence as an implicit "Go knock yourself out."

The resulting hourlong effort, *The Real Spider-Man: The Making of The Green Goblin's Last Stand,* was actually longer than the movie it covered, but it featured extensive interviews with Poole and his pals, plus outtakes, a deleted scene and some unused, often painful stunts. Completed in April 2001, Poole took his new production to the 2002 NoDance Film Festival in Park City, Utah, where it won the Audience Award for Best Documentary, and the Golden Orbs Award for Best Guerrilla Marketing. That summer, it was screened at the San Diego Comic Con, while a review in *Film Threat,* referencing the "making of" documentary of Francis Ford Coppola's *Apocalypse Now,* declared it "the *Heart of Darkness* of the comic book world."

When Poole began selling VHS tapes of it over the internet, he figured he'd make enough money to shoot a new movie. He didn't; instead, the doc flopped. With the advent of DVD-R burners, he rereleased it, this time giving the people what he knew they wanted: *The Green Goblin's Last Stand* as a free DVD extra. By this time, the *Spider-Man* feature films had started coming out, and among them, the years of bootleg tapes and the tiny, free version available over the Internet, interest in his fan film had already peaked; plus, the same bootleggers that sold VHS tapes of his movie copied the DVD-R edition and started selling it, too, so Poole still didn't make any money from the documentary.

However, that didn't mean that he was done with superheroes and death-defying stunts. In 2007, 20 years after he started making homemade Spider-Man films, Poole and his Alpha Dog Productions company went into production on *The Photon Effect.* The independent feature film, about a pair of radio tower engineers who gain superpowers after an accident on an experimental microwave antenna, found the 39-year-old writer/director/producer/stuntman working for the first time from an original screenplay.

"We shot a 108-page script in 30 days, which is fast," he says, "but I'm a different director today. I'd rather take the time to do things right, I have patience with actors, and I'm not intimidated by a big set. I used to want to keep things small and keep moving, because I didn't want to focus on the fact that I was in charge. Now I maintain calm and order so we can focus on the scene and getting the best shot."

Armed for the first time with HD cameras, a real budget, and real actors, Poole, at long last, became simply a filmmaker, without the caveat "fan" before the title. And that suits him just fine.

• • •

When *The Green Goblin's Last Stand* arrived on the Internet in the fall of 1999, it was already late for the late-nineties' fan film party. By then, fan productions were springing up all over the Web; it was a phenomenon spurred in part by the dot-com explosion of the time, but the main trigger was a *Star Wars* fan movie that had arrived a few years earlier. That short was unlike anything seen before, *Star Wars* or otherwise, and it changed fan films—and possibly the nature of the Internet itself—forever.

Troops was the first modern fan film—the one that brought the secret genre into the mainstream once and for all, blazing a trail for the use of consumer electronics and the Internet to create and publicize homemade, independent media.

The Internet distribution of movies, music, and more (whether legal or illegal) was about to become as easy as sending an e-mail, and *Troops* proved to be the taste test that got millions hooked on downloading. In short, it wasn't merely a brief visit to a long time ago in a galaxy far, far away; it was a premonition, a glimpse of any second now, right here.

9
Send in the *Troops*

Growing up on a small farm in Gilroy, California, Kevin Rubio was 10 years old when the first *Star Wars* film came out in 1977. Like many in Generation X, he was enthralled by the adventures of fellow farm boy Luke Skywalker, and inspired by the flashiness of the Hollywood creation; 20 years later, he knew a little something about the real Hollywood, as he worked as a self-described "below-the-line schmo" at the Fox Kids Network, toiling through the days as a cel animation archivist. Like many lifelong fans, in February, 1997, he got together with a few friends—Steven Melching, Dave McDermott, and David Hargrove—and went to see the *Star Wars* special edition rereleases, although unlike the average fan, he had the luxury of seeing the films in a deluxe screening room on the Fox lot.

For most of the millions who turned out to see the special edition rereleases, they were a fun way to revisit the past, seeing old friends like Luke and Leia back on a movie screen instead of cooped up on the tube. The difference was that unlike the past, when it was over, the millions went back to their lives and that was that. Twenty years on, *Star Wars* was no longer the greatest movie they'd ever seen. With two decades worth of entertainment ingested since then, the lifelong fans had grown more sophisticated, and with the onslaught of cable TV, the Internet, and other accoutrements of the modern, 24-hour media lifestyle, they had grown more jaded, too. When they were 10, nothing else had compared to *Star Wars*; now—and especially with the much-hyped addition of new computer-generated imagery (CGI) effects—the movie was comparable to anything, as a generation steeped in media suddenly recognized plot points "borrowed" from other classic films, found the line between good and evil perhaps too starkly drawn, and discovered that Luke Skywalker, formerly the generation's surrogate in the story, was actually kinda whiny.

Even so, there was still a lot in the films for adults to enjoy and consider. In the wake of seeing the original trilogy once again, it was in fact the faceless minions of the Empire—the stormtroopers—that caught the eye of Rubio and his friends.

Who was underneath those masks? Maybe they weren't completely evil. Maybe they were actually regular guys with families and bills to pay and next week's paycheck already spent. Maybe working for the Empire was just a gig with lots of stupid trodding around in armor to keep the boss happy. Maybe, to borrow a phrase, they were below-the-line schmoes.

Sitting around spitballing after watching *Episode IV: A New Hope* on the Fox lot, an idea began to take shape among Rubio and his pals. Initially, it wasn't even for a film, but for a different visual medium: a comic strip that would be pitched to *Sci-Fi Universe* magazine by Melching, Hargrove and McDermott.

"It was going to be called *Tales of the Death Star Scanning Crew*, a parody of *Tales of the Bounty Hunters* by Dark Horse Comics," Rubio says. "[Hargrove] blurted out, 'Hey, wouldn't it be funny if you crossed *Cops* with *Star Wars?*' And I thought, 'Oh, yeah, it would . . . and I happen to know enough people to pull it off.'"

Pretty quickly, the story jumped from being a comic strip to a short movie, and as the plot grew, so did the thought that went into it. *Troops* wasn't going to be merely a few gags strung together; instead, its humor would come from welding together the two wildly different genres of space opera and police documentary. The story's alternate history of why the Skywalker homestead was destroyed and how Uncle Owen and Aunt Beru died was a surprisingly snug fit into the movies' mythology. Ultimately, that irreverent reverence to the *Star Wars* canon gave the story a fun feel for the casual fan, and a patina of enticing plausibility for the hardcore enthusiast.

After they went their separate ways that day, Rubio stopped by the Fox Television library and borrowed a few tapes of *Cops*. "I went home," he recalls, "watched about four of them, wrote the script, and then started grabbing every friend I had in the business to help me do this."

Rubio needed help fast, because the film had to be made ASAP: "It was *Star Wars'* 20th anniversary, so there was a whole bunch of publicity around it, and I knew that if this could be pulled off right, there were enough megafans out there for this to get attention."

The best way to reach thousands of mega-fans, then, was to premiere it in July at the San Diego Comic Con International—the biggest comic book, science fiction and fantasy fan convention in North America. It would be the perfect launch pad—thousands of fans would be attending, and given the proximity to Los Angeles, many Hollywood behind-the-scenes folks would be there too, whether promoting a film or TV series, or just looking around for fun. Best of all, the convention's film program was one of its most popular features, so getting *Troops* into the lineup would ensure a splashy debut before a big crowd. The mid-July deadline would also come at a lull between the special editions' spring theatrical rereleases and their debut on home video that fall. It was almost too perfect; if they could get it done on time for the convention, *Troops* could take advantage of the newly revived fan interest without having to compete directly with the real movies.

And how could they not get it done in time? The San Diego Comic Con was still six long months away; surely that would be enough time to finish a 10-minute movie. Heck, there'd be time to spare.

Lining up a 20-person cast and crew was easier than expected; Rubio didn't credit his persuasive powers or even the Force, but rather the source material: People simply read the script and liked it, plus he pointed out that they might be able to network and get jobs from people who'd eventually see the project. "Essentially, we wanted to showcase our work to people in Hollywood and get jobs and agents out of this," he says. "That was the goal."

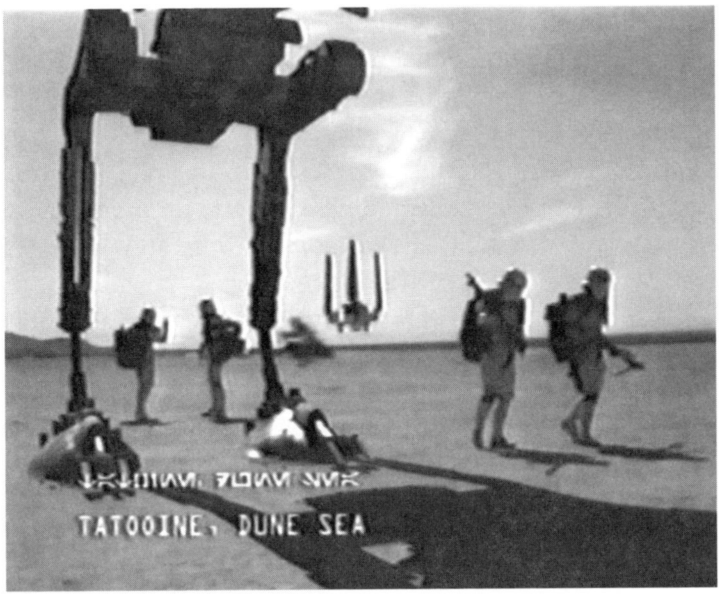

Shant Jordan and Patrick Perez handled the visual effects in *Troops*, thanks to gear they used daily for their real jobs, producing effects shots for the TV series *Babylon 5*.
(Courtesy of Kevin Rubio)

Getting professionals involved was crucial, however, because they would give the project a veneer that could lift it from being a simple home movie to something special. With that in mind, the first people he called, just three days after seeing *Empire*, were two effects gurus who eventually became coproducers on the project: Shant Jordan (pronounced "Shaunt") and Patrick Perez. Despite their heavy schedules doing effects for the TV series *Babylon 5* at Netter Digital Entertainment in North Hollywood, they instantly agreed.

While quality special effects would help anchor the film as taking place in the Star Wars universe, the sound would be equally important. *Troops* had to sound like the real thing, whether it was a Jawa speed-talking or a blaster blowing that Jawa's head off. This time, Rubio turned to Charlotte Fullerton, a friend who was a writer and producer for Fox Kids' on-air promotion department. "Kevin asked me to postsupervise *Troops* and direct the voice talent because of his deeply held respect for me as an artist and as a human being," remembers Fullerton, "and because he knew I could get his postproduction done for free."

With effects and sound nailed down, the next hurdle was actually the biggest: casting stormtroopers. Luckily, the fledgling director picked up a copy of the *Los Angeles Times* and spotted his future cast right on the front page, standing on line in stormtrooper costumes at Mann's Chinese Theatre for the Special Edition premiere of *A New Hope*. Rubio knew in an instant: These were the stormtroopers he was looking for.

The troopers, in fact, were five students attending a school that was already a part of fan film history—the Art Center School of Design, where Marv Newland had created *Bambi Meets Godzilla* more than 25 years earlier. Rubio had no idea how to find them, however, as the caption didn't give their real names. "I saw them and thought, 'Those are too good to be amateurs,'" he recalls. "I asked an effects friend of mine who was on the line that night if he knew who they were. He said, 'No, but they go to the Arts Center and two of them are girls and they're twins.' As luck would have it, my roommate at the time was head of admissions at the school, so I just asked her to track them down. I figured, how many twin girls can there be in a school who know how to vacuform [the process used to mold plastic] stormtrooper costumes? I met them at a party for the *Empire Strikes Back* rerelease, gave them the script, and the rest is history."

Soon, Eric Hilleary, David Max, Caleb Skinner, and twin sisters Kohar and Kenar Yegyayan were onboard for the film. As it turned out, they had been working for months on their stormtrooper costumes, artificially aging them to achieve the right dusty, worn-in look. Additionally, Hilleary not only appeared as two separate troopers and Boba Fett, but also became the art director/production designer, storyboarding the script.

Just two weeks after Hargrove first floated the *Troops* concept, Rubio had gathered enough support from professional and personal friends that production was slated for a day's work at El Mirage Dry Lake in San Bernardino County—a three-mile-wide dry lakebed in the Mojave Desert. Typically, El Mirage is used for TV and film shoots, camping, extreme sports, and driving cars really fast without any cops around to annoy one with trifling things like speeding tickets. For *Troops*, the remote location was ideal: it made a decent replica of Tatooine, and it was far enough from prying eyes to keep the number of onlookers to a relative minimum.

Production was set to start at 5 AM on a weekend morning, when everyone involved would meet in a local parking lot and trek out two hours to El Mirage. The assembled cast and crew was "a motley crew of long-haired cowboys, goateed artsy guys, two little people [for the Jawa costumes] and some grungy film students," according to the production diary of Marilyn Estes, who handled script supervision and robot wrangling that day. Despite coming up one car short for all the people and gear, the production managed to hit the road and by 7:30, the stormtroopers were suited up and ready to roll.

Given that they'd be shooting all day in the desert, everyone naturally dressed to be cool in the face of oppressive heat. Unfortunately, no one took into account that it was winter; they were greeted at El Mirage by 50 degree temperatures and a bracing wind that lasted all day. It was freezing. To top it off, the stormtroopers' costumes were cooled by the wind and the white armor reflected the sun, essentially refrigerating the cast inside the plastic outfits.

Armed with a typical, consumer-grade Sony TRV-82 Hi8 video camera, cinematographer Shona "Cricket" Peters captured the raw visual aesthetic of *Cops*, choosing a handheld approach that added to the you-are-there vibe, as the camera ran after stormtroopers on the move. Working with Peters were effects gurus Jordan and Perez, who studied each shot's composition, figuring out whether they could cover up the tell-tale signs of Earth—RV campers and parasailers—with the detritus of Tatooine, like Sandcrawlers and the Skywalker homestead.

Just like a major motion picture, there were moments where the money shot just didn't work out and the hasty answer was, "We'll fix it in postproduction." In this case, it was a Jawa who didn't fall down when blasted by an irked trooper; rather than reshoot the scene (and the actor), the CGI pros felt they could match the take with a computerized Jawa . . . that they would then blow to smithereens. In the finished movie, however, only the running Jawa's head gets blown off, as the actor comes to a standstill with flames sputtering in the space previously occupied by his noggin.

Like any low-budget film with a volunteer cast and crew, incongruities inevitably came up on-screen. During the Owen and Beru confrontation, attentive eyes will catch a motorcycle that rolled by in the background. Other anomolies are harder to spot, such as the fact that all the troopers wore lace-up shoes spray-painted white—except the one wearing white high-heels.

Slowly but surely, the cast and crew worked through the script's pages, although some moments, such as one where stormtroopers rode ATVs that would later be replaced by CGI *Return of the Jedi*–style speederbikes, had to be scratched. Nonetheless, the opening speederbike segment was necessary to the film, appearing under subtly menacing exposition ("I like the small-town feeling you get around here; I mean, we know everybody . . . *everybody.*"). The speederbike moment would be short, but it established the film's Star Wars credibility while simultaneously providing time for the *Cops*-style narrative; it couldn't be cut. As a result, close-ups of the trooper were shot on the back of Rubio's truck, ensuring that the landscape would be rolling by during the shot. Rubio returned to the area four weeks later and taped some pickup shots of the terrain rolling by to use for speederbike effects, breaking up the single monologue shot.

At the end of the long day, shooting was completed and the truly hardcore work began. Rubio still had his eye on debuting the short at the San Diego Comic Con, five months away. There were other issues to contend with as well: "Our original editor flaked on us, the effects supervisor found us a new one, then in the middle of effects work, Shant and Pat got caught up in a massive move with the effects company that they were working for, so the render machines that we were using were down."

By the time Rubio and editor David Foster had the rough cut of *Troops* complete, the months had screamed by, the San Diego Comic Con was only two weeks away, and none of the special effects or sound work was done. If they didn't pull together, they were going to blow the one big chance to give *Troops* the splashy debut it needed to grab Hollywood's attention.

During the editing phase, Jordan and Perez had been working on the models that would be used in the short. Initially, they'd

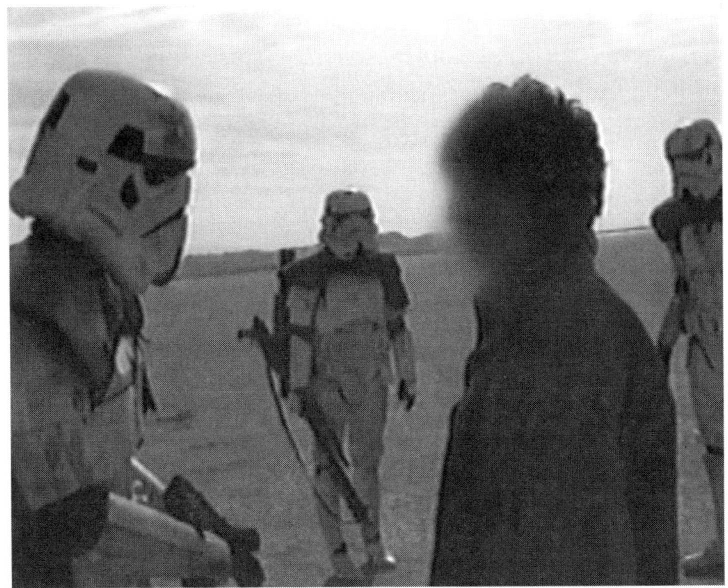

Parodying the TV show *Cops*, Luke Skywalker's Aunt Beru appears with her face blurred to protect her identity. Meanwhile, in real life, not all the stormtroopers in the cast were men—note the center trooper's high heels.
(Courtesy of Kevin Rubio)

planned to reproduce TIE fighters and the Jawas' sandcrawler by using computerized 3-D models that fans had posted to the Internet, but upon inspection found that the models weren't suitable. The only recourse, then, was the time-consuming task of building, rendering, and compositing their own. Using Lightwave 3-D, an off-the-shelf software package, and a then roaring 600 MHz DEC personal computer, the pair began to knock out the effects later than they'd originally planned—just three days before the convention; they would be gunning right up to the last minute. Inevitably, time ran out and some shots had to be abandoned, like a snippet ad-libbed for the opening credit montage, where a stormtrooper gave a ticket to an imaginary landspeeder, never to be CGI'd in.

Two weeks before the convention, however, the sound work was the main focus; it took roughly twice as long to handle *Troops'* audio as the visual effects because CGI was used in only a handful of short shots while audio played a role throughout the entire short—and it was uniformly all screwed up.

Forget about sounds like blasters and spaceships; no one could even hear the actors. The problem wasn't that they were muffled under stormtrooper masks; as Rubio concisely puts it, "We were in the desert with the winds blowing at 35 miles an hour. All you could hear on the audio was *wwwwwwwwffffff*!"

Fullerton took the project to Post Logic, a postproduction facility in Hollywood that had become her second home over the years as she wrote and produced promo spots for the Fox Kids Network. She and Rubio were depending on the help of sound designer Bryant Arnett (who soon after wound up on staff at Fox Kids) to make the film listenable. Arnett, according to Fullerton, "was responsible for all the kick-ass sound you hear in *Troops*—or don't hear, as the case may be. They say the greatest compliment you can get for sound is no compliment at all, and man, is that the truth."

When he agreed to be a part of the *Troops* crew, Arnett brought not only his audio acumen, but also his late-night, after-hours access to equipment far out of the reach of the average fan filmmaker. What he didn't have, however, was a clue about what he was getting into. "I've been a huge fan of *Star Wars* since I saw it opening night back in 1977, so it was a big thrill to work on something fun like this," he says, "but it ended up being a much larger project that I realized. I thought I would be bringing in audio from production, but we had to basically start from scratch. It turned out to be fun. I got some of the other guys from the studio to pitch in their time as well, because everyone really liked the Fox Kids folks and wanted to help out—and everyone was a big *Star Wars* fan."

While the visual effects were being created on what amounted to a very high-end home computer, the audio on *Troops* received treatment worthy of a major motion picture. The sound was edited using Avid AudioVision and the film wound up getting a stereo mix in Post Logic's Studio C, which housed a $500,000 Solid State Logic 6000E mixing console.

With everyone working late at night after hours, the movie's audio began to take shape, but time was running out, with the San Diego premiere just days away. Not being able to hear the dialogue was a disaster. Rubio had to make the most of a bad situation, but turned it around to work in his favor. With their connections at Fox Kids, Fullerton and Rubio knew many of the top cartoon voice actors in Hollywood; a few judicious calls later, the stormtroopers suddenly had some of the most sought-after throats in Tinseltown.

Fullerton directed the voice-over work while engineer Connor Moore recorded the talent over the course of a week when the actors were available; the results were stellar. The film's jokes became even more multilayered; one trooper's new accent, borrowed lock, stock, and barrel from the Coen Brothers' classic *Fargo*, added new humor as he intoned, "Now if you move again, I'm, ehhh, gonna shoot ya."

With the vocal tracks on the mend, the next order of business was to find Star Wars sound effects. They couldn't just put a Chevy Nova engine rumble under a speederbike and be done with it, so the sound effects, while seemingly minor, were crucial. They were also impossible to find.

The first place they looked was in a sound effects library—a collection of CDs containing different sound effects—that was commercially sold by Lucasfilm itself. Amazingly, there were no Star Wars sounds on it at all. "We looked at each other like, 'Uh oh; now what do we do?'" recalls Arnett, laughing.

> We ended up going through all three films, looking for places with sounds. Fortunately, Kevin and some of the others knew the movies so well that they were able to take us to places right away that they thought there were sound effects that played in the clear, but for the most part, it turned out that if they were in the clear, they were cut off quickly by music or dialogue. You could barely extract anything from the film itself. I had a record called *The Story of Star Wars* that I got back when I was 12 years old, which I dug out of my box at home and I actually found a few sound effects on it that were in the clear, like the TIE fighters swooping by.
>
> Then we brought in a Nintendo Star Wars game, plugged it in and actually used it. There's a segment in the game where you're on a speederbike and you cruise around. We figured that would give us a nice continuous loop of the

sound, but Kevin had to play the game for 15 minutes just to get up to the part where that sound effect happened—and then we had to make sure that we were recording right at the right time, because it's not like you can back the game up. So he's zipping along on the speeder-bike and there's all kinds of explosions going on as he's playing; he had to basically go through and kill everything in the game so that we'd have a nice little five-second chunk where he could just drive without any other noises. We wasted a lot of time playing the game.

Some laser fire sounds were also culled from the game and a few effects from other sound effect libraries were modified, while Jawa voices were handled by certain crew members who had impersonated the desert scavengers for years as a joke. The crew did their imitations, Arnett raised their vocal pitches a bit, and *voilà*—instant Jawa. Despite all that, however, the thing that Arnett was most proud of was the amount of foley work done for the production.

Foleying is a sound effects process—named after Jack Foley, an early sound effects editor at Universal Studios in the 1930s—where sound engineers record people re-creating a natural sound, such as footsteps in a hallway, the sound of a door opening or a person rummaging through his pockets. For *Troops*, they tried to re-create the sound of stormtrooper armor moving by recording the sounds of fabrics brushing together and other things, but it never sounded quite right. The only answer, it turned out, was to call in the Troops.

"They came into the studio in their full stormtrooper costumes, which were amazing," remembers Arnett. "Not only did they look great, but the costumes made sounds which were completely right for the way you'd think stormtroopers would sound—the movements, rattles of buckles and stuff. We basically foleyed the whole thing with them re-creating their movements, and it worked out great. It makes it seem as if the sound was recorded all live."

Progress was still too slow. Rubio had secured a space in the convention's film program to debut the short, but during that final week, the premiere kept drawing closer and *Troops* just wasn't done.

Dialogue was recorded, sound effects were obtained, and the final cut was completed 16 hours before the film was due to debut, but the visual and sound effects were still incomplete. After six months of hard work, hundreds of hours spent writing, directing, acting, recording, rendering, cajoling and more, it was all coming down to the wire—and it looked like time had run out.

The biggest problem was explosive—literally. Jordan and Perez had to create a series of explosions for a segment where the Jawas' sandcrawler is attacked by TIE fighters. The effect wasn't hard for them to pull off, as they'd done it many times on *Babylon 5*. No, the drawback was that there was no way to create and render the special effects, and then get *Troops* across Los Angeles to Post Logic for the audio crew to lay in matching sound effects—and still make the premiere on time.

Meanwhile, the audio crew itself was in upheaval—Arnett couldn't be at the studio for the final mix. Post Logic engineer Fred Howard stepped up to pinch-hit in the mix position and found that the rest of the crew was running on sheer adrenaline. "Kevin and Charlotte have such passion for what they do; it doesn't matter what they're currently doing, they attack it all," says Howard. "It was just really neat to watch them pursue it with such limitless energy. I saw Kevin and it was, 'OK, so you're up to 36 hours of not sleeping. You just don't need sleep, huh?' He just seemed to be able to swing with it."

Even with a new sound engineer in place, they still faced the main problem: there wasn't enough time for the special effects to be completed and then finish the audio work as well before the premiere the next day. Their answer, it turned out, was that instead of waiting to match the sound effects to the picture, they did everything backward. "I was going back and forth between effects and sound, editing both separately," Rubio recalls, "so I'd revert back to my animation experience and do frame counts. I'd ask Shant, 'How many frames is this shot? On what frame is the explosion? Where does it peak?' and so on. Then I'd go over to the postsound house and we would create sound-to-picture that wasn't there and hope that my frame counts were right and that it would all match up."

Working until 3:30 AM the night before Comic Con, Rubio,

Fullerton, and Howard took a leap of faith. Fullerton explains, "We did the final mix to an incomplete picture, because Shant and Pat were rendering the remaining CG shots like madmen, right down to the wire. They sent us timings of the missing CG effects, like the sandcrawler exploding, and we timed the sounds—the impact, crescendo, peak and tapering off of the explosion—to their time code numbers, without ever timing the sound to picture." When the mix was finished, the audio was sent to Jordan and Perez, who were waiting for their visual effects to finish compositing; once the computers were done thinking, the effects artists dropped the final audio mix onto the final cut of the film. It was a hell of a gamble—the perfect way to screw up all their hard work at the last minute—but there was no choice. If the sound was out of synch with the visual effects, it would be too late; there would be no time left to rework the effects and still make the convention.

On July 18, 1997, *Troops* premiered at the San Diego Comic Con International. By the time it came up in the film program's running order, the screening area was jammed; in a room that fire marshals said was allowed to hold 350 people, every seat was filled and there was no room to walk due to all the fans sitting on the floor; the film would be debuting to an overcapacity crowd.

Many cast and crew members were part of the audience, all too ready to see the results of their hard work. During shooting, they'd all felt they were a part of something unique, something special, but had they been mistaken? No one knew if the jokes worked, or if the setting, the costumes, or the special effects truly seemed authentic. What if the audio, slaved over for days, was out of synch with the visual effects? No one was certain—not even Rubio, the person who had dragged the short into existence through sheer willpower, the man who was counting on *Troops* to help him finally climb above the line and out of the cel art archive at Fox Kids. Six months after Hargrove had first brainstormed the *Star Wars* meets *Cops* idea, it all came down to this moment.

"That 'world premiere' screening at Comic Con was really the first time any of us who worked on it got to see the final piece," remembers Fullerton. "I had my fingers crossed; I knew there was going to be an explosion sound; please let there be something exploding on screen!"

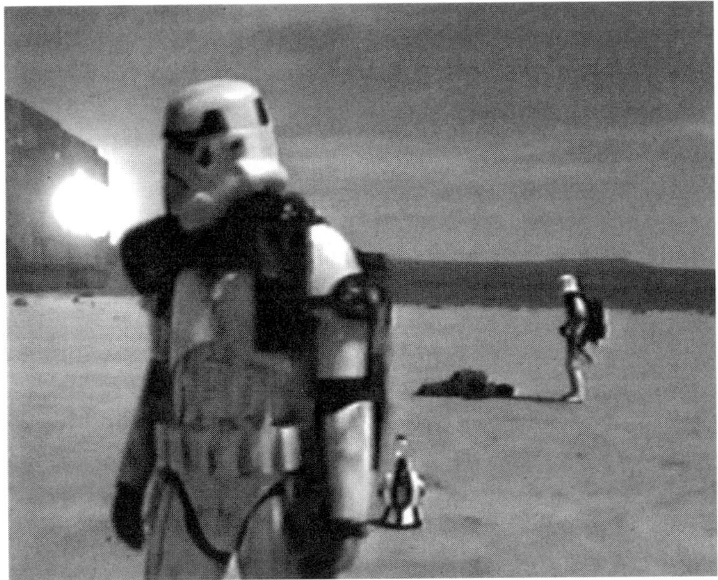

When the audio of the Jawas' sandcrawler detonating was mixed into the movie's soundtrack, the crew had to cross its fingers that the sound would match what happened on-screen. Note the cameo appearance of robot Tom Servo from *Mystery Science Theater 3000*. *(Courtesy of Kevin Rubio)*

When it was over and the audience began cheering, it was clear that *Troops* worked. The jokes made people laugh. The Speeder-bikes and TIE fighters made the audience murmur. The intricate ways that the story fit into the real Star Wars chronology gave them delayed chuckles 20 minutes later as they suddenly realized some of the plot's nuances. It was everything that the prototype of the modern fan film could hope to be.

The handful of Star Wars fan flicks that existed before *Troops* all looked like they were made by amateurs, usually because the special effects were impossible for regular people to re-create. Even a success like *Hardware Wars* had used flying steam irons and wafflemakers instead of Star Destroyers and battle stations, turning low-tech into its own cheap gag. While earlier fan films usually had some good humor about their humble, makeshift starships and such, in the end, they were essentially apologies to the fans: "Yeah, we don't have the money to do it right, but watch this and pretend it looks like the real thing."

Troops didn't make apologies; it looked like the real thing. A huge part of the short's power to wow audiences was the fact that it went toe-to-toe with the established Star Wars universe, serving up photorealistic vehicles and explosions. Rubio, Jordan, and Perez weren't hiding behind the cheap joke of dangling a purposefully terrible spaceship on a string; instead, they had stepped up with a Han Solo swagger, so confident in their effects that they even threw in a superfluous shot of TIE fighters heading for the death star to open the film—just because they could. Fans responded to the humor and clever plotting, but it was the look of the short that sold the Comic Con audience.

The crowd there, however, was just a fraction of the multitudes that would eventually see the short. Word slowly spread around Hollywood and copies started floating around, turning up at parties and special-effects production houses. Even the staff of *Cops* saw the short, and promptly sent *Troops'* producers hats and jackets sporting the show's logo; years later, they even stuck the short on a *Cops* DVD as a bonus feature.

Rubio started getting phone calls here and there about the production, and one was from a representative of Mark Hamill, Mr. Luke Skywalker himself. Hamill wanted to see the flick, so a screening was arranged. He dug it, as Fullerton later discovered when she worked with the actor—now a noted cartoon voice artist—on ads for Fox Kids Network: "Mark Hamill came in to read some Joker promos, and he's this total *Troops* fan! Who would've thought back when we were all kids carrying *Star Wars* lunchboxes and memorizing the making-of trivia that someday Luke Skywalker would be a fan of our work? How cool is that?"

Then George Lucas was rumored to have watched it during a lunch break while filming *Episode I: The Phantom Menace* in Tunisia. The upshot? He liked it. Soon Rubio was invited by model maker Tony Preciado of Industrial Light & Magic (Lucas's special-effects company) to screen the film at ILM and take a look at some of the things they were cooking up for *Phantom Menace*.

Considering that he'd played fast and loose with Lucasfilm's copyrighted characters and scenarios, it was a surprisingly warm response; the company had a somewhat prickly history with creative fans. In the early 1980s, Lucasfilm had sent letters to a number of fanzines in response to what it felt was improper use of its characters, threatening legal action if they didn't knock it off; Lucas had been livid to learn of X-rated fan fiction starring his PG characters. Months later, the Star Wars Fan Club, under the direction of the company and its legal counsel, issued a series of official guidelines regarding fan fiction, noting that it would support fans' efforts so long as they followed the rules. Even after *Troops*, however, the company still had a somewhat contentious relationship with fandom that suffered occasional flare-ups, such as a brief episode in 2000 where the company offered to host fans' tribute webpages on its own website—on the condition that any fan-generated content would become the property of Lucasfilm. *Troops*, however, had no problem being accepted by the company.

"As I understand it," says Rubio, "'Lucas the entity' is mainly worried about the portrayal of their material in a bad light. They don't want stormtroopers smoking cigarettes or peddling booze, and my film itself doesn't do any of that. I think we're very respectful of the original source material, and tried to make it as classy a production as possible. At the same time, it doesn't use one single bit of original *Star Wars* footage; everything was created from the ground up."

Helping publicize the movie early on, *Film Threat* gave *Troops* its "Underground Short Film of the Year" award, beating such stiff competition as the infamous Pam Anderson/Tommy Lee sex tape. While Rubio was starting to reap the rewards of his efforts, however, another homegrown Star Wars effort was getting underway that would kick *Troops* into overdrive: In September that year, TheForce.net debuted.

The fan-based website had grown out of a Star Wars page founded in 1996 by Texas A&M University roommates Scott Chitwood and Darin Smith. While Chitwood handled content, Smith was the technical guru, building the site from the ground up. By the time *Troops* was floating around fandom, Brian Linder was a manager on the site; e-mailing Rubio, Linder offered to host the film—a move that was technically audacious at the time.

While websurfers can now download massive amounts of data in seconds, in 1997 downloading a movie was a revolutionary—

and iffy—prospect. Having a 56K dial-up modem was like having a Ferrari attached to your computer, and most average users simply couldn't afford them. As a result, the 10-minute flick had to be split up into five heavily compressed Quicktime files that literally took days to download. When played back, the postage stamp–sized video clips were jumpy and blocky, sporting equally dodgy sound. Nonetheless, in February 1998, six months after the San Diego debut, *Troops* took on a new life when it was posted online. The segments were given their own section on the site—TFN Theater—and promptly became a smash hit. "It got around, but once we put it on the net," explains Rubio, "that's when things really shot out."

At TheForce.net, Linder was just as surprised as Rubio. "At first, I didn't think that many people would download the videos because of their file size," Linder told *Camcorder* magazine, "but I was wrong. We just put it up there, and the people found it. It was wild, amazing." In fact, after placing *Troops* online with no advertising about the flick, the site's visitors quintupled from 5,000 to 25,000 a day in under two weeks. Rubio cracked to the magazine, "It gets more hits that Jerry Springer's home page." Soon, *Troops* wasn't just news on the Net; *Newsweek* wrote about it, as did *Entertainment Weekly*; next the short was turning up on TV as CNN, *Access Hollywood*, and the SciFi Channel each covered the little film. Web traffic to theforce.net exploded—so much so that it crashed the site's server as thousands from around the globe tried to download the film simultaneously.

For many, *Troops* was the first form of media they'd ever downloaded from the Web, and the sheer popularity of it may well have inspired users to go hunting for more downloadable content, such as songs available in that newfangled format MP3. As a result, *Troops* became many users' first taste of getting quality content off the Internet for free, and that hunger soon fueled illegal downloading entities such as Napster and Kazaa. The success of *Troops* was a portent of the not-so-distant future, demonstrating on a massive scale how films could be instantly distributed for free around the world via the net, years before Hollywood began to fathom that this might be something to worry about.

In the meantime, Rubio's ultimate hope for *Troops*—that it would help get his foot farther in the Hollywood door—came to pass. Industry pros were amazed that Rubio had spearheaded such a professional effort on a budget of merely $1,200. Of course, that number wasn't entirely accurate, since everyone had worked and provided expensive professional equipment for free; if everything had been paid for, Rubio estimated, *Troops* would have come in at around $279,000.

It didn't matter, though; one producer enthused to *Entertainment Weekly*, "If he could do this with $1,200, what could he do for a million?" Another reason the budding director was so popular was that he hadn't tipped his hand, as an executive at MTV Films pointed out in the same article: "If you have three minutes of greatness, you're willing to give a person a shot to make a whole movie, with the hope that it'll be great. But if you've got 90 minutes of just-average stuff, then there's no leap to make. You've already seen what they're going to do with a feature."

Soon after, Rubio signed with the William Morris Agency and before long, was cutting deals to develop various TV series, adding to his resume as he went on to create a pilot presentation, *Alien Hunter*, for SciFi Channel; *Colossor*, a pilot for MTV; *Action Man* for Fox Kids; and *Storm Watch*, a pilot for the USA Network. At the same time, Rubio scribed a series of *Troops*-like *Star Wars* stories for Dark Horse Comics—eventually collected as the *Tag and Bink Were Here* graphic novel, named a top trade paperback of 2006 by the American Library Association—and an original title, *Abyss*, for the familiarly named Red 5 Comics.

A decade after *Troops* paved the way for the modern fan film, the short was still paying off for Rubio when he was named a writer—along with his old pal Melching—on Lucasfilm's all-CGI TV series, *Star Wars: The Clone Wars*. However, the gig wasn't nabbed solely on his *Star Wars* credentials—which now included being an official Stormtrooper after his induction into the 501st Legion, (a worldwide *Star Wars* Imperial costuming group) as an honorary member at the 2006 San Diego Comic Con. Instead, his recent history in animation was a factor, as he'd returned to the field in the mid-2000s as executive producer of *Duel Masters*, the U.S. adaptation of a popular Japanese Anime cartoon. And lest it seem that after all that hard work, no one else from the *Troops* crew landed a job for their work on the short, fear not: Nearly every episode of *Duel Masters* was written by none other than Charlotte Fullerton.

10
Good Times, Fad Times

Until the late nineties, fan films were barely known of outside of sci-fi or comic book fandom, but by 1998, they were ready to go to the big time, thanks to a perfect storm of factors: a groundbreaking piece of software; a generation of fans inspired by *Troops*; the hubris of the dotcom era; and the tidal wave of hype that preceeded *Star Wars: Episode One—The Phantom Menace*. The result was that 1998–99 witnessed the speedy rise and fall of what could only be termed "the fan film fad."

• • •

On June 29, 1998, while the fad was just starting to build up steam on the Internet, something happened that ensured homemade genre flicks would continue long after the craze was over. It was something that paved the way for YouTube, and to some degree, even the iPod. On June 29, 1998, Glenn Reid went to work.

It was his first day in the trenches for Apple Computer, and while he spent most of it doing the paperwork that accompanies the start of every job, the next nine months were spent leading a three-man team as they created iMovie, a consumer video-editing program that was noth-

Glenn Reid spearheaded the development team behind Apple's landmark iMovie software.
(Courtesy of Glenn Reid)

ing short of revolutionary.

Way back when Super 8 cameras reigned supreme, it was easy to edit a flick; film-splicing blocks were cheap and the cost of glue or tape to connect it all back together was negligible. When video cameras took over, however, the quality of home productions took a huge step backward, because there were only a few choices when it came to editing, and they all stunk. The best option was to somehow get access to a professional video editing system (it's no wonder that local public-access cable channels flourished during those years). Otherwise, amateurs had to make do, copying individual shots from one consumer VCR to another while riding the PAUSE button. Regardless of the method, the results were usually disappointing.

When video editing software arrived for personal computers in the early nineties, it was aimed at professionals—and it was priced accordingly. Typically, most computer-based video editing required a $3,000-plus PC and professional software like Adobe Premiere, which had a price of $600. There were a handful of consumer-level programs under $100, like Sony's MovieShaker, but their interfaces were clumsy and the results were often inferior. All of this meant that video editing—much like the original movie camera of the early 1900s—was essentially the province of professionals and hobbyists with enough money and free time to afford and learn the often complicated software. Glenn Reid's nine-month project changed that paradigm overnight.

When iMovie debuted on October 5, 1999, it was priceless—literally. The program was free . . . if you didn't count the $1,299–$1,499 Apple iMac DV computer that it came preloaded on. Using a simple interface, Reid's application brought basic non-linear editing to the masses. Users could edit, re-edit, add music, titles, and transitions intuitively, and unlike previous linear (tape-to-tape) methods, if they made a change, they didn't have to start all over again from the top. In one swift stroke, iMovie democratized video editing for everyone; if you could afford a Mac, you could polish your home movie to a nice, respectable shine.

The iMovie program did more than just revitalize home videos, however; it gave the iMac superpowers in the eyes of consumers. The original iMac, released a year earlier in October 1998, was Apple's first hit in years, and the ailing company seized that success like a drowning man lunging for a life preserver. The iMac racked up sales of 2 million computers in a year, but time moves quickly in the computer industry; when it came time to prove that the computers were still relevant a mere 12 months after their debut, iMovie and the new model iMac DVs were placed directly in the public eye, front and center.

Apple CEO Steve Jobs was at no loss for words when it came to the program, telling industry analysts the following July, that "iMovie is huge! We believe that desktop movies are bigger than desktop publishing. We know a lot more people who want to make a movie of their family than want to put out a newsletter from home. . . . iMovie has been a huge hit; there are more of those we're working on." Some of those hits included iPhoto (which Reid also shepherded), iTunes, and the lifeboat that grew into a cruise ship, the iPod.

In the short term, iMovie's success powered iMac sales, but looking at the big picture, it revolutionized home computers and, more important, society's view of how a computer fits into daily life. People now purchase home computers expecting to see some form of video editing software in a feature list on the side of the box; what started as a pleasantry of added value, like power windows on a car, is now often a given. The personal computer is expected to be a Swiss Army knife for creativity—a flexible tool that will accommodate whatever its user wants to do, whether it's to make a movie, touch up photos, create music, build a website, or write the Great American Novel.

When iMovie was released in the fall of 1999, the fan film fad had already peaked, but the program nonetheless provided a springboard on which thousands of backyard auteurs could explore their own creativity. All they needed was the software and a modern video camera, since camcorders, too, had kept up with the times, moving to digital media with the debut of the DV and miniDV formats in the later nineties. iMovie became the final link that would allow people with the most basic of tools to create their own movies—and they needed it; in many cases, amateurs had already completed every aspect of their fan films except the editing, having been inspired by *Troops* a year earlier.

The original *Star Wars* had opened up the imaginations of a generation of kids, inspiring them to dream that maybe they could create their own space epics someday, but *Troops* reignited that dream, imbuing it with a new immediacy that infected thousands of fans. The stuff of idle daydreams was no longer a wish about the one-in-a-billion chance to make a Hollywood movie; now it was the first step to a handwritten *Star Wars* script to be shot on a camcorder with friends. Maybe you weren't George Lucas, and maybe your special effects department was a bedroom PC, but it didn't matter—you could do it if you really tried. Kevin Rubio and his crew had shown it was possible to reverse engineer *Star Wars,* and now anyone with enough patience and determination could roll their own Force flick.

While average fans became inspired to make their own Star Wars flicks to share with each other on the Internet, however, many of Rubio's fellow "below-the-line schmos" decided to make their own *Troops*-like "calling card" movies in hopes of catching Hollywood's eye. Semipro efforts started popping up, like *Swing*

Blade (a fake trailer combining *Swingers* and *Sling Blade*), *Evil Hill* (Dr. Evil of the Austin Powers movies in a dreadful *Notting Hill* takeoff), and *Pearl Harbor II: Pearlmaggedon* (in which asteroids from director Michael Bay's *Armageddon* rain down on his follow-up, *Pearl Harbor*).

While the fan films were unauthorized, nonprofit ventures, they were created by professionals and had big budgets to match. It was a gamble that usually didn't pay off, too; out of the pack of semipro flicks that followed in *Troops'* wake, only one hit the jackpot for its creator: *George Lucas in Love.*

• • •

Working at 3-OH!-05 Creative Advertising, a production house specializing in movie trailers, administrative assistant Joe Nussbaum was itching to direct his own calling-card short, and decided that the latest Oscar-winning best picture, 1998's *Shakespeare in Love,* was ripe for a parody. The film, which finds Shakespeare inspired to write *Romeo and Juliet* based on people and events surrounding him, could easily be transposed to the current day; after toying with versions about Stephen King and Joe Ezsterhas (the screenwriter behind tawdry fare like *Showgirls* and *Basic Instinct*), Nussbaum and friends/cowriters Tim Dowling and Dan Shere hit upon Lucas, a man who had inspired all of them to enter the movie biz.

Soon, they were shooting a seven-page script, following the iconoclast Lucas (played by Martin Hynes) as a USC student in 1967 who struggles to write a final script that will allow him to graduate. Surrounded by friends and enemies that resemble various Star Wars characters, Lucas eventually finds his muse in the form of Marion (Lisa Jakub), a woman leading "the student rebellion." While there were plenty of jokes for sci-fi fans, the charming short showed range, proving the director could handle romantic comedy as well. The on-screen chemistry he created must have worked—Hynes and Jakub wound up as an item for a time.

Nussbaum originally budgeted for a $10,000 film, to be paid for with an inheritance from his grandparents, but the cost quickly ballooned to two-and-a-half times that amount, as a funky dorm-

George Lucas in Love, a 10-minute fan film that parodied *Shakespeare in Love*, was a sensation, at one point outselling *The Phantom Menace* on Amazon.com.
(Courtesy of Amusement Park Productions)

room set, an 18-person orchestra paid under the table and other costs came along. At the same time, corners were cut by convincing Panavision to loan them a 35mm camera, getting the 40-person cast and crew to work for free, and editing the flick on the sly after-hours at Nussbaum's day job. The short was cut in a week, sound and music took another 10 days, and soon the nine-minute tale was complete, just three weeks after shooting.

A total of 300 VHS copies were made and distributed to contacts around the industry, but the tapes quickly took on a life of their own. Looking back, Nussbaum says, "When we made it, we foolishly didn't take into account its appeal to *Star Wars* fans. We were only hoping—at best—for it to appeal to the people who might hire us." It turned out, however, that everyone wanted to see it—and not just in Hollywood. In short order, there was coverage on CNN and NBC, as well as write-ups in *Entertainment Weekly* (which gave it an A+), the Associated Press, *Variety*, *USA Today*, the *Hollywood Reporter,* and elsewhere. Soon it was being shown at festivals, on the SciFi Channel, on foreign TV, and even by airlines, but the key sign of achievement was that Nussbaum landed a feature directing deal with DreamWorks.

A now-defunct website, Mediatrip.com, spent $1,500 for the rights to put the short online, where it garnered more than 150,000 viewings in three weeks; Nussbaum took the Mediatrip money and spent it on film prints to show at festivals. When *George Lucas in Love* was eventually released on home video, it moved 50,000 VHS tapes and another 20,000 DVDs—a feat that found the fan film even outselling *The Phantom Menace* on Amazon.com for one week. And the icing on the cake was that the real George Lucas liked it so much (Steven Spielberg sent it on to his pal after watching it at DreamWorks) that he sent two letters to Nussbaum, praising the film as "the life story I wish I had." Never one to miss an opportunity, the budding director hid one of the letters on the fan film's DVD as an "Easter egg" for viewers to discover.

After all the various deals, *George Lucas in Love* eventually grossed over $50,000—a fact that nearly invalidates it as a fan film since, by their nature, fan productions are nonprofit ventures. While making money was the last thing on the director's mind when he created the film, when the opportunities came, they were legally feasible. Nussbaum and his cowriters had been careful not to violate any copyrights, and Lucas himself, as a public figure, was fair game, so the film could be released. As Nussbaum told the *New York Times,* "What is it they say? If three people tell you you're drunk, you'd better sit down? Well, if four Internet sites tell you they want your movie, you'd better put it on the Internet."

George Lucas in Love accomplished Nussbaum's vocational goals like a charm, yet jump-started his career only to leave it idling in the driveway. The director spent most of the next five years making commercials for the likes of Nike and Kellogg's while he was attached to seven different feature films, waiting for any of them to get the green light.

Looking back, he feels that could have been avoided: "There is one thing that I would have done differently very early on: When the short was still at the height of its buzz around town, I would have pushed my agents to get me into rooms with actors and actresses. I met with tons of producers and studio executives—and that was great—but it's the in-front-of-the-camera talent that really makes this town work; if I could have hooked up with even just one or two actors with name value and an affection for the short, I probably could have gotten a project off the ground much quicker." When he finally got to make his feature directing debut, it was with MGM's 2004 tween flick, *Sleepover*, which was followed by the million-plus-selling, direct-to-DVD *American Pie* sequel *The Naked Mile*, and 2007's fairy-tale update, *Sydney White*.

"*George Lucas in Love* always gets a positive reaction and has continued to help me get work, even now after having done three features," says Nussbaum. "Early on, when I had done about a dozen commercials, it would frustrate me that I was getting hired solely off the short and not off the strength of my new work, but I learned to embrace it. In this business, it's so hard to get hired at all that if you have something that's well liked, ride it as long as you can. I can laugh at myself about it, but whenever I meet someone new and they say, 'I loved your film', I always know they mean the short."

• • •

George Lucas in Love hit Hollywood just as *Phantom Menace* hype was at its peak in June 1999, but fan films had been a buzz across the Internet for more than a year by then. When *Troops* had appeared online in 1998, plenty of its viewers began searching the Net for other fan productions, but most were nearly impossible to find—and, if you'll indulge me, that's where I came in.

In 1998, I founded the first website devoted solely to fan films, Mos Eisley Multiplex. Taking the name from the spaceport town where Luke and Obi-Wan meet Han and Chewie, the site quickly became the place to find Star Wars fan cinema. In a pre-YouTube world, there weren't any easily searchable movie websites; if you wanted to watch fan films, you had to go endlessly spelunking through search engines like Yahoo and HotBot with fingers crossed that you'd find something, so the Multiplex began as a list of links to movies that were online. Soon I added fan film news,

In *George Lucas in Love*, Lisa Jakub and Martin Hynes portray the famed filmmaker and his muse, Marion (named after the character Marion Ravenwood from *Raiders of the Lost Ark*).
(Courtesy of Amusement Park Productions)

filmmaker interviews, links to fan-film articles elsewhere on the Web, and, as a sign of the technological barriers that people faced putting video online, a placement service to help match up films with websites that were willing to host them. That problem would vanish virtually overnight with the debut of YouTube in February 2005, but seven years earlier, posting video on the Internet was an expensive, arduous proposition.

Word quickly spread, and soon the site was extolled in the *Los Angeles Times*, the *San Francisco Examiner*, and *USA Today* (which named it Hot Site of the Day), as well as magazines like *Total Film* and, oddly enough, *CMJ New Music Monthly*. A few radio morning shows chatted about the Multiplex, as did, for some reason, an evening TV newscast in Eden Prairie, Minnesota, but most of the site's coverage, understandably, came from the Internet, including E! Online and the Internet Movie Database.

All that coverage drove plenty of visitors to the Multiplex, so I scoured the Web to find more flicks to add. There were few at first, but with the hubbub surrounding *Troops*, things changed quickly as older, pre-Internet Star Wars productions started popping up online. Soon, brand new ones turning up, too, quickly churned out by fans seeking their moment in the sun. By the time *The Phantom Menace* hit theaters in late May 1999, dozens of efforts were appearing online every week; in fact, the sudden gold rush was so overwhelming that by the summer of 1999, it threatened to choke the format to death. After 70 years of existing as an underground movement, fan films had suddenly become a fad.

• • •

Of course, there's nothing wrong with popularity; while numerous fan flicks over the years had come close to achieving mainstream success, none had ever broken out the way *Troops* had. The rub was that 95 percent of the "me too" movies that followed in its wake were terrible—and they were everywhere on the Net.

Even these days, with the fad long since over, the me-too mentality continues to a degree, with some fans taking an almost mercenary approach to how they expend their fandom energies—and it has little to do with commenting on or altering the original franchise of their affection. Henry Jenkins, director of the Massachusetts Institute of Technology comparative media studies program, explains,

> There's a hunger that many of these people have to create, to be part of a shared mythology that is not about a struggle over the meaning of the text, but is simply over "I'd like to contribute to this, I've got creative talents, this is what interests me." And increasingly, as I talk to younger fans, I'm seeing that they sometimes choose to create stories in particular universes not even because they're fans of that universe, but because that universe will generate the most traffic, the most viewers for what they produce. Right now, a lot of young people are working in Harry Potter [fan fiction]—that's a flexible enough world that a lot of stories can be told through it, but they also know if they tell a Harry Potter story it will attract a lot more viewers than if they tell a Torchwood story. That choice, of creating for community and using that outlet as a space to tell stories that are important to them, is a different way of thinking about what it means to be a fan. . . . You could say that's about publicity, but that's an understanding of publicity in a very narrow sense. It's not like total narcissism in which I simply want to

> be famous for being famous. These communities are generating content for complex reasons, and they like that content to have some circulation and some influence, to reach people who may be interested in that content.

That point of view wasn't limited to amateur filmmakers during the fad, either; the 1999 explosion of fan films coincided with the height of the first dot-com era, as plenty of overcapitalized, underutilized websites were scrambling to attract customers in any way they could. Numerous savvy Web marketers realized that hosting a Star Wars fan film was an easy way to draw traffic to your dot-com, so they threw together amateur shorts as fast as they could. Take, for instance, the now-defunct DailyMovies.com, which proved it took little time, money, effort, or thought to videotape a Jar-Jar Binks toy being run over by a car, then pop it online and litter the Internet with missives to come see *Killing Jar-Jar*. Clearly even less time was spent considering whether anyone would actually want to watch such dross.

It was inevitable, however. What might look like an influx of also-rans jumping on the bandwagon was actually something more: growing pains. Until that point, there had never been a true public awareness of fan films; after all, here was a film movement so underground that most participants didn't even realize other people were making these movies, too. The rise of the Internet changed that, though, and while there were still serious technical and financial barriers to overcome in order to put a fan film online, the Web was providing a sense of community to this unusual strain of indie filmmaking for the first time. Thanks to the high profile of *Troops*, it just happened to be a community that a lot of people suddenly wanted to move into.

Fan films were becoming a "vernacular culture," a term used by scholars to describe a cultural form created and organized by regular folks, a hobby that grows organically, created by people instead of manufacturers; for example, video games are a pastime that was created by companies, while graffiti art and Civil War reenactments are hobbies that qualify as vernacular cultures. As noted by Kris M. Markman in her essay "Star Trek, Fan Film, and the Internet: Possibilities and Constraints of Fan-Based Vernacular Cultures,"

> Some current work in cultural studies suggests . . . that vernacular cultures provide alternate understandings of cultural history, and that they may offer opportunities for change and liberation that mass culture does not provide. However, [Kent A. Ono and John M. Sloop in their essay "The Critique of Vernacular Discourse"] stress that vernacular cultures should not be assumed to always be emancipating per se, because they may in fact reproduce some of the same oppressive features of the dominant culture. In their view, vernacular cultures are mixed in their opportunities for resistance and change.

That's exactly what was happening to fan films in 1998 and '99; the public fell in love with the homemade movies because they provided different ways to look at feature films that everyone already knew by heart (*Troops* was a letter-perfect example of an "alternate understanding"). Also, the fact that Star Wars fan productions—far and away the subject of most fan films at the time—even existed was irreverent and liberating, simply for the fact that they didn't originate from Lucasfilm. However, once fan movies suddenly exploded across the Internet, a loose fan film community soon formed, and with it came slowly realized, often unspoken consensuses on what constituted a fan film, "good" flicks versus "bad" ones, the "right" way to achieve certain ends (one of the most argumentative online forums at TheForce.net concerns ways to create lightsaber effects), and so on.

Quickly, this wild frontier of creativity developed its own etiquette and organization, in many ways imitating "oppressive features of the dominant culture"—that is, the real movie biz. That speedy maturity was accelerated by the influx of beginners and dabblers drawn by mainstream media's sudden interest in the fledgling vernacular culture, but with organization and growing self-awareness, a binge of fan films ensued—and with it came four clichés that would choke the fan film fad by the end of the millennium.

11
From Chaos to Cliché

Today, it's fairly easy to spot a fan movie made before the rise of the Internet, and not merely due to technical limitations apparent in the productions. Before the fad, most fan filmmakers didn't know about each other and had never seen a fan film, so they had no preconceived notions about what their movies should look like, what they should be about, or how they should be produced. As a result, many pre-1998 fan flicks have unique perspectives and creative values. They were made for audiences of tens, not tens of thousands, and since no one was watching—especially hypercritical fan-filmmaking peers—the films had a certain sense of freedom. For instance, distinctive efforts such as Pewter Joe Flynn's *The Odd Star Wars Couple*, Pez D. Spencer's *The Star Wars*, John Hudgens's *The Empire Strikes Quack,* and Matthew Ward's *Death of a Jedi* were all made before Kevin Rubio's landmark *Troops*. However, what's creative and innovative in one set of hands is dull and derivative in another, so each one of these shorts anticipated a major fan film cliché that emerged during the 1998–99 Star Wars fan film fad.

+ + +

The Odd Star Wars Couple, produced by the Glendale, California–based filmmaking collective Pewter Joe Flynn, was deceptively straightforward. The 1997 short simply recast Neil Simon's classic play/movie/sitcom *The Odd Couple* with Chewbacca as nebbish Felix Unger and Darth Vader as überslob Oscar Madison. It could be argued that they were cast against type (really, wouldn't loose and wooly Chewie work better as Oscar and the sharp, straight lines of Darth flatter a Felix?), but the short still worked on a number of levels.

Following the sitcom's format, the three-minute fan film is comprised of a "teaser" scene that sets up the rest of an episode that's never shown, followed by a remake of the show's opening credits. Throughout the teaser, a laugh track howls at aggressively weak jokes about Felix's Wookie opera club and Oscar's helmet getting featherdusted; while the opening credits are jammed with good sight gags, the "unfunny" scene is a riot, too, thanks to its purposeful awkwardness—and in turn, it provides a unique commentary on the success of *Star Wars*.

By combining the biggest movie of the 1970s with one of the most popular sitcoms of the era, the short highlights the contrast between the two sources: a predictable comedy with predictable jokes versus a then-revolutionary space opera. While it's affectionate toward the creations of both George Lucas and Neil Simon, it also seems to suggest that the overwhelming success of *Star Wars* might have been due to a lack of true creative competition. If *The Odd Couple* was typical of popular entertainment in the seventies, how could recycled gags about two divorced men living together compete with X-wings, lightsabers, and the like?

Ironically, the Pewter Joe Flynn members intended the short to be a commentary, but on an entirely different, far more oblique subject: big media's tepid attempts to cater to their age group by crassly using totems of their youth as window dressing. As PJW leader Kurt Ramschissel puts it, "[Our film] goes hand-in-hand with all the ridiculous stuff that we've all gotten tired of—the Gen X films where they reference *Schoolhouse Rock*, *The Brady Bunch*, *Puffinstuff*, and all that crap."

Between this short and *Troops*, a simple blueprint for the

"mash-up" fan film was created, copied by plenty of others: Combine *Star Wars* with something completely different and there's your movie. Their results were rarely as well conceived, however, because most fan filmmakers saw the concept of a mash-up as an end to itself rather than a vehicle to explore an idea.

Take, for instance, one of the more heavily promoted fan films of the period: *Park Wars: The Little Menace*. Created by Lincoln Gasking, cofounder of the movie news website Countingdown.com, the short was an exact remake of the trailer to *The Phantom Menace*, except it starred characters from the cartoon series *South Park*. Gasking says his inspiration for the short came from "the fact that when [I was] watching the trailer, all the characters seemed to match up in my mind." Unfortunately, that appeared to be the sole basis for the fan film—whereas *The Odd Star Wars Couple* commented on the banality of the 1970s and *Troops* created an alternate timeline for beloved characters, *Park Wars* merely presented a Cartman-esque Yoda, and while that might bring a chuckle of recognition, real laughter requires real jokes. By mimicking the original so closely, the short confused imitation with satire and elicited shrugs as a result. It wasn't alone in that mistake, however; to be fair, plenty of fan efforts—and, indeed, Hollywood productions—make that mistake all the time.

One filmmaker who recognized that trap was Jeff Allen, a self-described "HTML monkey," then in his midtwenties, living in Atlanta. When not glued to a computer at his Internet development job, Allen's favorite hobby was build stormtrooper costumes. Once he built a few outfits, however, he and his buddies needed excuses to wear them, and it didn't take long to come up with a good one—shoot a fan flick. Allen settled in on spoofing the work of slacker-film director—and noted *Star Wars* enthusiast—Kevin Smith, whose breakthrough came with the 1994 indie classic *Clerks*. The result was *Trooper Clerks*, a shot-for-shot remake of the Smith film's trailer, featuring stormtroopers looking after a convenience store on the Death Star.

The flick painstakingly re-created the cheap, grungy look of the original film, but was no shoddy endeavor. "All in all, it cost about $1,000 U.S. to shoot," says Allen. "The costumes nearly killed me, because we had to custom build seven of them. A

Jeff Allen paid tribute to the classic slacker indie film *Clerks* by parodying its trailer with *Trooper Clerks*, a shot-for-shot trailer remake featuring Star Wars stormtroopers.
(Courtesy of Jeff Allen)

stormtrooper costs just over $200 in materials alone; Greedo ran about $100 after we rigged him up with pyrotechnics—which never made it into the film."

Unsurprisingly, the flick was very popular with Smith's legion of fans; when Allen sent a copy—and a prop helmet—to Smith's production company, ViewAskew, the faux trailer was quickly posted on one of the organization's websites. Smith himself comments, "I was amazed at the amount of effort they put into that, especially the attention to detail. If you compare it to the original *Clerks* trailer, they're really close."

Despite the hard work, the short played much like *Park Wars;* it supplied a few amusing clips—C-3PO asking a stormtrooper, "Do you want to have sex?" is surely a classic fan film moment—but was ultimately unfulfilling. Recognizing an opportunity to expand on the idea, however, Allen decided to make a full-fledged *Trooper Clerks* fan film, taking an unusual approach. Given the money poured into costumes and sets for the trailer, most fan filmmakers would've recycled them for a new flick, but Allen changed

Taking the *Trooper Clerks* concept one step further, Allen created a full-fledged short, but changed media from video to Flash animation.
(Courtesy of Jeff Allen)

media altogether.

Instead, he put his computer skills to work, creating a Flash-animated *Trooper Clerks* cartoon. The new short was brilliant, pairing up the creations of Lucas and Smith with deceptive ease, as the titular clerks schemed to get the blueprints of the Death Star into rebel hands, thus ensuring, through twisted logic, that they wouldn't be fired from their convenience store jobs on the Empire's space station. The characters may have looked like they were in the *Star Wars* universe, but they walked, thought, and swore (and swore) like the myopically self-absorbed denizens of Smith's movies.

However, while Allen had come to realize that strict imitation wasn't terribly interesting, many wannabe directors continue to this day to jump headlong into that mistake, so in the quickly coalescing world of fan films, mash-ups became the first major cliché.

• • •

It wasn't the last—another soon-to-be-threadbare formula was the action figure movie. As Henry Jenkins of MIT has noted in his book *Convergence Culture*, "The mass marketing of *Star Wars* inadvertently provided many of the resources needed to support [fan film] productions," adding that "a significant number of filmmakers . . . have turned toward those action figures as resources for their first production efforts."

Throughout the late seventies and early eighties, plenty of kids used toys to make their own stop-motion animated versions of Lucas's space saga, but it was *The Star Wars,* made in 1994 by Pez D. Spencer (aka Troy Durrett), that took the concept of the action figure movie to the ultimate level—thanks to its structure, which was dictated by the merchandise it exploited. The short was a collector's fever dream, an experiment in metastorytelling, a commentary on the commercialization of *Star Wars* and an insular artistic conceit taken to the extreme—far more than the sum of its (plastic) parts.

Working with fellow slacker/record-store employee Lance Robson, Durrett put his film degree from the University of South Florida–Tampa to use by reenacting the original 1977 movie using toys, a card table for a set, and desk lamps with T-shirts wrapped around them for lighting effects. Thanks to years of haunting flea markets, Robson was able to bring a massive Star Wars toy collection to the table—literally—as he evoked his own degree in graphic design, setting up shots for the largely static film. Although they reenacted most of the story with action figures, the final assault on the Death Star was handled with footage of the rare *Star Wars: The Arcade Game* home video game cartridge, produced by Parker Brothers for the Atari 2600, the first landmark video game console. Arguably, this could be considered one of the earliest examples of machinima, a film genre in which video game settings and characters are used for performances or to tell a story, rather than for the intended purpose of playing the game.

While the visuals were informed by vintage toys, however, so were the audio and structure of the movie; its narration, music, dialogue, and sound effects all came from a 45 RPM record that was part of a now vintage children's read-along book-and-record set ("Turn the page when you hear R2D2 beep!"). On the seven-inch vinyl record, the two-hour movie was reduced to a 10-minute summary that skipped major plot points, all breathlessly retold by a hokey narrator aided by (terrible) voice actors.

Robson explains, "The fast pacing of the read-along book, along with the awful-slash-great voices of the stand-in actors, paved the way. The comedy was so easy to achieve; as we shot and watched the preview on a monitor, it was a total gas. We didn't shoot and critique; we just let the scenes happen. We let go and the inner child took over."

By sticking to the strict confines of the record's narration, the flick was short and to the point, enjoying an editorial focus that many fan films lack, but, more important, the brevity underscored their minimalist take on the space epic, highlighting their film's inherent lack of nuance, tone or even "actors" with more than one facial expression.

The toys, record, and video game had all been adapted from the feature film, and each piece of merchandise was a reductive symbol that stripped *Star Wars* down to its most basic, bare-bones essence. The short, then, drew from all these polymorphic interpretations of the original, weaving them together to create an adaptation of the memorabilia instead of the original movie from which they were derived. The result is a fan film that is the cinematic equivalent to a cover of a cover song. If literary critic Roland Barthes argued in his essay "The Death of the Author" that readers must divorce a story from all the surrounding material from which it originates (the storyteller's background, intentions, etc.) in order to truly interpret it, here was an unusual, if accidental, example.

Acknowledging the primal feel to the whole endeavor, the filmmakers named their production *The Star Wars*—placing emphasis on the *The*—because that was the original working title for the feature film. It was wholly appropriate, too, because the fan flick plays like a rough draft of the real thing, as if it was made solely so it could fall through a gap in time and land in the lap of George Lucas circa 1973, ready to be fleshed out into something more substantial.

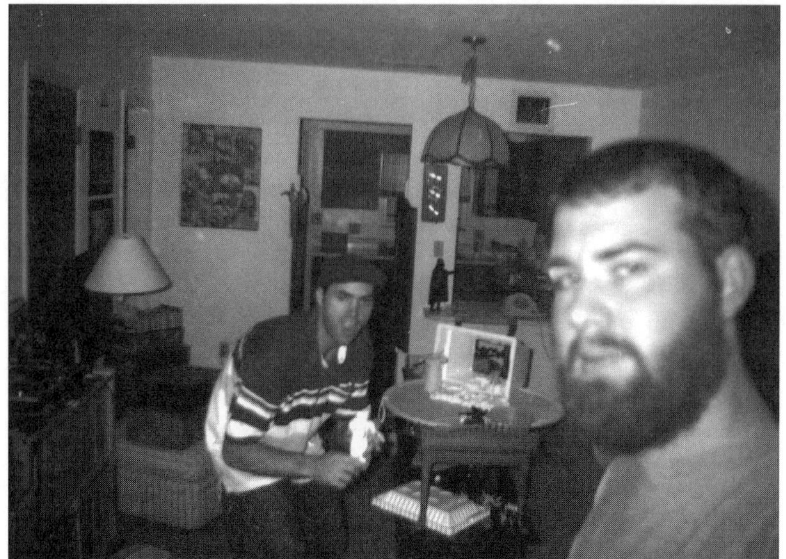

Pez D. Spencer, a.k.a. Troy Durrett (left), and Lance Robson created *The Star Wars*, a remake that used merchandise for everything, from "actors" to sets to the narration. A sequel based on *The Empire Strikes Back* (shown here in production) was never completed. *(Courtesy of Eye Splice Creative)*

Most folks who saw it, however, just thought it was cool; Dead Kennedys lead singer Jello Biafra bought a copy, and underground surf band Man or Astro-Man? hired Durrett to tour the world, screening the short and other "found footage" before concerts. Durrett was psyched: "To have the perfect audience in a new city or country, every night, to show the video we created, was the most unique way to distribute art and be witness to the reaction every night. The experience traveling with Man or Astro-Man? was the greatest."

The Star Wars was hardly one of the first toy-based movies to be made, but it likely was one of the first to be made by Generation Xers once the age group was old enough to have a nickname. When the Star Wars fan film gold rush began in 1998, plenty of other action-figure adaptations followed, but none with the force (if you will) of Durrett and Robson's version. There were promising ideas like Corn Pone Flicks' *The Empire Strikes Back by George Lucas, Age 9*, which killed off Luke at the Battle of Hoth, and an unfinished serialization of *Shadows of the Empire*, an official novel that takes place between *Empire* and *Return of the Jedi*, but both were undone by their sheer length and occasionally incoherent storylines (*Shadows* was later fully adapted in 2006 as a 100-minute action figure movie by Portuguese fan filmmaker Milton Soares Jr. voiced in his native tongue with broken-English subtitles). Taking the action figure film to its logical extreme in the late nineties, however, was *Star Wars: Figure Edition*, a tedious two-hour reenactment of *A New Hope* starring toys, which was never placed on the Internet due to its length.

By far the most popular action-figure movies of the period were created by Seattle architect and hobbyist filmmaker Evan Mather. Producing a series of Star Wars–related fan films between 1997 and 1999, Mather quickly made a name for himself in the early days of downloadable movies on the Internet. The first 30-second effort, *Kung-Fu Kenobi*, landed online in June 1997, followed by *Quentin Tarantino's Star Wars*, the short that catapulted him to prominence in February 1998. "I was looking for another film to do, and this one literally popped into my head," he explains. "I had done films with Star Wars action figures, and I had done films which mimicked other directors' styles—Scorsese, Allen, Lynch—and decided to blend the two concepts together."

The shorts were widely acclaimed, garnering press in places like *Wired*, *Esquire UK*, and the *New York Times*; *Newsweek* called them "clever" while MIT's Jenkins wrote "Mather's films . . . represent a no-holds-barred romp through contemporary popular culture."

In truth, the shorts—devoid of coherent plots—mainly featured lots of disco dancing; a bisexual Lando Calrissian trying to get it on with anything that moved; extreme flatulence; and endless scenes of figures getting kicked in the crotch (and, on a personal note, when find yourself thinking, "*America's Funniest Home Videos* does that so much better," you can only hope you've reached the nadir of book research—but I digress).

What Mather's figure flicks lacked in narrative sophistication—because, much as in real life, a little flatulence goes a long, long way—they made up with often stunning visuals, providing a primer on how to compose a shot for maximum effect, even when the cast is miniature. Given the shorts' great look, it's not too surprising that Mather wound up being courted for a time by Hollywood agents, eventually creating the impressive opening credit sequence for the Chris Gore–scribed feature *My Big Fat Independent Movie*. With the onslaught of toy-based fan flicks coming from all corners of *Star Wars* fandom at the time, however, there was no denying that the action figure movie had become the second big fan film cliché.

• • •

Few fan filmmakers have been at it as long as John Hudgens, a paragon of the Southern sci-fi convention scene. Today, he's known in the fan film world for his reality TV parodies like *The Jedi Hunter* (spoofing *The Crocodile Hunter*) and *Sith Apprentice* (the Imperial Emperor à la Donald Trump forces Darth Maul, Darth Vader, and Count Dooku to compete in a talent contest), but his first well-known effort appeared in 1991—and didn't feature any original footage at all. *The Empire Strikes Quack* was a "dub," a video art form that synchs audio from one source to visuals from a completely different source. In this case, the basis for the short came from Warner Brothers' classic 1953 cartoon, *Duck Dodgers in the 24-1/2th Century*—a loose mockery of *Buck Rogers* serials, starring Daffy Duck in the title role with Porky Pig as his sidekick, squaring off against the Roman-helmeted Marvin the Martian. Hudgens took the cartoon's complete audio, and then draped a collage of footage from the Star Wars trilogy over it so that Luke mouthed Daffy's dialogue, C-3PO was voiced by Porky, and so on.

There was no rhyme or reason to the choice of visuals, bouncing between the original trilogy films like a pinball out of control, but the cumulative result was undeniably funny. The silly voices from cartoon legend Mel Blanc undermined the dramatic Star Wars visuals; most pointedly, the usually foreboding Darth Vader was effectively neutered once viewers heard the odd nasal whine of Marvin the Martian emanating from that dark mask. Similarly, the *Duck Dodgers* audio inadvertently peeled a few layers of smooth Hollywood veneer off Star Wars to highlight some of its debt to Buster Crabbe's 1939 *Buck Rogers* movie serial, which Lucas likely saw at USC in the 1960s.

Assembled slowly over the course of a year using footage from home video, the short was shown to raucous crowds at sci-fi conventions, and soon a handful of bootleg copies had gotten out and made the rounds among fans. It was hardly the only dub effort—others estimated to be from the same period include *Apocalypse Pooh,* which mashes *Apocalypse Now* and *Winnie the Pooh* cartoon footage together, and an unnamed short where the cartoon band the Archies (who were credited on the real-life 1969 number-one hit, "Sugar Sugar") perform "Anarchy in the UK" by the Sex Pistols. *Quack* was likely one of the first Star Wars–themed dubs though, and it definitely became the form's best known example.

By the time fan films exploded on the Internet at the end of the 1990s, Hudgens was already toying with the idea of shooting original fan shorts with friends, starting with the brief but critically lauded *Crazy Watto,* a pseudo–used spaceship ad starring the owner of the young, enslaved Anakin Skywalker in *The Phantom Menace.* Encouraged by the fake ad's success—it eventually was shown at the 2005 Cannes Film Festival—Hudgens followed up with numerous efforts, including *Jedi Hunter* and *Sith Apprentice,* both of which won the Audience Choice Award at the 2003 and 2005 Lucasfilm Star Wars Fan Film Awards, respectively. Those successes, in turn, spurred him on to produce a feature-length documentary on fan films and their surrounding culture.

Hudgens' flicks had started with *The Empire Strikes Quack,* but in an ironic twist, while hundreds of fan films were popping up on the Web in the late nineties, he was determined to keep *Quack* off the Internet, fearful that Lucasfilm wouldn't appreciate his cavalier use of its footage. As a result, *Quack* was usually only seen at sci-fi conventions.

Fewer people may have seen the short as a result, but they were definitely taken by it, making the dub one of the most influential fan productions of the era. In 1994, NYU film student Curt Markham made his own short, *Beer Wars,* as a result: "I read an article about *The Empire Strikes Quack,* and thought of doing something similar with the characters Bob and Doug McKenzie from *SCTV* and *Strange Brew.* I first showed it in my editing class;

most of my classmates were foreign students who weren't familiar with the material, so they didn't really understand it." Echoing Don Glut decades earlier, Markham adds, "The teacher didn't quite get it, either, and wanted to know what the film 'meant.' Angry, angst-ridden films were the fashion at that time, and making any other kind of film meant selling out."

Markham's flick appeared online in the 1998–99 fan film explosion, and then came the deluge: Dozens of dub shorts began appearing online, with approaches ranging from the collage style of *Quack* and *Beer Wars* to comedic redubbings of movie trailers—most popularly the teaser for *The Phantom Menace*—which, more often than not, were woefully unfunny.

Taking the concept to its zenith, with questionable results, was *Star Wars: A Newfangled Hope* by Bob West, a Los Angeles–based prop builder, who redubbed the entire length of *A New Hope* in the spring of 1998. "*What's Up, Tiger Lilly* was probably the main inspiration," he explains. "I wrote a complete script, but while we were recording, we quickly found some sections that just didn't work. The biggest example of this is the scene where R2D2 is captured by the Jawas. In the script, I had all the Jawas who were hiding behind the rocks talking, but we figured out that it would be funnier to keep the Jawas quiet, since you can't see them anyway, and just add the music from *Deliverance*."

Despite their popularity, it didn't take long for dubbed productions to be excommunicated from the fan film scene, and to this day, many online forums for fan filmmakers delete messages pertaining to the use of footage from feature films. Part of this is a legal consideration to ensure that the forums don't encourage piracy, but an unspoken disdain for dubs is at play as well.

Dubs had quickly become the no-effort entry into the fan film fad—why bother writing, costuming, shooting, and editing a movie when you could dump a movie clip of Yoda into a PC, affect his voice, and curse like Samuel L. Jackson with a stubbed toe? That lack of commitment was also often reflected in their writing, which usually betrayed any extensive effort being put forth. There were exceptions, but it was largely another example of what happens to any fad when the barrier of entry is lowered to the point where anyone can jump on the bandwagon, and thus came the third fan film cliché: the unfunny dub flick.

• • •

Decrying a fan film for a perceived lack of creativity or the way it was executed would seem to miss the point of amateur filmmaking—after all, these productions are products of the learning process, even if they mimic the original or other fan films, perhaps too closely.

"It's never mere copying," remarks Jenkins. "Even the worst fan story never simply copies the original—it's always adding something to it. You may not value what it adds to it, and they may be misguided in the choices they made of adding something, but it is always about expanding the universe in some direction that reflects the interest of a particular fan. It's additive, it's creative, it's generative in terms of what the contribution to the original material should be."

The drawback, then, was that while plenty of fan filmmakers added something to the Star Wars genre, their films tended to be the same thing over and over. Nonetheless, the fact that there were enough fan efforts online that clichés could be called out meant that the genre was growing into a vernacular culture, that fellow filmmakers were watching and learning from others' efforts, and that people were judging them with increasingly raised expectations.

Still, the oppressive sameness could be stifling. Anyone making a fan film at the time was making a Star Wars flick—as if no other franchises had ever been produced—and as a subset of those fan films came the one cliché to rule them all: the plotless duel in the woods, featuring the filmmaker's buddies flailing about, whacking each other with lightsabers née broomsticks.

Dozens of saber fights have been made throughout the years, and to team that up with another hoary cliché, they're almost all a dime a dozen. One of the few significant ones at the time was *Death of a Jedi*, created by Matthew Ward, then a student at Savannah College of Art and Design in Savannah, Georgia. Shot in January 1997 as an assignment for his Introduction to Film and Video class, Ward's wordless short was simply a brief duel between Darth Vader and an unknown Jedi (later named

Dei Jeigh, since he was played by a pal/aspiring turntablist whose stage name was DJ Jedi). "The shoot took only two hours to complete," explains Ward. "We were running all around each other, getting as many different camera angles as possible. We only had one camera, and time was very short. Worst of all, it was freezing and my actors were going numb. Once I was in the Avid suite, editing was easy; with all the different takes, I actually made the duel much longer than it was really intended to be."

The short got an A and that was that—until the summer of 1998, when Ward landed an internship at George Lucas's special effects company Industrial Light & Magic, which was neck-deep in producing *The Phantom Menace* at the time. There he wound up working for technical director Louis Katz in Rebel Unit, a group of 10 technical directors doing final effect shots, such as modeling, texturing, lighting, animation, and compositing with live action. "Matt loves to talk about 'Matt,'" kids Katz, "so he told me about his *Death of a Jedi* immediately." Intrigued and sensing an opportunity to teach, Katz had Ward load the short into a computer and start upgrading it with letterbox cropping and rotoscoped glowing lightsabers created with Adobe After Effects software. Posting the short online when he returned to school that fall, Ward played up the film's history—after all, few fan films pass through Lucas's own company—and garnered praise from fans and some attention from the press as a result.

After graduation, Ward was able to parlay his internship into a full-fledged job at ILM, and wound up working on a number of *Star Wars* prequels before leaving the company to work on various films, including both sequels to *The Matrix*, Spielberg's *War of the Worlds*, and Robert Zemeckis's *Beowulf*.

Despite being completely devoid of a plot, the popularity of Ward's flick among fan filmmakers served to highlight a growing issue in fan films, one that mirrored a longtime problem with Hollywood—namely, that there was an increasing emphasis was on effects instead of story. While it's natural that someone primarily interested in teaching himself special effects software would focus on that aspect of production, bombastic visuals without a coherent plot still add up to the old benchmark: sound and fury signifying nothing.

A few fans definitely had something to say, however, and started using homemade cinematic efforts as something other than paeans to their favorite franchises; instead, they ushered in the emergence of what might be called "the protest fan film."

• • •

If *Troops* put the modern fan film on the map, 1998's *TIE-Tanic* burned a hole through it. The funny, angry screed, took fan cinema to a new place: the realm of cultural critique.

Up to this point, fan films had been a declaration of love; even parodies like *Hardware Wars* had been made with deep and obvious affection. *TIE-Tanic,* a short that mashed together redubbed footage from *Titanic* and *Star Wars* with new material, poked fun at Lucas, but this time, it was no friendly gesture. If fan films were a baseball game, this flick was the bleachers—angry, drunk, and funny as hell. Using the amateur medium as a forum for voicing discontent, the movie was a protest, a political statement, a seductively fun love/hate argument with no resolution. Most of all, it was a howl of protest by fans angry about everything that they felt was wrong with the Star Wars films, from money-milking rereleases to irritating Ewoks.

At the time, *Titanic* was the new kid on the block, well on its way to becoming one of the most popular movies ever, but in *TIE-Tanic,* the movie was seen as nothing more than a threat to Star Wars' dominance of pop culture. The short starts with a redubbed conference room scene aboard the Death Star (you know, the one where Grand Moff Tarkin makes Darth Vader stop choking the guy).

Arguments break out among the military as Tarkin announces that "Lucasfilm has bumped up the release of the new [*Phantom Menace*] trailers," until Vader steps in: "Don't be too proud of this technological photoplay you've constructed. The ability to control the medium for 20 years is insignificant next to the power of a good chick flick." Taking no chances, the Empire (Lucasfilm) attacks the S.S. *Titanic*. New CGI spacecraft are worked into *Titanic* footage, such as a squad of TIE fighters and, cleverly, an AT-AT Walker from *The Empire Strikes Back*, lying in wait on the famed iceberg. Lasers fly as chunks of the ship are blown to smithereens, and Ewoks—the overweight teddy bears from *Return of the Jedi* detested by fans—run wailing across the screen, covered in flames. The short ends with a final, massive explosion that throws R2-D2 sky high, as if to suggest that on a boat filled with cute and cuddly elements of the two biggest movies ever, only the stubby robot was worth saving.

The little flick is largely played for laughs, but it has an angry nature. The tone is different right from the start, in that Lucasfilm—the entity behind all that is Star Wars—is portrayed as evil. Lucas's independent studio isn't the rebels going up against the establishment of Hollywood—as it is often portrayed in big media—but the Empire itself, focused on one thing: complete dominance, regardless of whether it is box office records or filmgoers' hearts and minds. Moreover, this Empire is willing to do anything to appeal to base interests, as noted by the pointed redubbing of certain lines to suggest that Lucasfilm is enslaved to demographic studies, while Vader rattles off Lucasfilm's home video marketing accomplishments at the drop of a hat. It was rare for fans to so publicly call out Lucasfilm's penchant for rereleasing the same movies repeatedly, rather than producing new flicks—and doing so using the company's own footage only served to rub salt in the intended wound.

In reality, of course, the short didn't even nick the Star Wars saga, much less wound it. *Titanic* went on to become the highest-grossing movie ever ($1,835,300,000 worldwide), and the Star Wars franchise hasn't done too poorly in the meantime. *TIE-Tanic,* while one of the best satires to emerge from the period, didn't make much of a blip on the cultural radar; today, it's hard to find, even on the Internet with the proverbial long tail where everything is always available. Nonetheless, the short paved the way for fans to use their films as soapboxes, creating an opportunity to explore what they thought was wrong with the franchises they clearly loved.

Taking that sentiment to the vitriolic extreme, there's Earl Newton's 2004 effort *Fall of a Saga;* pandering to the truculent fanboys left disenfranchised in the wake of *The Phantom Menace,* the short's existence provides vivid proof of Yeats's observation,

"We fed the heart on fantasy; the heart grew brutal on the fare." The fan film finds a corpulent, plaid-workshirted George Lucas sitting alone inside a hotel room in the midnineties, struggling to write the prequel that the whole world is demanding from him. Suddenly, there's a knock at the door, and his old producer shows up. Turns out that back in the day, Lucas begged him to help make the original trilogy; now the protégé forces Lucas to pay up the debt—by writing *The Phantom Menace* as badly as possible. Why? Well, the producer is Satan, of course, and Lucas sold his soul to make the original film.

At 20 minutes, the flick is 15 minutes too long, and though intended as a jibe, its plot implies some vicious insults—that Lucas's success isn't his own; that he has no soul (and therefore his films are soulless); that he'd be the kind of chump to actually make that deal; that the Star War movie series that some fans treat like religion is in fact the work of the devil; and that *The Phantom Menace*. a flick that, whether good or bad, Lucas clearly sweated over, was written as poorly as possible. That's a lot to lay at someone's feet simply because you didn't like a movie.

To average filmgoers with only a passing interest in Star Wars, films like *TIE-Tanic* and *Fall of a Saga* can be easily dismissed as boorish and inconsequential, interested in nothing more than taking a few cheap shots. For those within fandom, however, these shorts were couriers for heady political statements—cries, à la *Network*, of "I'm mad as hell and I'm not going to take it anymore!"

Of course, fans did take it, just as they always had. The *Star Wars* prequels continued with great monetary success, if only moderately better critical reception. As they were released, Fandom duly—sometimes begrudgingly—went to see them, but while the films were popular, the franchise's place as a critical pillar of science fiction and media fandom had taken a blow, a fact readily evident by the end of 1999.

Suddenly, the fan film fad was over. Coinciding with the turn of the millennium, with the fall of Star Wars, and with the cries of overfunded websites drying up and blowing away at the end of the "dot-bomb" era, regular people's desire to make their own paean to summer blockbusters was over. Thanks to *Troops* and *George Lucas in Love*, fan films had become closely identified with

The Phantom Menace, so as the prequel fell from grace so did the vernacular cultures associated with it.

As a result, even my own creation, the Mos Eisley Multiplex, slowly ground to a halt. When the fan film fad burned itself out, the number of new flicks fell off, too, providing little to add to the website; rather than keep it going, I simply gave the site away to a fellow hobbyist. While I felt like I was abandoning my baby, it was good to know the Multiplex would go on, and I looked forward to seeing how my little website would change in the years to come. Instead, the Multiplex got a cool-looking redesign that removed all the news, interviews, and services, leaving just a list of links to movies. After that, it was never updated, and as time crept by, it became a decrepit husk—an aged site filled with broken links and rusted Web design. One day, I decided to visit my old Multiplex, curious to see if anything had changed—and it had: my baby had vanished, taken offline for eternity.

Although the fad flamed out with the turn of the millennium, it was a good—and necessary—turn of events. The passage of time allowed editing software to mature, and for the blunt disillusionment caused by both *The Phantom Menace* and the dot-com collapse to fade into memory. Of course, fan films didn't vanish from the face of the earth—instead, with the dissolution of Star Wars' stranglehold on the media, fan filmmakers suddenly realized that there were other franchises ready to be explored.

There was a new challenge ahead for the genre: If the entire fan film fad could be wiped out by a single bad feature film, perhaps it was possible to save an entire series of bad feature films with one good fan film.

12
Comic Con-troversy

Sandy Collora was frustrated. A muscular guy with a tightly shaved head, he'd moved from New York to Los Angeles as a teenager in the 1980s to attend college, but dropped out to work full-time at Hollywood's creature-building Mecca, Stan Winston Studios. There he learned at the feet of masters, working on sci-fi and fantasy movies like *Total Recall* and *Men in Black*, as well as designing the logo for *Jurassic Park.* Eventually striking out on his own, he began to make a name for himself sculpting figures for toy companies, as well as creating fantasy maquettes—small, expensive, scale models of comic-book characters and such, sold in comic shops and by the Franklin Mint. By the time he turned 30, Collora was doing well, running his own company in Huntington Beach, California, and surfing every day. He was still frustrated, however, because like the rest of Los Angeles, what he really wanted was to direct.

He started with a creature-laden, live-action short, *Solomon Bernstein's Bathroom,* and followed up with a few sample TV ads and music videos, self-financed in hopes of landing paid gigs. While his visual work got better and his sample reel got longer, he was only getting the occasional assignment for things like Japanese soft drink ads, and by 2002, it was clear: to jump-start a film career, he'd have to make a splash, creating

Bodybuilder Clark Bartram donned a pitted cowl, based on Alex Ross's artwork, for Sandy Collora's *Batman: Dead End*. *(Courtesy of Montauk Films)*

something that would get his name out there.

While Collora had been sweating it out making his short movie and ads, the fan film fad had both come and gone. During that time, there had been a handful of cases where fan filmmakers landed movie jobs; overall, however, Hollywood had ignored the influx of fan productions, and perhaps understandably so. Almost all of the efforts during the fad years were *Star Wars*–related, showing no variety, and to professionals who had spent their lives making movies, even the best fan flicks were nothing but amateurish junk, from the acting to the direction to the equipment and the budgets.

Collora noticed, however, that fan films got incredible support from, well, fans, not to mention decent attention from the press. If franchise devotees could rally behind such homespun efforts, what would happen if someone made a professionally produced fan film—and what if that someone was Sandy Collora? As a lifelong comic book fan, it didn't take long for the idea to emerge: he'd make a Batman movie. "It seemed right; it *felt* right," says Collora.

"Batman is such a great character: dark, brooding, complex. He's tough, man. Calculated, cunning . . . just cool."

And "cool" was one thing Batman hadn't been in a while, having last graced the silver screen in 1997's box-office bomb *Batman & Robin*. The unsatisfying movie series had always owed more to hype and stunt casting than comic books, so by the time that fated production had come along—the fourth *Batman* feature film in just eight years—the public had wised up and moved on. The franchise had been milked dry, and Hollywood abandoned the carcass to rot while comic book fans were left to mull over what might have been had the studio decided to follow the darker, more dramatic vision of the Dark Knight that graced comic pages every month.

Collora was one of those fans. He began mapping out *Batman: Dead End*, a $30,000 short that would present the flawed hero as mad, bad, and dangerous to know. He needed to put the archvillain Joker in there, but given his own background, Collora decided to bring something else to the table—namely, characters he'd worked on in feature films. Certainly he'd spent enough time detailing the title character's costume during the production of *Predator II*, so he could do one of those. Soon, the big baddie from *Alien* was added to the genre goulash, too. There was some precedent for the idea—there had been both *Batman vs. Predator* and *Aliens vs. Predator* comic books, and the latter eventually became a series of poorly received feature films—but the cross-pollination of a trio of Billion-dollar franchises was something that Hollywood suits would never allow in real life. If Collora could shoot it to look like a clip from a big-budget action feature starring the Dark Knight mixing it up with the Joker and two of genre cinema's most potent bad guys, it would be nothing less than a fanboy fever dream. The cherry on top would be to debut the flick just like *Troops*—at the annual comic- and movie-fan destination, the San Diego Comic Con; now *that* would get attention.

"No, I didn't do it for the buzz," Collora recalls. "I did it to *do it*. I love Batman; I wanted to see him real—done like in the comics." Of course, to say you spent $30,000 just "to do it" is a bit disingenuous; plenty of people talk about what they'd do if they made a superhero movie, but few go ahead and shoot one, and fewer still allot themselves such a budget. Pressed on the point, Collora rebuts, "No guts, no glory. . . . I pitched stuff for over two years; there was some interest, but ultimately, nothing happened, [so you've] gotta make your own dreams happen. No one's gonna do it for you."

One thing *Batman: Dead End* wasn't, however, was a protest fan film, although it could certainly be misconstrued that way. Sure, he was presenting a fan's take on the character, and yes, it was considerably darker and more aggressive than the Batman feature films, but unlike *Fall of a Saga*, this was no vulgar gesture to Hollywood. "I did it more like, 'Hey guys, why don't you try this,' or 'Let *me* try this with your money,'" Collora comments, laughing.

Regardless of how it would be interpreted, the filmmaker had his work cut out for him. While keeping up a full schedule of the art and design work that paid the bills, Collora spent six months readying for a four-night shoot in April 2003. Mere weeks into the prep, however, things took a serious turn for the worse: "My mom was diagnosed with cancer in December 2002. Merry fucking Christmas."

Collora was shaken: "It was the hardest time of my life. I'd work 12 to 16 hours a day, then go hang with her in the hospital while she was getting chemo." While his mother Joann's cancer made a Batman movie seem insignificant, she insisted that he keep plugging away: "You can't let anything get in the way of your dreams; Mom wouldn't have that."

Despite the situation, Collora pressed on, casting the two speaking roles of the film, Batman and Joker. The brooding hero's shoes were filled by Clark Bartram, a bodybuilding model and occasional workout show host who billed himself as "America's Most Trusted Fitness Personality." Assuming the lion's share of the dialogue, however, was Josh Andrew Koenig as the Joker. The son of *Star Trek* (and eventual fan film) actor Walter "Chekhov" Koenig, he'd played various character roles on TV over the years, but remained best known for his work as "Boner" on the eighties sitcom *Growing Pains*.

With the stars cast, Collora began bringing in friends to build costumes, and asked his longtime mentor, sculptor Henry Alvarez, to create Batman's cowl, basing the design on comic artist Alex Ross's well-known depictions. Meanwhile, fight choreography began; the crux of the film would be a down-and-dirty street brawl between Batman and a Predator, so Bartram began rehearsing with stunt coordinators one day a week for two months prior to filming. Before long, the cast and crew headed to an alleyway in North Hollywood for an arduous shoot.

It may have been grueling for the cold, rain-soaked team—the movie takes place during a nighttime downpour—but they were prepared. Collora had storyboarded every shot of the 35mm film, and between the rain towers, lighting rigs and stunt equipment, the production wasn't the typical "Let's grab a video camera and shoot down the block" fan film.

Soon after, the footage was handed over to editor Toby Divine; working with Collora and an Apple Mac running Final Cut Pro, he quickly assembled the final eight-minute short, and created a promotional DVD that could be handed out to industry types who might express interest in the film. Rounding out the disc, Divine also cut together a behind-the-scenes documentary; twice as long as the film it covered, it was by turns fascinating—seeing how the slick flick came together—and wince-inducing, such as when Collora offers, "There's moments in the evolution of any art form that redefine the boundaries of what's possible in that particular medium, and I think this film is one of those moments."

Batman: Dead End didn't redefine cinema, but it did establish that Collora was a visual stylist; the film looked amazing. Unencumbered by the burden of plot, the story was simplistic--Batman fights the Joker, then the Alien, then the Predator, roll credits—but still took a dramatic risk in its envisionment of the Joker, knowingly cut from broad swaths of gay stereotypes. Koenig played the scoundrel mincingly, preening but pissed, and while never explicitly stated, the fact was easy enough to discern. If handled poorly, the portrayal could have come across as a clumsy demonization of homosexuality, but instead made for a challenging, different spin on a tired villain. After all, what would strike greater fear in the heart of an arch-conservative superhero like Batman? A gay interpretation only served to create a greater dichotomy between the two fun-house mirror opposites.

Josh Andrew Koenig's aggressive take on the Joker was miles away from his best-known role, "Boner" on the 1980s sitcom *Growing Pains*.
(Courtesy of Montauk Films)

While Collora had limited directorial experience to depend on when he made the film, he leaned on his natural ability to hustle once it was completed. Having done some creature work for Kevin Smith's *Dogma* years earlier, Collora got *Dead End* into the director/comic book writer's hands and soon got an endorsement in return: "Possibly the truest, best Batman movie ever made." Artist Alex Ross, whose artwork inspired many of Collora's visuals, also weighed in, remarking that it was "Batman the way I've always wanted to see him." As the San Diego Comic Con drew near, the director "leaked" stills from the film to the Ain't It Cool News website, getting the site to plug where and when people could see the flick at the convention. Ross, too, plugged the short during a panel at the Comic Con, and the end result was that the room was packed when the film screened at 3 PM on July 19.

To say it went over well would be an understatement. The audience went berserk; when the Alien and Predator made their unexpected appearances, that just piled on the fanboy hysteria even more. The short was the surprise hit of the convention, so much so that Collora was asked to screen it again that night as the kickoff to the Masquerade—the massive annual costume party. Screening your fan film for 5,000 hardcore comic fans isn't a bad way to build buzz, and the following Monday, Collora's agent fielded more than a few phone calls about the flick. The budding director wound up with a number of meetings around Hollywood, but perhaps surprisingly, none of them involved lawsuit-wielding lawyers from Warner Brothers, home to the Batman franchise.

To his credit, Collora had been careful to point out at every turn that he wasn't selling the movie or distributing it, but that said, the short had already somehow landed on the illegal P2P downloading service Kazaa before he'd even screened it in San Diego. Still, Collora remarked quite openly that he expected to eventually get a cease-and-desist letter about his fan film, and that wasn't just hyperbole—he had good reason to be concerned because DC Comics and its parent company, Warner Brothers, had a history of going after fan films.

• • •

Just a few years earlier, a fan had incurred the wrath of the DC Comics legal department when he put a hot-rodded, homemade Superman movie on the Internet. Just as Stuart Basinger revived his teenage Bond film, *Moonraker '78,* in the 1990s with the help of modern technology, Marc Kimball, a motion graphic designer for TV commercials, dug out a 15-minute Superman film that he'd started in 1980 but had never completed. The college project, featuring 20-year-old Kimball running around in a leftover Halloween costume, was radically revised into *Superman, The Super 8 Movie: Special Edition*—a title that underlined his intention to send up big Hollywood productions. While he and his friends only spent four days shooting around Boston in 1980, starting in January 1998 Kimball spent the next two-and-a-half years slathering the aging silent footage with 147 special effects shots created on an Apple G3 computer.

"It was my 'ship in a bottle' project," notes Kimball. "I made it for fun, but also to test my skills and learn; I hate doing tutorials—there's nothing like real problem solving on projects. I storyboarded the missing visual effects shots, added digital CGI graphics to existing shots, then treated them in After Effects to look like old Super 8 film. I also created 40 shots digitally to finish the movie, including adding digital legs to a medium shot of me and rotoscoping out scratches I'd made in the film to create bolts of electricity from Vendicon, the super–bad guy trying to kill Superman."

Kimball posted a trailer online in June 2000 when he was close to completing the flick, and fans took notice; when the full film went online that September, it instantly hit 3,500 downloads a day. Despite the fact that it was clearly a homemade labor of love and not a bootleg summer blockbuster, DC's legal department sent him a cease-and-desist letter within four days.

"I was surprised because of all the Star Wars fan films out there [that were made without issues]," he comments. "I just appeared in a handmade Superman suit, it was all original music and selections from stock music libraries, and I created all the logos and effects from scratch instead of taking them from other movies. I didn't have any advertising on the website, and I would never have sold it or made money on it; that would have been wrong, and I respect DC's ownership of Superman."

DC's "C&D" didn't put it that way; the cease-and-desist letter pointed out that he'd used the character without permission in an unauthorized production, and demanded that the film and website be taken offline at once. Kimball eventually went on to make *Star Wars* spoofs and an original sci-fi short, but faced at the time with DC's demands, he didn't see any options for the Superman fan film. "I immediately shut it down," he told a reporter at the time. "I'm one guy against a wall of cash. If they wanted, I'm sure they could have done a lot of damage to me."

• • •

A mere 36 months later, times and attitudes toward fan productions were starting to change. Sandy Collora never received a cease-and-desist letter from DC or Warner Brothers; instead, he got a plethora of press, meetings with movie execs about a remake of *The Creature from the Black Lagoon,* and a William Goldman–scripted *Shazam* flick (both which were never made) and plenty of fan and hate mail in fan forums across the Internet. The buzz around the film was huge; it was the summer hit that no one could find and everyone wanted to see. If success is measured in dollar amounts, sure, the short itself never made a profit (by necessity), but in late 2004, Hollywood auction house Profiles in History gave some indication of the film's impact when it sold one of the screen-worn Predator costumes for $8,000.

With all the buzz generated, the months that followed the 2003 Comic Con were unquestionably Collora's time to shine—but the moment was bittersweet at best: A week to the day after *Batman: Dead End* debuted, his mother, Joann, lost her battle with cancer.

"She hung on to see it finished . . . she saw the film and knew I could do it," Collora remembers. "Life, man; nothing hits harder than life. It's not about how hard you can hit, but how hard you can get hit and keep moving forward."

That learned tenacity turned out to be necessary, however, because while the filmmaker had finally made his big splash, it didn't result in a directing gig. While he cavalierly told interviewers at its debut that *Dead End* would be his only fan film, after a few months it emerged that he'd changed his mind and was putting together a sequel of sorts: *World's Finest*. By now, Collora had made the point that he could create a superhero short, so the impetus was different this time.

"*World's Finest* was really for fun," he recalls. After the reaction to *Dead End,* "Everyone was fired up to do it again. When I didn't get a deal after a few months, we were like, 'Let's do another one!' OK, write another check." Collora didn't have enough money to do a complete short, so instead he poured $12,000 into a four-minute faux trailer for a superhero feature. Bartram was Batman once again, joined this time by Michael O'Hearn, a four-time Mr. Universe, as the Man of Steel himself, Superman. The short, then, stitched together colorful moments among the heroes, their alter egos and Superman's coterie, including Jimmy Olsen, Perry

Michael O'Hearn, a four-time Mr. Universe, played Superman in *World's Finest*, a fan film follow-up directed by Sandy Collora (right).
(Courtesy of Montauk Films)

White and, of course, archnemesis Lex Luthor.

While some dialogue hinted at the merest threads of a plot (and intriguingly so—an unwitting corporate merger between Luthor's LexCorp and Batman's Wayne Enterprises? A love triangle among Clark Kent, Lois Lane, and Bruce Wayne? Bring it on!), it wasn't clear whether Collora had a complete story in mind or was merely creating a collection of cool moments. "It was a little bit of both," he admits. "Those [clips] were more experiments than anything else, to see if the traditional comic vision of those characters could work on film." While the short left armchair critics still undecided as to whether Collora could direct straight dramatic scenes, *World's Finest* showed he didn't have to lean on bleak, atmospheric lighting and nonstop brawling to make an entertaining short.

In fact, though shorter and having less of a through-line, plotwise, the pseudotrailer was far more fun than its predecessor. The short played to everyone's strengths—the bodybuilders looked manly, the supporting cast carried most of the dialogue, and film editor Toby Divine, who'd cut *Dead End*, got to show off tricks he used at his day job as a trailer editor.

When the short started coming together, Collora began spreading the word that he was working on a new production set in the DC Comics universe—and this time, fanboy culture took notice.

• • •

Since Comic Con the previous summer, *Batman: Dead End* had spread around the world, propelled by word-of-mouth, bootlegs, the Internet, and Collora's marketing smarts. While he'd made a name for himself in certain circles, the director had virtually single-handedly resurrected fan films after the fad years had left the form a desiccated wreck. Ironically, while *Troops* had propelled fans to make countless Star Wars flicks, now amateur auteurs were making Batman movies left and right, inspired by *Dead End*.

As a whole, fan films were (and largely remain) stigmatized by the cliché that they were produced only by teenage comic book/sci-fi nerds. Even as he proudly labeled himself a fan filmmaker, Collora, too, bought into the stereotype, as he stated in an interview on iFilm.com, "I get fed up with this attitude of, like, 'Oh, you have to be some 17-year-old kid with a video camera to make a fan film,' and I think that's just crap. You can be a 34-year-old fan and working industry professional, and still make a fan film. I don't think there should be any boundaries there."

He wasn't alone in that opinion, however, because when the 2004 San Diego Comic Con rolled around, *World's Finest* was listed in the fan-film programming, but this time it was joined by other movies, too, that clearly aimed to catapult their creators into the professional ranks of filmmaking—and just happened to be Batman related. Among the flicks on the bill were *Batman: Madness* by Aaron Schoenke and *Grayson* by John Fiorella. Schoenke, a college intern at Sony Studios, had made a string of Batman shorts since the start of the 2000s, and his 40-minute *Batman Beyond: Year One* had actually screened alongside Collora's *Dead End* at the 2003 Comic Con. A year later, Schoenke was looking forward to returning with a new movie, building on his own momentum while taking advantage of the heightened fan film awareness that *Dead End* had created.

Similarly, *Grayson* was bound to benefit from the rising popularity of fan productions, although it took a different route as a five-minute fake trailer for a film focusing on Batman's sidekick, Robin and his alter ego, Dick Grayson. Shot on weekends over the course of 10 months, the $18,000, 16mm short was an instant hit among comic fans when it finally landed on the Internet, thanks to a slick look, smart editing, and the wisps of a plot that found a bearded, adult Grayson investigating the murder of Batman, convinced that Superman had done the deed. Topping it off were appearances by the Green Lantern, Wonder Woman, the Joker, Bat Girl, Commissioner Gordon, Catwoman, the Penguin, and the Riddler. Unlike most pseudo preview fan films, though, *Grayson* was based on a 120-page screenplay Fiorella had written in 2002. While he'd begun working on his short before *Batman: Dead End* debuted in 2003, the filmmaker was likely influenced by Collora's game plan, as *Grayson*, too, appeared as a promo DVD, complete with a half-hour "making of" documentary. The effort eventually paid off, however, as the film was downloaded over nine million times; received praise from comics biggies Neal Adams, Jim Lee, and Alex Ross; and even got an A- from *Entertainment Weekly*.

Also on the Comic Con fan film bill that year was none other than Dan Poole, returning to the fan film fold 12 years after he'd made *The Green Goblin's Last Stand*. In those dozen years, his Spider-Man epic had taken on legendary status among cult movie fans, so his decision to shoot *Last Call*, featuring the Marvel Comics character Wolverine, was not made lightly. It was, however, made due to the buzz surrounding *Batman: Dead End*.

"When Sandy Collora hit the scene, everyone was talking him up," says Poole, "and I remember thinking, 'Yeah, it's very cool—obviously it looks phenomenal—but it is, after all, a short and it's not a real narrative. But everyone was suddenly 'fan films, fan films,' and then *Grayson* came along, and again, it looks great, but it's just a trailer. Even though it looks cool and the eye candy's fun, where are the characters? What's going on? None of these are actual stories. So I remember thinking, 'You know what—what could I do these days? What could I do with the tools I have now?' It got me all fired up to do something." The result was violent, vintage Poole: Wolverine walks into a bar, a fight breaks out, Poole cheats death as he does a somersault off a second-floor balcony.

With all these high-powered productions lined up on the same bill, the fan film slate of the 2004 San Diego Comic Con was set to be unprecedented. Between Collora and Poole, there were the genre's all-stars, and Schoenke and Fiorella were among its strongest up-and-comers. The convention was primed to become a turning point, a quintessential moment that would raise the form to new heights in front of not merely an influential audience of über-fans, but also the countless media outlets covering Comic Con. Ready to sandblast the nerd-with-a-camera cliché off fan movies for good, the weekend would, in hindsight, be seen as nothing less than the Woodstock of fan films.

And then it was cancelled.

• • •

In late June, less than a month before the convention, the various filmmakers were informed that the San Diego Comic Con was scrapping its fan film program; organizers had been contacted by the legal department of Warner Brothers, the parent company of DC Comics and home studio to the various Batman and Superman feature films. As David Glanzer, director of marketing and public relations for the Comic Con, explained to Comics2film.com, "Comic-Con International received a letter in early June from Warner Brothers requesting that we honor their intellectual copyrights by not screening films which may infringe upon those copyrights. Needless to say, we have complied."

While the announcement came almost at the last minute, Warner Brothers' move is said to have been in the works for some time, as excitement over *Dead End* had continued to rise in the wake of the 2003 convention. As the 2004 event approached, Warner Brothers reportedly took on Schoenke as a consultant on the matter, getting his input as a fan filmmaker.

"I've been in contact with Warner Brothers' legal team ever since [I began making Batman fan films], just to make sure everything was legal," notes Schoenke. "I don't want to piss them off; I know a lot of fan filmers go out there and say, 'We're gonna show Warner what it's really like.' I'm like, 'You really shouldn't yell at your hopeful future boss like that.' The previous year, when my film and Sandy's film were there, it caused a pretty big uproar;

Warner Brothers reportedly consulted with Aaron Schoenke in 2004 on how best to handle the wave of fan films featuring its characters. *(Courtesy of Bat in the Sun Productions)*

Warner Brothers didn't realize these films were as popular as they were, and they called me, asking, 'What should we do about it? What's the best thing to do?'"

According to Schoenke, the concern was not that the shorts were becoming well known. Rather, since Comic-Con International charged admission to the convention, the organization was effectively profiting from the fan films, even though they were presented "free" to all attendees. "Warner Brothers doesn't want any money made off the films—they don't mind fan films at all and that's why they haven't shut any one of them down," he explains. "You can find hundreds of films online and Warner Brothers doesn't really care; Warner Brothers actually really likes them, and they're not looking to stop fan films. Back then, they got a bad rap for some reason—'Oh, they hate fan films, they want to shut them down.' Well, technically, if you're making money, you are doing something illegal, so you can't fault 'em for that."

For the rest of the filmmakers whose shorts were scuttled at the San Diego Comic Con, however, it came as a bitter blow. Speaking years later, Poole is still frustrated by the turn of events: "They decided to bow to studio pressure to stop showing fan films [and] pulled the plug. I think that helped sour my idea of fan films in general, because Comic Con wasn't behind it, which is kinda sad. It's a comic book convention—it's for comic fans—but it's been co-opted by pop culture and the studios so much that they're going to do whatever's popular or politically right."

Faced with having spent money not only on the film but its promotion—not to mention travel expenses for attending a convention on the other side of the country—Poole did what little he could to get *Last Call* some attention. "We had a screening at a local bar, but afterwards, I came back to reality," he says. "I realized, 'You know what? There's no point in this anymore. No one's ever gonna get a contract or a job from a studio based on a fan film. You can't market them, can't sell them, can't do anything with them and they're never going to go anywhere. The studios will never sanction or acknowledge them. Why am I spending my money? Why am I wasting my time?' So after *Wolverine* in 2004, I just moved on." For Poole, that meant shooting his own original indie feature, *The Photon Effect*, three years later.

• • •

Three weeks after the convention, Schoenke passed a loosely worded statement, reportedly from Warner Brothers, to Superherohype.Com, stating that the studio had decided to give noncommercial fan films a pass. Why would a multi-billion-dollar company issue a press release via a fan as opposed to one of its media relations departments? "That actually came from them," swears Schoenke. "There wasn't an official released statement, because then it's Warner Brothers coming out and saying 'We support you guys' and . . . they legally can't do that. So their statement was; by having no statement, that was their statement.'"

Perhaps so, but a quiet "nonstatement" of support is the same thing as a statement of no support, and both Warner and DC Comics subsequently avoided going on the record concerning fan films in the years that followed.

Asked directly at New York Comic Con in 2008, however, Paul Levitz, president of DC Comics, broke his company's silence on the topic, stating definitively, "We're against anything that monetizes our assets and our copyrights without our permission. We are not against things where people use our assets if they don't do anything monetarily with them."

The confirmation was revolutionary. In the space of a scant few years, DC had gone from sending lawyers after amateur filmmakers to giving permission to openly use characters worth billions of dollars without fear of legal reprisals—a truly staggering corporate mind shift. Ironically, because of the monetization issue, Warner Brothers and DC Comics were now permitting the movies to be placed on the Internet where they could be seen by millions of people, yet weren't allowing them to be screened for infinitely smaller—but likely more appreciative—audiences at conventions. In the end, however, while they were deprived the opportunity to hear a live audience applaud their work, most fan filmmakers came out ahead.

• • •

Sandy Collora, however, did not come out ahead. As might be expected, he took the scrapping of the fan film program as a far more personal affront. As he tells it, "Warner Brothers contacted the Comic Con director of programming and said, 'No Sandy Collora films.' They thought it would be unfair to not show mine and show others, so they just banned them all. That was a sad day; *World's Finest* at the Con the following year after *Dead End* would have been nuts."

The year before, Collora had arrived at the convention with dozens of *Dead End* promotional DVDs to hand out; when he hit the show floor a year later, however, he claims it was a much different story:

> They were pretty vigilant about *World's Finest* not seeing the light of day at the Con that year. Warner Brothers was getting very nervous; they'd seen the reaction to *Dead End*, knew *World's Finest* would go through the roof and they

> were doing a lot of press there for *Catwoman* [a disastrous comic book flick starring Halle Berry]. You tell me, which film was better—my three-minute trailer or that crapfest?
>
> We were forbidden to hand out copies at the con; I had a WB guy following me around the whole three days I was there. He actually came up to me at one point and said that he was stunned at how many people recognized me and asked for autographs, DVDs or pictures.

Warner Brothers revived the Dark Knight on the big screen the following year, with 2005's critically and commercially successful *Batman Begins*, a film that Collora enjoyed, but for which he also claimed some credit: "I did all their homework and took the risk for them. I proved a dark Batman could work. They never even dreamed of doing anything like *Batman Begins* until after the overwhelming success of *Dead End*."

If the fan film had an effect at Warner Brothers, it was more likely as proof that *Batman Begins* director Christopher Nolan was on the right track with his dramatic vision of the character. Nolan had signed on to revive the franchise in January, 2003, a full six months before Collora's short debuted, and intended to go with a darker slant from the start, telling *Variety* at the time, "He is the most credible and realistic of the superheroes, and has the most complex human psychology. His superhero qualities come from within. He's not a magical character."

Despite having the debut of *World's Finest* derailed, things still looked to be on the upswing for Collora; that summer found director Guillermo del Toro (*Pan's Labyrinth, Hellboy*) linking up to produce the fledgling director's first flick, but that was not to be, nor were a few other concepts Collora pitched around Hollywood in the years that followed. While it seemed that his good luck was turning, however, those career frustrations paled next to what happened in July 2006.

"I was rear-ended by a drunk driver going over 100 miles per hour," explains Collora. "My car flipped four times and I ended up in the hospital for a while with four broken ribs, a collapsed lung, internal bleeding, a major concussion, and 217 stitches and staples; I almost bought it. The doctor said it was a 50/50 chance that I'd ever walk again; it took almost six months to recover, with lots of physical therapy. It's been a tough few years."

Collora was determined to land on his feet. The man who once declared that his fan film had redefined the medium had been humbled by how life had played out. A full four years after *Dead End* had debuted, he admitted to the Silver Bullet Comics website, "There were a few projects that kinda got close, I guess, but to be blatantly honest, for some reason, it just didn't happen for me. I tried harder than anyone I know, but no one would actually pull the trigger and give me a job—so now I'm doing it myself."

And indeed, as this book goes to press, he is busy in post-production on *Hunter Prey*, a low-budget, sci-fi/horror feature plotting intergalactic military against creepy monsters. Not leaving anything to chance, Collora has cowritten the script and handled all the art design, and had jumped back into the director's chair, aiming to finally prove that his fan films were only a taste of things to come.

13
Witty in Pink

Perhaps the biggest irony of the 2004 ban on fan productions at the San Diego Comic Con was that fan films *were* screened at the convention. In fact, they played to a packed house with a foot-stomping, cheering audience, and after the films were shown, the filmmakers who were responsible weren't hectored, but honored, by Hollywood. Underlining just how differently media companies could react to fan-produced content, Lucasfilm used the convention to host its third annual Official Star Wars Fan Film Awards.

Created in 2002, the awards (later renamed the Star Wars Fan Movie Challenge in 2007) were conceived as a collaboration between George Lucas's film empire and AtomFilms.com, a website for Internet movie shorts. The annual contest would highlight the best efforts, providing a way for the website to draw new visitors in the form of curious fans (a full 40 percent of the site's traffic was generated by the contest during the first year), while the *Star Wars* franchise gained considerable publicity within fandom as well as mainstream media. Not only did the various submitted films play on AtomFilms.com, but the 2002 winners were screened on the SciFi Channel in a Kevin Smith–hosted special (in later years, top flicks were shown on a different cable network, Spike). Meanwhile, winners took home both a golden trophy of R2D2 and C3PO and a cash prize of up to $2,000, depending on the category in which they won, the most coveted being the creatively titled George Lucas Selects award, chosen by . . . oh, you get the idea. Marking the first official acknowledgment that fans were creating their own films, the contest was an interesting idea—a mixture of "if you can't beat 'em, join 'em" mentality, a very public showing of largess and, to some extent, a measure of damage control.

By 2002, despite the fallout of the fan film fad, a steady stream of Star Wars fan films had been coming along for five years and the writing was on the wall; they simply weren't going away. Clearly, fans were undaunted by the threat of legal repercussions and simply didn't care whether they had permission to make the shorts. As a result, the creation of the contest could also be interpreted as a smart marketing move that tried to mold the vernacular culture of *Star Wars* fan films: By making Lucasfilm's permission valuable, the company began guiding fan filmers in directions that would best benefit the franchise.

The contest's rules stated that only parodies and documentaries were allowed to enter. While Lucasfilm was ostensibly lending its consent to production in those genres, both forms are protected by the First Amendment, and could therefore be produced regardless of the corporation's approval. Both are traditional forms of "transformative" works that provide new ways of looking at existing works that belong to someone else. In the academic essay "Copyright Law, Fan Practices and the Rights of the Author," Rebecca Tushnet notes that courts have been increasingly protective of "'transformative' unauthorized uses against copyright owners' allegations of infringement," later adding that "the legal concept of transformative use denies the author the authority to control all interpretations of his text. . . ."

Noticeably missing from the contest's mix, however, were dramatic fan films. While they were eventually permitted in 2007, five years after the awards had been established, the initial omission caused no end of consternation for many amateur filmmakers who had toiled on flicks in previous years only to find they now couldn't be submitted as entries. The decision made sense, though; it was well within Lucasfilm's rights to want to expand upon the Star Wars universe as it saw fit, so allowing fans to try their hands at adding to the saga's overall canon would be a mistake. For instance, one well-known fan effort, 1999's *The Dark Redemption*, details how the infamous plans for the Death Star wound up in Princess Leia's hands. While there are actually several versions of that same concept within the official Star Wars canon—mostly due to multiple video game plots where the player attempts to steal the plans—it's ultimately up to Lucasfilm to decide which story is "the one."

Unusually, *The Dark Redemption* became the only known fan film to receive a cease-and-desist letter from Lucasfilm. The 20-minute movie was made between November 1997 and June 1999 for a fan film contest (judged by Lucasfilm, no less) held at Force 3, a sci-fi convention held in Melbourne, Australia. The showy flick sported eye-popping effects, a $6,000AU budget and a large cast that included Australian TV personalities, plus actor Peter Sumner reprising his minor role as a Death Star lieutenant in *Episode IV: A New Hope*. "We didn't start approaching people to work on the film until we had a watertight script that fitted neatly into the Star Wars universe," notes executive producer Warren Duxbury. "We put five months of research into the script to keep it true to the whole universe, so I think the script was the turning point for the majority of people's interest."

That included the media—the short was heavily publicized in TV news stories and local papers, but ultimately was beaten by another flick whose director, Justin Dix, happened to be the contest's coordinator. His *Bounty Trail* won 10 of the 14 fan film awards that evening; coincidentally, the award statues were all made by Dix, too, who went on to land a job building droids for the real *Star Wars* productions of *Attack of the Clones* and *Revenge of the Sith*, when they filmed in Australia.

The creators behind *The Dark Redemption*, on the other hand, received a cease-and-desist order, informing them that they'd better take down the film's website or else. "I am pretty sure that [Lucasfilm] tolerated what we were doing only for the course of the Melbourne competition," Duxbury grumbled to fan website Echo Station. "They contacted us after the production was completed and the competition was over. The whole team have fully supported the decision to shut down the site; however, the film is 'out there' now, just like other fan films and fan fiction."

At least one Force 3 attendee liked it, however: Hugo Award–winning novelist Timothy Zahn, who was a guest of honor for the event. Within the "expanded universe" depicted in the various Star Wars novels and comics, no non–movie character is more beloved by fans than Zahn's creation, assassin and Mrs. Luke Skywalker, Mara Jade—and *The Dark Redemption* marked her first appearance off the printed page.

"It was weird to see one of my characters on-screen," Zahn admits. "It was a *good* weird, though. It was a very professionally produced film, and I thought they got Mara pretty well. I think there's been at least one other Mara in a fan film, but I generally don't have time at conventions to sit in the screening rooms, so I'm not even sure if I've seen a complete other film with Mara in it."

While *The Dark Redemption* made a splash, dramatic fan films were nonetheless excluded when the Official Star Wars Fan Film Awards debuted a few years later. As Jim Ward, vice president of marketing for Lucasfilm, told the *New York Times* in 2002, "We love our fans. We want them to have fun. But if in fact somebody is using our characters to create a story unto itself, that's not in the spirit of what we think fandom is about. Fandom is about celebrating the story the way it is."

This time, it appears Lucasfilm tried to get more bees with honey. Rather than threatening fans with draconian "thou shalt not"–type rules, the contest prizes were just the right incentive to keep things on the straight and narrow. By providing a high-profile forum for the fan filmers—and the possibility that their work might be seen by Lucas himself—they were greatly encouraged to follow the rules, thus ensuring that their films would be eligible for consideration. Why knock yourself out and spend lots of money to make a film that couldn't be in the running? The lure proved too irresistible for most Star Wars fan filmers, so while the contest didn't have a chilling effect per se, some interpreted it as a cleverly suppressive move.

Possibly aware of that position, Steven Sansweet, Lucasfilm's director of fan relations, told Wired.com in 2004, "There is plenty of room for fans to express their own feelings and opinions. We believe our core fans are responsible for the continuing popularity

Henry Jenkins, Director of the MIT Comparative Media Studies Program.
(Courtesy of MIT)

of the series, and we want to encourage them. Our intellectual properties are there for you to play with, but we expect you won't try and make a profit or use our characters in a salacious way. Having that wide-open frontier serves as a self-policing mechanism for the fans, who are really appreciative of being included."

Not everyone was included, however. MIT's Henry Jenkins notes strenuously in his book *Convergence Culture* and in various essays that the contest's policy of only allowing parody and documentary works excluded the two main categories that would be favored by female fan creators—vidding (homemade music videos made with movie footage) and dramatic stories. Discussing the issue, he remarks,

> the fact that Lucas has allowed certain modes of fan cinema to gain public visibility and rejected others, has strong gender dimensions. . . . Even the fact that it's a contest speaks to the male side of the equation, because women have had

> shared [vidding] showings; they've tended not to do contests. The notion of fandom as a competition as opposed to a collaboration would break along gender lines.
>
> So when Lucas says you can do documentaries or parodies rather than fan fiction or reappropriated images, that's a schism that reflects those taste preferences. . . . The overall amount of parody is produced by men, and in part, this has to do with a particular emotional dynamic: Parody is a way of acknowledging and distancing one's self from the content, whereas fan fiction is a way of bringing about an emotional closeness to the content, of getting inside the heads of the characters and exploring their emotional lives. If you prohibit fan fiction, but you allow parody, the overwhelming number of people participating in the competition will be men.

While Jenkins acknowledges that Lucasfilm's policy change in 2007 to include dramatic fan films is "a step in the right direction," he points out that "it's vidding that's really the female form of response and the one that's going to be hardest for Lucas to embrace, because it involves the direct repurposing of their content." In fairness, it also involves entities outside of Lucasfilm—various tentacles of the music business—that would have to give permission (and receive royalties) for their songs to be used in a corporate-sponsored vidding competition or showing. In that light, such an event might well be fiscally impossible, and that doesn't even address the feasibility of obtaining permission for vidding's sometimes controversial pairings of music and content.

While not everyone was pleased with the contest, overall, it was still a political success, and that wasn't lost on other companies, including Warner Brothers, which was reportedly trying to figure out what to do with its own fan film issues. While the 2004 San Diego Comic Con found the Star Wars franchise honoring its top fan movies, Warner executives are said to have been elsewhere onsite, trying to figure out how to set up a similar plan, according to Aaron Schoenke:

> At Comic Con that year, we met in this really weird, small,

> little DC booth, and a lot of the heads of those departments in DC and Warner Brothers showed up. We tried to work on something, and realized there weren't enough hits on the fan film side, because obviously there's way more *Star Wars* fan films out there than there are Batman ones. There's been a handful of Star Wars ones that are really nice and you can appreciate the artisticness of the film, but there's been only, what, four Batman fan films that are really worth a damn? There just weren't enough active fan filmers; I guess if there'd been more talent out there, we would've had something.

Star Wars clearly did have something—not only did Lucasfilm get a huge response to its contest, but the company began its own internal contest for employees as well, completely unrelated to the AtomFilms coventure. The Backyard Film Contest, affectionately known as the BFC to insiders, is a yearly contest for Lucasfilm employees to help them get in touch with their inner amateur filmmaker. Created by ILM managers Tom Martinek and Colin Campbell, the contest was conceived as a way for staffers in the ILM digital effects facility to get back to their roots, making slapdash, retro genre flicks.

The homemade shorts are created each year under strict guidelines: The movie must be under ten minutes, cost less than $100, and only use effects that could've reasonably been done with a Super 8 camera back in the day (i.e., they can shoot on video and use computers during editing to simulate whatever effects could have been achieved with Super 8 film). While entrants are required to make genre flicks, it's no surprise that fan films turn up from time to time, such as *Tar Tar Binks: His Last Episode*, a 2006 entry by Anthony Shafer, a lead technical director at ILM who, depending on the project, also serves as a CG sequence supervisor. The five-minute flick sports plenty of jokes and scenes that will warm a Jar Jar hater's heart—let's just say the Golden Gate Bridge figures prominently.

"It was very well received and didn't cost more than $50—mostly for props and gas," explains Shafer. "*Tar Tar* was filmed almost entirely in San Francisco, in and around the Presidio

Lucas Digital Arts Center Campus." Cowriter Jason Long recalls, "It was an adventure to shoot it. We got lots of looks carrying this doll through the city, but there's no room for embarrassment when you have to ask people to interact with the doll to get your shot. All the actors are real people, doing their real jobs, so it's a 'reality movie' of sorts. Only a cab driver refused to participate; everyone else seemed to enjoy the opportunity to act with an action figure in front of two guys with a handicam."

That kind of enjoyment isn't limited to San Francisco, judging from the immediate success of the Official Star Wars Fan Film Awards in 2002. The awards were handed out at a big screening/award ceremony that was part of Celebration II, an occasional Lucasfilm-sponsored convention, held that year in Indianapolis, Indiana, to promote the release of *Star Wars Episode II: Attack of the Clones*. A whopping 244 films were submitted for consideration. Among the inaugural class of winning films was *Troops*, which was honored with a special "Pioneer Award"—the same tribute that was given the following year to an absent, conflicted Ernie Fosselius for *Hardware Wars* when the awards moved to the San Diego Comic Con. Perhaps unsurprisingly, *George Lucas In Love* earned Joe Nussbaum the Awards' third Pioneer trophy a year later in 2004.

They weren't the only longtime fan filmmakers to be heralded during the nascent beginnings of the awards, however; for two years running, a prize went to Trey Stokes, who hadn't made a fan movie since he directed *Moonraker '78*. Right around the time that his pal, Stuart Basinger, was putting the final touches on their James Bond extravaganza 25 years after they'd begun production, Stokes was taking the Official Star Wars Fan Film Awards by storm. In 2003, he landed the George Lucas Selects award for his short, *Pink Five*, and then followed it up a year later with the rarest of beasts—a sequel arguably better than its predecessor. *Pink Five Strikes Back* was rewarded with an Audience Choice Award in 2004, and while it marked the end of his awards streak, it was only the beginning of his and Pink Five's adventures. Soon, the character would achieve a truly unique place in sci-fi history, going where no other fan film creations had set foot before.

• • •

After heading to the West Coast in 1978 to learn filmmaking at USC, Stokes had embarked on a multifaceted movie career, working in visual effects (*The Polar Express, Starship Troopers*), puppetry (*Batman Returns, Team America: World Police*), and special effects (*The Abyss, Species*). However, what he really wanted to do—here it comes again—was direct.

It was that desire that led him to an Internet video series called *Alien Dog* in early 2001. Having nothing to do with extraterrestrials or canines, the doomed series was ahead of its time, produced in the wake of the dot-com blowout at a point when downloading video to your PC was still a hassle. The daily show was typically a three-to-five-minute improvised vignette that would star one—or on a good day, two—actors. Since the cast and crew were all volunteers, the series churned through people on both sides of the camera pretty quickly. As a result, when Stokes answered an ad, aiming to build up his directing résumé, he was welcomed with open arms. His "audition" was to edit an episode featuring actress Amy Earhart, a distant descendant of famed aviatrix Amelia Earhart. The resulting short went over well, and soon the director and actress were a team, with Earhart charming the camera while Stokes worked behind it, taking on direction, cameraman, and editor duties. During their year on the project, the pair built a rapport that often found them going from brainstorming session to a completed, edited episode in as little as two hours. Ironically, while Stokes landed the job in part because he owned a computer with video editing software, he had to shoot all his episodes using borrowed video gear. It wasn't until early 2002, months after *Alien Dog* had died of natural causes (no money and even less public interest) that he finally bought his first video camera.

"I'd just gotten it and wanted to use it on something," Stokes recalls. "Meanwhile, a friend of mine had a fighter pilot costume and a blue screen he'd been using for a demo project, so I tried to come up with something Amy and I could do with them. I had a few ideas, but I kept coming back to that one."

"That one" is *Pink Five*, a five-minute hoot that follows a Valley Girl behind the controls of an X-Wing attacking the Death Star.

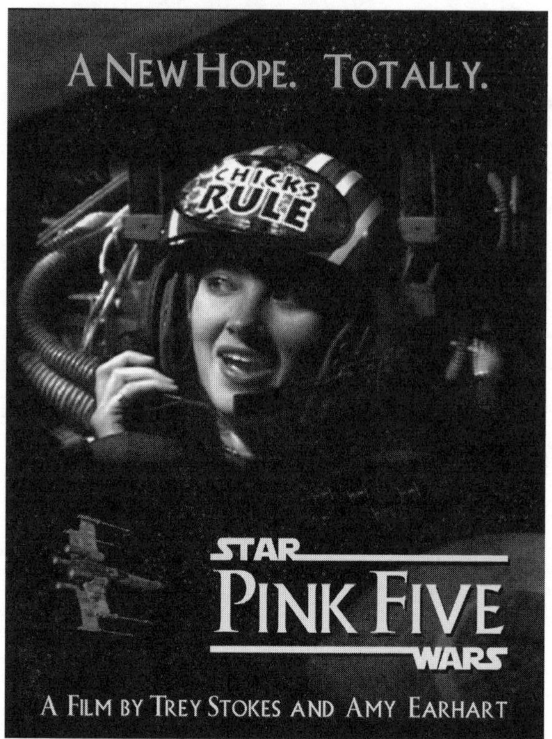

A NEW HOPE. TOTALLY.
CHICKS RULE
STAR
PINK FIVE
WARS
A FILM BY TREY STOKES AND AMY EARHART

Amy Earhart, "Stacey" in *Pink Five*, had no idea what her character was talking about when she shot the film. Ironically, neither did Stacey.
(Courtesy of the Truly Dangerous Company)

Merrily chirping, "They said today, everybody gets to fly," Stacey/ Pink Five is unprepared—and unconcerned, cluelessly chitchatting with her R2 droid ("Dude, the fat guy totally just blew up . . . no big loss; he was always hitting on me anyway"). Soon, she's flirting with Han Solo over the radio until she unknowingly sets the real film's climactic events in motion.

"When we made *Pink Five,* I wasn't aware of the phrase 'fan film,'" says Stokes, "so to me, it was another short I was making with Amy; this one just happened to have Star Wars in it." The flick played to the duo's strengths, in large part because they'd had a year's practice at making single-actor shorts. Earhart knew how to carry a scene by herself without it feeling like a monologue, while Stokes was adept at keeping things moving visually, helping gloss over the fact that only one actor was on screen. While the result became one of the most popular fan films around, however, *Pink Five* was never meant to seen by anyone.

"Trey lied to me, OK?" laughed Earhart in a documentary a few years later.

> He said *Pink Five* was never supposed to see the light of day; it was a test. He called me: "Amy, I got this screen, right? And I got this helmet. Do you have a couple of hours?" I said, "Sure, Trey." So I literally rolled out of bed, I didn't have a stitch of makeup on my face, I was super tired, and Trey picked me up and handed me this little four-page script, like "I just wrote this." I read it, and I didn't know how to pronounce words in the script, like "Tatooine," I didn't know who the smuggler guy was, I didn't know what the basketball reference was. So he was explaining it to me in the car on the way to the studio, and we shot it in two hours—and a monster was born!

Peppering the script with ad-libbed slang ("'That smuggler guy is totally crushing on me' is all Amy," says Stokes), Earhart ran through the story a few times, alternately giving the character a Texan torpor, an urban attitude, and a Valley vapidity. Oddly, by not understanding all the jokes, Earhart delivered a better performance since her character wasn't quite up to speed with her surroundings either.

Happy with the results and the opportunity to try out the new camera, Stokes went home and began editing, combining Earhart's different takes to create a spunky vision of Stacey who wasn't dumb so much as cheerfully oblivious. Next, he used rudimentary visual effects created in Adobe Premiere software to place his heroine in space; they were rough and he wasn't proud of them, but they'd do for a project that would only be seen by a few friends.

That is, until a few months later when he heard about the first awards being held by Lucasfilm and AtomFilms.com, and a second, unofficial contest at iFilm.com. On a whim, he submitted *Pink Five* to both, but only heard back from iFilm, which promptly featured the short on its front page the same day that *Star Wars:*

Episode II—Attack of the Clones opened, garnering 15,000 views of his film in 24 hours.

"We had a great run on iFilm," Stokes recalls, "and then a year later, I got an e-mail from Megan O'Neil, who'd just become AtomFilms' VP of Filmmaker Relations. Whoever had her office before left a big cardboard box of tapes—and ours was on top of it. She wrote me saying, 'It's kind of cute, why do we have it, and can we show it?' I said I had no idea how it got in the box, and yeah, they could show it, but could we still enter it in this year's contest?"

O'Neil agreed, and Stokes was excited—until he watched *Pink Five* again and couldn't bear his lousy visual effects. Having just purchased new software—Adobe After Effects—he kept the same edit of the film, but tore out all the previous effects, learning the new program on the fly as he raced to upgrade the short by the submission deadline (Ever the perfectionist, Stokes has further upgraded the effects numerous times since).

> "We got in a year late," he recalls, and suddenly there was this popularity that we weren't prepared for. Winning got us a lot of attention. Lucas did a pretaped announcement for the awards ceremony, and his line was something like, "The winner of this year's George Lucas Selects award is a quirky little film that retells the Battle of Yavin in a very different way: Trey Stokes with *Pink Five*." I'm told he had the damnedest time trying to say my name, so somewhere there's a reel of outtakes of George Lucas mangling my name over and over. Winning it was fun, especially because Amy was in complete shock. It felt like I was able to give her a gift: Here you go—2,000 people applauding for you, all 'cause you made a video.

As a result, the short became an online hit, viewed by more than 2 million people. In Hollywood, when a sci-fi film is a hit, that usually means a truckload of sequels are on the way. Earhart and Stokes, however, adamantly refused to even consider the idea, figuring that they had nowhere to go but down, inevitably frittering away whatever credibility the award had imbued upon

Celebrating with their trophies after the 2003 Official Star Wars Fan Film Awards were (L to R) Amy Earhart, "Stacey" in *Pink Five*, which won the George Lucas Selects Award; John Hudgens, director of *The Jedi Hunter*, which took the Audience Choice Award; Mark Rusciano, director of *Carbonite*, which nabbed the Skywalker Sound Award; and Trey Stokes, also of *Pink Five*. Hudgens and Stokes had fan film pasts, as Hudgens made *The Empire Strikes Quack* in the early 1990s, while Stokes had directed *Moonraker '78* some 25 years earlier. *(Courtesy of John Hudgens)*

them. In early 2004, however, they got a call from a higher-up at Lucasfilm, asking if they were planning to make a sequel. Stokes responded that a new *Pink Five* was simply out of the question; besides the threat of failure, he was already working 12-hour days on a feature film, Earhart was juggling both a waitress gig and college, and the contest deadline was only a month away. And OK, they'd do it.

The way to top *Pink Five*, they decided, was to make sure they didn't repeat themselves; having Stacey pilot a snowspeeder in *The Empire Strikes Back*'s Battle of Hoth simply wouldn't fly. The answer was to emphasize story over shtick this time, going so far as to even include character development for their thought-free Valley Girl.

"It'd been two years since the first one; Amy was now 25, and I think she naturally brought more maturity to the character, but we were moving to a different movie anyway," says Stokes. "And it's like *Empire*, which is dark—we had Stacey come in a little tweaked, and get more pissed by obstacles as the movie progressed."

As a result, *Pink Five Strikes Back* finds Stacey crash-landing on Yoda's home planet of Dagobah, secretly training with the diminutive, green Jedi and the ghost of Obi-Wan Kenobi while an off-screen Luke Skywalker, unaware of her presence, completes his own schooling in the ways of the Force. Stacey remains as perky and self-involved as ever, irked that her lightsaber doesn't match her outfit, but things get increasingly worse for the heroine, while Yoda and Kenobi spend their time bickering like an old married couple.

While hurried, the second production was far more ambitious than the simple camera test that was *Pink Five*. The cast and crew (this time there was a crew!) had to shoot on location in a boggy area next to a noisy freeway; an R2 droid and a movie-quality Darth Vader costume had to be located and borrowed; Yoda's home—and the little master himself—had to be built; and a variety of visual effects had to be put together. Whatever hardships the production entailed, however, they paid off when *Pink Five Strikes Back* garnered its Audience Choice Award a few months later during the 2004 Star Wars Fan Film Awards ceremony at the San Diego Comic Con.

While the success was a thrill, it did have one downside: If the sequel had been a dud, there wouldn't be a demand for yet another *Pink Five* fan film. Instead, it had become a hit and now they were obligated to their fellow fans to make a final movie, placing Stacey into the periphery of *Return of the Jedi*.

The concluding tale required a fair amount of brainstorming, which Stokes did with Chris Hanel, an effects artist on *Pink Five Strikes Back* and extended house guest in the director's spare bedroom. Hanel had gained some renown within amateur filmmaking circles for his 2002 movie, *The Formula*, a 50-minute flick about making a fan film that took its title from one character's criticism that most homemade Star Wars flicks boil down to the same cliché, noted back in chapter 11: the plotless lightsaber fight in the woods.

Aiming to avoid those sorts of issues, the pair concocted a massive story line for *Return of Pink Five* that they knew would be foolhardy to attempt. Stokes recalls, "We wrote a lot of script, but figured we'd cut 90 percent of it, saying, 'OK, we'll write a Battle of Endor scene with Ewoks and stuff, but there's no way we could pull that off.' But then we didn't cut anything, which was something we didn't expect to happen, because who watches a 45-minute fan film?"

To make it more manageable for the crew and viewers, the story was broken into three volumes: the first segment finds Stacey escaping from Jabba The Hutt's palace only to wind up spilling rebel secrets to the evil emperor, while the second installment follows her covertly helping the Ewoks clobber the Empire on Endor. And as for how the *Pink Five* saga winds up in the final chapter? Well, that would be telling.

If such a complex tale sounds impossible to tell on a microscopic fan film budget, it was. Extensive green-screen work was done to place the heroine on the Death Star battling Darth Vader for the emperor's amusement in *Volume 1,* while sets and elaborate costumes were employed to evoke Jabba's palace, down to a life-sized statue of Han Solo frozen in carbonite. Meanwhile, *Volume 3* featured a massive number of visual effects—in truth, far too much for Stokes and a few friends to take on by themselves. Some quick thinking on Hanel's part, however, landed them a visual effects team of 20 budding professionals using the latest software to churn out shot after shot for the production—and for free, no less. The team was actually a class of students at the Florida-based Digital Animation and Visual Effects School, where Hanel had now become a student. Using the film's complex effect requirements as a classwide final project for graduation, the school gave its pupils a taste of life in a real effects-production environment, tackling all aspects, from scheduling and budgeting to producing shots and meeting deadlines.

The downside to all this detail and heightened production value was that the final story took years to complete; *Volume 1* hit the Internet a full two years after *Pink Five Strikes Back,* in the spring of 2006, and the subsequent volumes trickled out slowly in the years that followed. The waits were inevitable given the scope of the production, but Stokes was undeterred; for him, the epic fan film hadn't become an obsession but a challenging puzzle.

The cast and crew of *Return of Pink Five* went on location, shooting in California's redwood forest, just like the original *Return of the Jedi* production.
(Courtesy of the Truly Dangerous Company)

"I didn't think we could do the Battle of Endor in *Volume 2*, and then we started to explore it," he says.

> I realized, "If we go to the redwood forest to shoot, there are people who are willing to show up with stormtrooper costumes, C3PO, and a Wookie suit, and we can get the permit for the forest. It *almost* makes sense to do it." But that meant we had to get them on trucks, drive them 300 miles north, put them up in hotels and it was pricey.
>
> I regretted the cost when I did it, but then I looked through the viewfinder, and in front of me I saw Han Solo, Princess Leia, Chewbacca, and stormtroopers, all running around in the redwoods. And I thought, "Maybe this was worth doing after all."

• • •

Plenty of other people thought it was worth it, too, as Stacey has become the most popular original fan film character ever. Fans have done everything from drawing *Pink Five* cartoons and writing fan fiction to dressing as the space cadet for Halloween and sci-fi conventions, to modifying Barbie dolls to create Stacey action figures. The character has gained a tacit Lucasfilm stamp of approval, too, not only garnering the awards, but also appearing on both a trading card and in a coffee table book, *The Star Wars Vault,* as a prime example of fan films—but all that has little to do with why she's so popular.

Rather, Stacey appeals to fans because she has a strangely familiar ring: Most of us know (or *are*) people ditzy enough to act like Pink Five if they were magically dumped into an X-wing. Trade her spaceship for a VW Beetle on a fast-moving freeway, and she'd fit right in, cheerily gossiping on a cell phone while doing an incredibly bad job of driving, all the while wishing she was somewhere else. And that's key: What makes for a heart-pounding movie climax in our existence is no biggie in hers; for Stacey, it's another day at the office. Her absolute disinterest in surroundings and situations that have thrilled millions of moviegoers is a deliciously ironic laugh.

It would be easy for the character to come off as whiny or irritating, but she doesn't, and that appealing nature is largely due to Earhart, who brings an innocent joy to the character. If, as children, fans of the series are meant to identify with Luke Skywalker and his journey to manhood, older fans can appreciate Stacey and her conversely childlike enthusiasm, mired in the very adult venue of war. In many ways she seems to be more like Luke than his separated-at-birth twin sister, Leia, although they do have their differences: Stacey and Luke are both naive and blindingly optimistic, but whereas Luke is anxious to jump headlong into becoming a Jedi over the course of three films, Stacey is loath to leave her small concerns behind, yelling at Yoda—"I'm sick of you people and your freaky religion and your stupid, dirty planet, when all I really want is a pedicure and a latte, and is that too much to ask?"

The cumulative result of the *Pink Five* trilogy is a gentle pinprick that deflates the extreme seriousness of the *Star Wars* saga while simultaneously injecting an additional layer of humanity into its story as well—a humanity that is perhaps more readily recognizable than seeing Luke at the end of *Return of the Jedi*, celebrating the anarchic destruction of all government by hanging out with ghosts and teddy bears in a tree fort (which, come to think of it, sounds pretty childish—scratch that "journey to manhood" thing after all).

While millions of people have enjoyed Stacey's exploits, however, there's one notable devotee who bestowed an accolade on the fan film franchise that dwarfed even the George Lucas Selects award: sci-fi author Timothy Zahn made Pink Five part of the official Star Wars canon.

"Canon" describes the official universe of the Star Wars saga and everything in it, while fan creations like Pink Five are considered to be part of what fans call, well, a "fanon." Zahn, then, took an unprecedented step with his 2007 novel, *Star Wars: Allegiance*, which takes place between *A New Hope* and *The Empire Strikes Back*. Deep in the book comes an unexpected moment that finds a young rebel pilot named "Stacy" [*sic*] flirting with that smuggler guy. The two-page cameo might be an innocuous in-joke, but it still had the effect of ripping the goofy X-wing pilot from the realm of fanon and making her as "real" in that make-believe universe as Luke and Leia themselves.

"'The mention of Pink Five in *Allegiance* is partly an homage to all of the fan films that are out there, bringing the whole fan film area into the *Star Wars* universe as best I could," says Zahn. "Having seen some of the movies and met some of the fan film people, it was nice to be able to do a little something to let them know I appreciated all the work they'd done."

If fan filmmaking is in some ways an adult version of kids playing with action figures in the backyard, then this was the ultimate "parental"/canon affirmation of the "kids"/fans' storytelling abilities. By engendering such a level of acceptance for the fan effort, it was a mighty feedback loop that said, in effect, "You derived your story from ours; we derive our story from yours."

It wasn't the first time Zahn had incorporated unusual sources into his franchise books, having included material from disparate Star Wars products into previous novels:

> With the *Thrawn Trilogy*, I used a bunch of the West End Games gaming materials in the book, and I learned afterwards that that the gamers really appreciated it. They had felt like they were at the children's table of Star Wars, so to speak, and by having some of the stuff they'd been playing go into an official novel, it kind of brought them to the adult table. Then, when I did *Specter of the Past*, I sneaked in a couple of references to Disney's *Star Tours* ride for the same reason—and then with *Allegiance*, I thought I'd have a shot at bringing the fan film group to the adult table as well. It adds a little excitement when the book comes out, too: "OK, how long will it be before somebody notices this?"

One person who saw it right away was Trey Stokes, who already knew that Zahn was a fan. "I met Trey at the San Diego Comic Con," explains Zahn. "I had seen a screening, and loved it. The way it was written and Amy's performance were just spot-on for me, and it was just a joy to watch. When we met, I asked if there was a possibility of getting a DVD, but he was all out. Trey said, 'Just a second,' ran over to a friend who he'd given a disc to, conned him back out of his copy and gave it to me on the spot."

That turned out to be a lucky break, as Zahn wound up with reference material for the cameo. "Well, she only has about two lines, so writing it wasn't exactly a problem," he chuckles. "I just visualized her sitting in that cockpit, yapping away at her R2 droid. I'm fairly good at voices, I think—at picking out Han or Leia, for instance, and how they would talk—and I don't think Pink Five gave me any problems. I'll find out from Amy next time I see her, whether she feels I found the true essence of her character or not. So far, most people have been rather neutral or favorable about it. It's such a small thing that if you don't like it, it's pretty easy to ignore.

"And," he adds playfully, "it's not guaranteed that it's *that* Stacey—you never really know."

14
Women on the Verge of a Hubris Takedown

While Amy Earhart's performances were the highlights of the *Pink Five* movies, her appearance in them at all was something of an anomaly, because generally few women act in fan films, and even fewer take part behind the scenes.

Maybe the lack of actresses isn't that surprising; fan filmmakers have always aimed to replicate Hollywood, and perhaps they hew closer than they know. In feature films and on television, male characters outnumber females roughly 3 (2.71) to 1, according to researcher Stacy Smith of USC's Annenberg School for Communication, working with the Geena Davis Institute on Gender in Media. That's a stark contrast to the 2006 U.S. Census, which found that females make up 51 percent of the country's population.

Fan films are likely reflective of their viewership's demographics, however. According to Emarketer.Com, in 2007, 97.2 million U.S. women went online—51.7 percent of the total online population. However, only 66 percent of those women actually watched videos—and, therefore, potentially fan films—on the Net, compared to 78 percent of male websurfers; as a result, the male minority was watching the majority of online video. Backing that up, a 2008 study on women and digital lifestyles found that men are 1.5 to 2 times more likely to download movies and TV shows from the Internet, whether from peer-to-peer sites or legal sites like iTunes.

With women giving fan films the short shrift, one can't help but wonder if it's in part because so few fan productions feature women in prominent roles. Given that the media often views fan filmmakers as "nerds with cameras," the obvious jab is that there's no women in fan films because the guys making them don't know any.

The dearth may be just as well, because while most fan films attempt to mimic feature films in style and production value, Hollywood's often two-dimensional depiction of women in genre films can trip up even the most earnest fan director. Poorly written dialogue in a fan film may make you groan, but homemade depictions of Hollywood-style sexuality can get downright uncomfortable, and can be potentially offensive to some viewers. Fortunately, you don't see much of that; maybe the male directors feel that they can't shoot it without it reflecting back poorly on everyone involved, or perhaps they just can't find any female friends willing to tart it up on camera. Either way, most fan films avoid sexuality altogether by making each woman "one of the guys," single-minded in her butt-kicking toughness and utter sexlessness.

One of the rare exceptions is New Jersey–based Blinky Productions, the ad-hoc shingle of comics enthusiast Chris Notarile. He spent most of his twenties making dozens of fan films—many of which feature himself clad in head-to-toe spandex as goofball superhero Blue Beetle—but unquestionably, the most popular Blinky productions are centered around female characters. Niki Notarile, his wife, has suited up as the villainous Catwoman many times, while friend Tawana Manion has become something of a fanboy favorite, depicting platinum-haired Power Girl, a distant relative of Superman whose costume features a circular neckline that plunges lower than the ocean floor. Whereas most fan filmmakers dance around sexuality, Notarile jumps right in, and though his flicks are typically PG in tone, he's nonetheless unafraid to let his female characters come off as sexy.

"I never had any intentions to make predominately female-heavy films," notes Notarile. "It just turned out that way, though sex sells and Power Girl and Catwoman are very marketable characters for a very male-heavy audience. Guys like my films 'cause I

Niki Notarile (left) and Tawana Manion often appear in Chris Notarile's fan films as Catwoman and Power Girl, respectively. *(Courtesy of Blinky Productions)*

show hot chicks in skimpy outfits, but girls like my films because all my characters are capable beings, not morons or stereotypes. Also, I show all my females in power—and if they aren't in power, they will be before the movie is over."

For instance, take *I'm Power Girl, Dammit!* The short features Bizzaro, Superman's evil, dimwitted doppelganger, fighting Power Girl—if you can call a conflict where she whips out a cell phone halfway through it a fight. In a tidy bit of spin control, Power Girl's sexuality comes up in the film expressly because Bizzaro is such a childlike brute; when he refers to her as "Boobie Girl," it's not an insult—the idiot really thinks that's her name. Similarly, her response isn't one of indignation or outrage, but of sheer exasperation. She's not embarrassed by her costume, but doesn't want to be defined solely by her bodily attributes, either. By mocking the reason that most of his audience will watch the flick, Notarile gets to have it both ways, providing a small commentary on society while still serving up what fanboys want most:

> I don't like to objectify my female characters so much as I like to put a spin on how they are objectified. I try more to show that my women are aware of the objectification of themselves and explore how they deal with that, whether they use it to their advantage or not. Catwoman uses her sexual-

> ity often with false pretenses. She acts sexy in front of men to throw them off guard, and when the moment is right, she strikes. She can hold someone hostage and be very sensual, but when need be, she can be a stone-cold bitch, which is great. Power Girl, on the other hand, is funny because she has the body of a hot chick, but she could honestly care less. I show Power Girl as a tomboy with feminine charm, and I think there are a lot of girls who might identify with the idea, "It's OK to be you, but it doesn't mean you have to hide your femininity either" I think that's what Power Girl represents: being yourself no matter what anyone else says.

Notarile isn't the only one exploring those concepts through fan films. Trade in those superpowers for big guns, color the hair brown, keep the "hot tomboy" premise, and you get Lara Croft of the best-selling Tomb Raider video game series. Croft was portrayed by Angelina Jolie on the big screen in a pair of critically loathed feature films, but in the fan movie world, the gunslinging heroine was embodied by an entirely different actress—Valerie Perez—in the 40-minute 2006 flick *Tomb Raider: Tears of the Dragon*.

As resourceful as the heroine she portrayed, Perez was key to the production not merely because she was the film's lead but also due to her real-world abilities. An IT analyst with a degree in neuroscience, Perez created all the CGI visual effects in the film, helped develop its premise, produced the flick, handled location scouting and—since she's a certified fire safety officer for film and TV production—set off all the film's explosions. For Perez, who grew up outside Los Angeles as the only child of a single, working mom, the appeal of making a fan film came from an entirely different place: "I needed something to draw me out of my shell . . . while also improving communication skills that were pretty underdeveloped from growing up a lonely kid."

The ever-confident Croft wound up being a persona that Perez would try on like a costume—which, in turn, was how she got into fan filmmaking. Interested in using Adobe Photoshop software to alter pictures of herself as Lara Croft, she had friend Nick Murphy, then a recent film school grad, take some shots of her. He suggested that they shoot a Tomb Raider music video, and Perez returned that they do a short film instead. Three years and $3,000 later, the film was completed, nabbing Murphy his first director credit while getting pictures of Perez plastered all over the Internet as well as UK tabloid *The Sun* and her own four-page spread in U.S. B-movie magazine *Femme Fatale*.

Despite the press focusing on her looks, Perez was less concerned about objectification of her character and more interested in ensuring that Croft didn't come off as a saint—something that was accomplished by blowing away plenty of bad guys. "I had to draw the line [to] not overly glorify my female character," she comments. "Selling a beloved character short is by far the biggest no-no on Hollywood's part that fan films try to correct."

The basic premise of the film, like most Tomb Raider games, finds Croft in search of an ancient artifact. As a result, she explores caves in the desert for a while, goes deep into an urban industrial area to take down a mobster and his heavily armed crew, and then explores a different set of caves and tunnels to find her treasure.

Given the variety of colorful and distant locations, it was up to Perez, wearing her producer hat, to keep things moving throughout the three-year, part-time shoot. "I welcomed the difficulties of limited resources and the creative troubleshooting of production," she recalls. "You tend to be shorthanded on a fan film, especially due to scheduling trouble, but there can be instances where you have a dozen friends watching, particularly if you're shooting a fight scene. Thankfully, that was the case one night in a rough part of Oakland, where there was safety in numbers."

According to Perez, roughly half the film's crewmembers were women:

> Most of the females that participated were easy to get interested because they were already fans of our main character, and half the actresses were Lara Croft cosplay [costuming] models I knew. Our [female] music composer came forward on a *Tomb Raider* chat forum after having previously developed scores inspired by the video game. Women's interest to take part in or lead their own production seems to catch on fastest by seeing more and more prominent examples of women in fan film cast and crew roles. Demystifying the

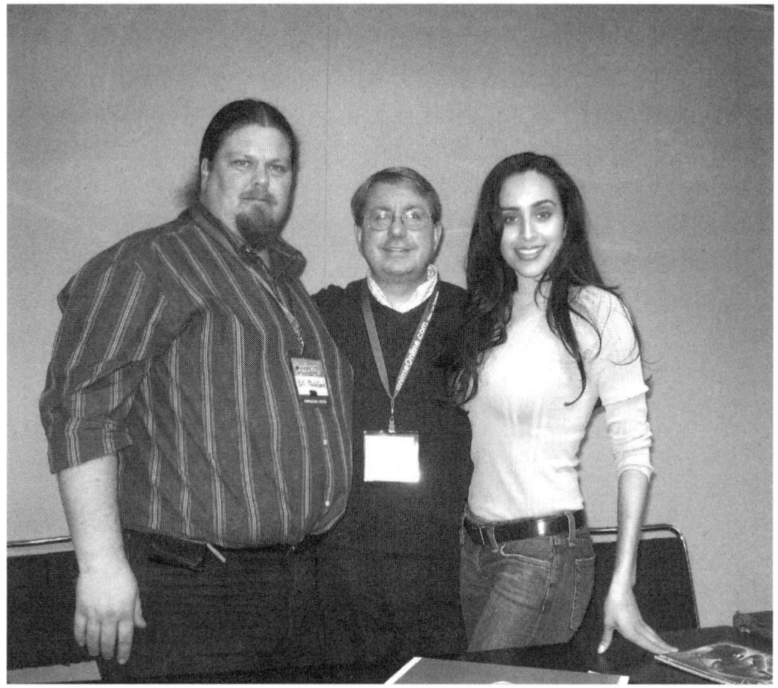

Valerie Perez's *Tomb Raider* fan film led to her being hired to portray comic book character Paula Peril in a short directed by Bill McClellan (left) that was written by *Peril*'s creator, James Watson (center). *(Photo by the author)*

> process and spreading around a few filmmaking how-to's makes a big difference to those sitting on the fence.

The experience that Perez gained from the production paid off a few years later when she recounted some of her efforts to James Watson, head of Atlanta-based indie comic book publisher Atlantis Studios. Putting her acting and pyrotechnic abilities to work, Watson produced a film short based on his company's comic book, *Paula Peril,* starring Perez as the title character, a Lois Lane–style reporter who gets into terrible scrapes.

"We looked into doing a live-action short, *Paula Peril: Trapped in the Flames,*" explains Watson. "What we found out was that it costs as much to create a five- to 10-minute film as it does to do one issue of a comic book. It's amazing what fan film people are doing with no budget and no hope of revenues; they're doing stuff that's better than a lot of what Hollywood is doing, so our thinking was, 'Is there a way we could make that happen for [our] characters?'"

While Perez was unusually involved behind the scenes in her movies, she wasn't interested in directing, and that's the case with most women in fan films, resulting in another instance where fan efforts mirror Hollywood. In 2007, only 7 percent of the Directors Guild of America's membership—roughly 1,000 out of 13,400 members—were female directors.

Francis Ford Coppola once opined, "To me, the great hope is that now [that] these little 8mm video recorders and stuff have come out, some people who normally wouldn't make movies are going to be making them, and, you know, suddenly one day, some little fat girl in Ohio is going to be the new Mozart and make a beautiful film with her father's camcorder. And, for once, the so-called professionalism about movies will be destroyed—forever—and it will really become an art form."

While not stated in the most respectful manner, Coppola's "great hope" sounds *exactly* like amateur filmmaking—so if fan films can be made by anyone, why are there so few women making them?

In truth, there are plenty of women interested in telling new stories with established characters; they just tend to take one of two different approaches—vidding and writing.

As mentioned previously, vidding is the practice of creating homemade music videos using footage from a movie or TV series. More specifically, they're videos made to illustrate relationships between characters. Often, they show controversial couplings—for instance, to imply an unspoken love between Harry Potter and cruel Professor Snape. While it started as slide shows in the 1970s, vidding evolved quickly, jumping to VHS videotapes in the early 1980s, a medium that allowed themes to resonate more deeply.

In *Enterprising Women: Television Fandom and the Creation of Popular Myth*, ethnographer Camille Bacon-Smith writes of encountering fan-created *Starsky & Hutch* and *Magnum P.I.* "song-tapes" in 1985, noting, "Songtape artists use popular songs like 'Stand By Me' and 'By Your Side' together with rescue scenes from the source products to emphasize the hero's need for supportive companionship." Songvids don't replace voices as they do in dubs (fan shorts comprised of TV or film footage with new dialogue from another source), but there's no question that they have the same intended effect: to create an alternate story line through the juxtaposition of content and context. However, they're generally excluded from fan film culture, and considering that virtually all vidding practitioners are women, that's a notable omission.

The other way women approach storytelling with established characters is to write fan fiction—to such an extent that "fanfic" is just as much a girls' club as fan films are a boys club. The popular website FanFiction.net, covers amateur scribblings in most every media fandom possible, but almost all its stories are written by women—and they write a lot. The site has literally hundreds of thousands of fan stories in the Harry Potter category alone; compare that with the relative handful of Potter fan films. If women are so clearly inspired to create new stories for beloved characters—like those in the Potter books, for instance—why do they, by an overwhelming majority, choose one form of artistic expression over another?

"Most women are more comfortable as writers than as filmmakers," explains Andrea Richards, author of the upbeat, how-to tome *Girl Director*.

> It's not because we aren't technically adept or capable of being directors, but because women have been taught from an early age to play a supporting role. We still live in a society that is often uncomfortable with women in positions of leadership and power, so women squander their own talents on the work of others. When I do workshops with girls and talk about making movies, the majority of them all want to be actors. They don't necessary know what a director is, and once they find out, many still can't envision themselves in that role.
>
> Think about the picture that comes to mind when we even say "Director." You see Steven Spielberg in a baseball cap or D. W. Griffith in his riding boots with a bull horn. You don't imagine someone who looks like Sofia Coppola. It's not that women don't have the skills, experience and tal-

> ent to direct feature films; it's just that the people who hire directors are less comfortable imaging that person as female. We love the boy wonder or the moody auteur, and sadly, a woman just doesn't fit that mold, even when she *is* a moody auteur, like Agnes Varda, or a girl wonder like Coppola. The main reason why I wrote *Girl Director* wasn't just to tell girls the info they needed to make a movie; it was to get them thinking as directors. The first part of that is envisioning yourself *as* a director—someone who has a story and the authority to tell it. After that, learning how to operate the tools is cake.

As if to underscore that point, it's exactly what happened for an Orlando-based dolphin trainer and one-woman Harry Potter movie studio. Erin Pyne was a big fan of J. K. Rowling's books—enough so that she ran the local fan club, sang in a novelty "wizard rock" band, and wrote a book on Potter worship, *A Fandom of Magical Proportions: An Unauthorized History of the Harry Potter Phenomenon*. Given her expertise, in 2004, a coworker, Tim Balko, ran his fan film script by her, and soon Pyne was an associate producer on *Sirius Black and the Secret Keeper*. While Balko directed, Pyne was making costumes, securing the location (a dumpster behind a strip mall), casting the extras and showing the film at The Witching Hour, a 2005 Potter academic symposium held in Salem, Massachusetts. "After the experience of the premiere," she recalls, "I was addicted to the emotional response of others to the project I worked on—I wanted more."

That led to her writing and directing her own Potter pictures—*The Marauders' Worst Memory* and *The Potter Prophecy*—which fleshed out stories only briefly mentioned in the original Rowling books. While Pyne had learned the ins and outs of fan moviemaking on *Sirius Black*, helming her own films was an altogether different experience: "It can be difficult for women to achieve the authority and respect it takes to be a director without seeming overbearing. Many women find it hard to step into a male-dominated role, especially when working with other men. I tend to create a collaborative environment in which anyone can throw out ideas and creativity is appreciated. I enjoy organizing and thrive on controlled chaos."

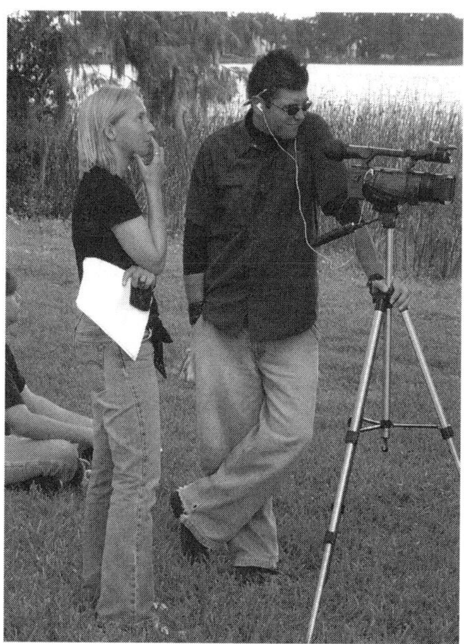

Erin Pyne wrote and directed *The Marauder's Worst Memory*, working with cinematographer Ken Guzzetti, who became her codirector for the follow-up flick, *The Potter Prophecy*. *(Courtesy of Quill and Cauldron)*

Helping create that chaos on *Marauders* was a cast plucked from the West Orange High School Drama Club, a limited $500 budget and only two weekends available to shoot—a fact that made the production an "all hands on deck" affair: "Generally, artists have many talents, and sometimes people discover they can do something they never thought they could when given the task. I learned how a 10-foot space can become a large cave, how to build a door out of foam and fiberglass, and how dedicated a group of young actors could be."

With a trio of Potter productions under her belt, Pyne had some different ideas for future projects, including one that she hoped would raise acceptance of fan movies among women. "There are so few women in fan films, most likely because, on average, more men are interested in the sci-fi and fantasy genre than women, and most fan films are based on that genre," says Pyne. "Fan films could be made for young women about their issues and interests. I have a script in which a woman fantasizes about being heroines from different films to escape her dreary life.

I think women can identify with wanting to emulate the idealized images of women and how it affects how we feel about ourselves."

• • •

The idea of exploring the lost corners of a sprawling epic was appealing to another female fan filmer: Dawn Cowings, who with her husband, Shane Felux, created one of the best-known fan films ever—2005's *Star Wars: Revelations*. In the fan production world, the 40-minute film was nothing short of a blockbuster. Within 48 hours of its release on the Internet the film had been downloaded more than a million times; within four months, that number had risen to 3 million. Meanwhile, Cowings and Felux wound up giving interviews on CBS, CNN, MSNBC, G4, CBC, and other networks, as well as becoming the subjects of countless newspaper and magazine articles around the globe, with Slate.com opining that their film was "just as good as—and often quite better than—the cringe-inducing *Star Wars* movies of recent years."

Kudos like that didn't come easy, however, which made the story of the mom and dad from Bristow, Virginia, who poured $20,000 and three years of their lives into *Revelations* all the more unlikely.

The young couple had always been sci-fi fans, and Cowings had long practiced vidding. "That's an area that is more strongly associated with women," admits Cowings. "The idea of [marrying] fast edits and storytelling to an appropriate song to underscore your fandom is definitely a labor of love."

Every so often, they talked about how they should put her degree in TV and film writing and his degree in acting and directing to good use by making a movie together, but after three years of marriage, nothing had come of it—until one day, Felux bought a Canon XL1-S miniDV camera on eBay for $3,500. They'd made the investment, now they had to put up or shut up; she had three months to write it, and then he'd direct it. Cowings began scripting with friend Sarah Yaworsky, and the result was an epic tale of two Jedi sisters being hunted across galaxies by an evil female disciple of the emperor.

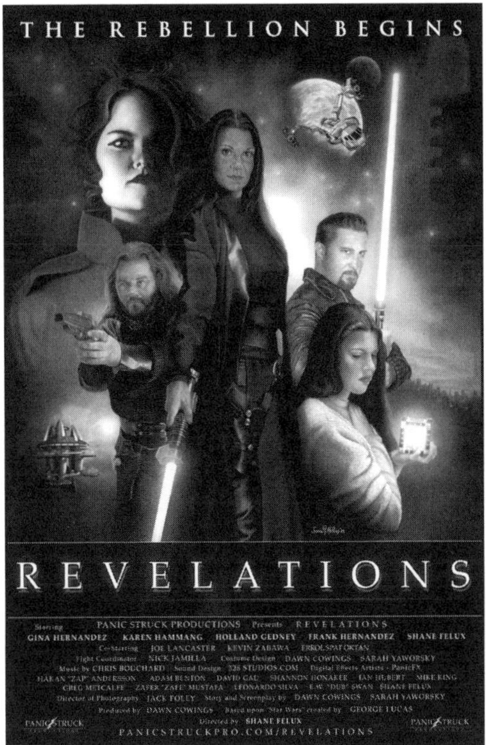

Star Wars: Revelations, a 40-minute, $20,000 fan film written by Dawn Cowings and Sarah Yaworsky, was directed by Cowings's husband, Shane Felux.
(Courtesy of X-ile Pictures)

"We decided to make it women simply because we were tired of seeing *Star Wars* fan films with male leads," recalls Cowlings. "Our story could easily be substituted with men—although it would make the love interests a bit awkward. We were lucky with the *Star Wars* universe because you don't have to explain how a woman can come by such strong fighting skills. In a typical action movie, any man can pick up a gun to defend his family and it's understandable, but a gun-toting woman? You almost always have to explain why a woman would know how to use a gun."

Script in hand, they dubbed themselves Panic Struck Productions and began a slow, steady trudge toward their goal. "We had so little money, and in order to make a movie, you need an army," says Felux. "Casting was, 'Hey, you can walk and talk; wanna be in my movie?'" It wasn't a question to be taken lightly: their friends, Frank Hernandez and his wife, Gina, took on major roles, only to find themselves driving four hours each way from Jackson, New Jersey, to Virginia every two weeks throughout the production.

Most of the budget was spent on food for the cast and crew; otherwise, costs were kept as low as possible—a feat that required creativity. Felux, a government graphic design contractor, built a website for a company that owned a rock quarry in exchange for shooting a desolate prison planet scene there. Meanwhile, info from the Virginia Film Commission helped the couple find professionals willing to work for free in order to build their résumés. "The most people we ever had on set was 160," Felux recalled, "and to feed them and to shoot 32 setups in six hours was rough. Towards the end of production, we had pros who would bring $50,000 worth of gear for free, just because they liked how we ran things. We'd learned how to treat everyone well and get things done."

"Getting things done" included recruiting amateur special-effects whizzes; posting to CGI hobbyist forums, they found more than 30 artists from the United States, Sweden, the United Kingdom, Canada, Australia, and Lithuania who were willing to pitch in. That, too, was slow going; given that everyone involved was working on the project in their free time, a five-second shot could take up to two months to complete. Artists would log into a special server, download edited footage, and get to work using software packages like Autodesk 3ds Max and Maya, NewTek LightWave 3D, Terragen, and Bryce. A shot would get passed around for notes and adjustments until Felux could finally incorporate it into the movie, editing in Adobe Premiere Pro on his 3.2-GHz Pentium 4 home PC, outfitted with terabytes of storage.

While the massive project started out small, it grew and grew, taking on professional aspirations in the process—but it was still a hobby. "It can put a strain on your marriage, because I work nine to five, maybe eat, and then work until one to two in the morning every night," says Felux. "I am really, really tired. It's very difficult, because it takes time away from the family."

And it *was* a family. Their first son was born in the middle of the three-year production; by the time the film was completed, there was a second newborn in the house. As *Revelations'* expenses

Felux (far right) got permission to shoot a prison planet scene inside a rock quarry in exchange for building a corporate website for the location's owner.
(Courtesy of X-ile Pictures)

continued to spiral skyward, Cowings became a stay-at-home mom. "The $20,000 built over three years, and that's basically credit card debt and eventually a home equity loan," says Felux, who admits that sometimes making *Revelations* didn't seem like the brightest idea.

"There was a point where I wanted to quit; I couldn't do it anymore. It was so hard, and then we saw this *Star Wars* documentary called *Empire of Dreams*—and we had the same problems as George Lucas! He was overbudget, over schedule, the film looked like crap, some of the cast and crew didn't believe in it, the studio wanted to pull it; it's amazing *Star Wars* got made at all. And that gave me hope because I realized, 'If this guy can do it—and he had it much worse that we did—we can do it.' So we finished the movie."

Completion meant that it was time to hold a premiere party—and incredibly, that was another $15,000. Nearly 200 people had volunteered to accomplish the impossible, and recognizing that the film never could have been made without them, the couple invited everyone to a massive, world-premiere screening at the Senator Theatre, a historic, art deco, 900-seat movie palace in Baltimore. The premiere was festooned with stormtroopers, limos, searchlights, and press, and then followed by a gala blowout that benefited the Make-A-Wish Foundation. The evening was a huge success.

As *Revelations'* costs had started going through the roof, by economic necessity, the film wound up becoming a calling card to Hollywood. The flurry of press and TV appearances that followed only helped to raise the film's profile even more, though, because the couple cannily debuted their epic a month before the release of 2005's *Revenge of the Sith* in order to ride on its coattails of hype.

The added attention had a downside, however, as it meant the film received a greater scrutiny from fans as a result. "I believe that the movie was judged a lot harsher than one with two guys in the backyard wielding toy lightsabers," says Cowings. "I've read a lot of comments where people think it's the worst crap they could have envisioned, or they hate the fact that the leads are female. I've also received e-mails from people all over the world who feel it fits beautifully into the canon and are more satisfied by it than the actual movies."

And her husband's review? "It's my first film and it shows. I'm proud of what we did with what we had, even though it's pretty bad—but not bad for a bunch of nobodies with nothing making their first film. I learned and grew a lot." For all the media attention lavished on the film, however, its director only landed two gigs making low-budget music videos—and only one was a paying job.

Meanwhile, Felux found he had a nagging sense of failure. Despite *Revelations'* popularity, the media attention and an unfathomable number of downloads, Lucasfilm told the press that George Lucas hadn't seen the flick, and of course, it couldn't be entered into the AtomFilms contest because it was a dramatic story. Adds Felux, "I'm friends with some AtomFilms winners and I always felt they saw it differently—like, 'You don't have a trophy; yeah, it's a serious film, but can you do comedy like we do?' The contest inspired me in the beginning when we had started making *Revelations*, and I realized I still wanted to enter and win; I wanted Lucas to see my film."

The result was that roughly a year after *Revelations* hit it big, Panic Struck Productions took the 2006 Official Star Wars Fan Film Awards by storm, snagging both the Audience and George

Lucas Selects awards with *Pitching Lucas*. A new, breezy short about clueless TV execs suggesting awful ideas for a *Star Wars* TV series, the film was a comparative walk in the park for Cowings and Felux, since it "only" took four months and $2,400 to make. The lower price tag was a break, too, as they welcomed their third son into the world less than a month after the film won.

Pitching Lucas, it turned out, was the short that put the husband-and-wife team over the top. *Revelations* had garnered industry interest, but only from B-movie outfits offering deals that were ridiculous. "I'm not 20, I have a career already, I make good money and my family comes first, so I'm not going to sell my soul to make a movie for the first person that comes along," says Felux.

One of the latter people to come along, however, was from Stage 9 Digital Media, a nascent Internet division of ABC/Disney. Stage 9 had expressed some moderate interest while Panic Struck Productions was producing *Pitching Lucas*, but when the short took the top awards, that lit a fire under the company to seal a deal with the couple. Soon Cowings and Felux were renaming their company X-ile Pictures, and working away on *Trenches*, a sprawling 10-part miniseries to be released on the Web.

Written once again by Cowings and Yaworsky, and directed by Felux, the sci-fi thriller follows battling armies on a decrepit planet who must unite against a big, ugly-mugly monster. Ironically, the first day of shooting found the filmmakers back on location in the rock quarry used in *Revelations*. Returning to it for the first time in years, they found the site was familiar, yet all brand new—because the quarry floor was now 30 feet lower than the last time. Much like their amateur status, their old stomping grounds had simply vanished into thin air.

15
The Future of Fan Films

Fan films are the spawn of movies and reality TV.

It was inevitable, really. Fan movie production had been growing for 70 years when it finally hit the mainstream at the end of the 1990s and bloomed into a full-fledged vernacular culture; now its future is tied to a number of other trends that also gained momentum around the turn of the millennium.

The late nineties marked the arrival of the so-called digital lifestyle, where laptop computers, camcorders, cell phones, digital cameras, BlackBerries, the Internet, iPods, and the rest were now within reach constantly, keeping folks company every living, breathing second. Manufacturers decided that people needed to be entertained and "connected" 24/7, and the incessant barrage of electronic sidekicks hurled at consumers ever since has ensured that's the case. Today, 180 million people in the United States use the Internet regularly; 230 million Americans are cell phone users and more than 25 million of them use a smartphone like a BlackBerry or iPhone.

Coinciding with the rising demand for content to fuel all those electronic accoutrements came the demonetization of scripted entertainment. Why pay for HBO just to watch *The Sopranos* if your pal can burn a DVD off his Tivo? Why spend $20 to go to the movies if you can download them opening weekend for free? As bandwidth restrictions eased and the economy began to falter, unlawful copies made simple economic (if not moral) sense to many people.

As scripted entertainment stumbled, there was a simultaneous onset (or onslaught) of *unscripted* entertainment—reality television. The format proved that people will watch just about anything, and even more so if it involves preening amateurs making mistakes every few seconds. Gone was the perfection of Hollywood stars, the infallible hero; instead we got a story with two simple outcomes. If the little guy triumphed, he conquered adversity. If he failed, we chuckled, thrilled that we weren't the idiot humiliated in front of millions.

And all this brings us to fan films, because a fan production is the ultimate result, the middle ground, the crossbred offspring of scripted and unscripted entertainment.

All fan films feature characters and stories we've seen a million times before, but here they're seen through the undistorted lens of reality. That's not a pair of Jedi slashing it out with lightsabers on a far-off planet—it's two guys from New Jersey wearing bathrobes in the woods as they wail at each other with sawed-off broomsticks. That's not Spider-Man casually swinging between skyscrapers overhead; it's a dude hanging from a rope who's gonna crack his skull open if his hands get too sweaty.

Capturing raw moments like these and turning them into a fan film has never been easier, thanks to the digital lifestyle. Regular people now have everything they need to make an amateur epic, from the camcorder (or camera phone) to the editing software that came with their laptop to an instant distribution network via the Internet. Certainly, they have the desire—the average person watches 4 hours and 35 minutes of TV a day—so why *wouldn't* they want to try making it themselves? They also have the conceptual knowledge, too, because with that much immersion, everyone has absorbed on some level how a show is visually constructed: Tape your pal running down the street dressed as The Flash, cut to a close-up of his foot landing on a banana peel, cut back to your master shot as he slips and winds up in traction. *Voilà*—instant entertainment . . . and perhaps a medical lawsuit. It really is *that* simple—and yet, of course, it's not.

Fan films are, by their nature, flawed films. No one can make a $200 million summer blockbuster for 20 bucks, try as he or she might. To watch a fan production, then, is to watch a string of compromises one after another, from the story, casting, and locations to effects, editing, and the final product. The resulting flick might take place in a fantasy world, but it's inexorably grounded in stone-cold reality. It's that very fact, though, that can unwittingly catapult a homemade superhero movie far past a $200 million flick when it comes to trifling aspects like value to our souls—because while a big-budget feature film uses tone, scripting, and design in an effort to entertain and hopefully arrive at a greater truth, the $20 movie has been mired waist-deep in truth since the moment it was conceived.

That simple truth is that it's an imperfect world. Many of the Hollywood movies we flock to are just collections of overprocessed, prepackaged images buffed to a glimmering sheen; the fan productions that aim for that kind of slickness, though, usually wind up slipping on it instead. As a result, viewing a fan film can often be a far more compelling experience, largely because watching a scrawny, teenage Indiana Jones is to watch ourselves. Inevitably, the kid is hopelessly out of place, mismatched to the tasks laying before his character, yet he passionately follows the old axiom to "fake it 'til you make it" in the face of utter ludicrousness. That's not an Indiana Jones plot; that's our lives, that's *us*! None of it makes any sense, but the kid in the fedora plods ahead anyway, and that's what makes him a hero: his quixotic devotion to the faint hope that we'll buy into him being a champion, and not just for a moment but for the length of the film. That narcotic mix of desire, innocence, and bravado? Now *that's* something to believe in!

It's the same story behind the camera, too; often it's the director's first time trying to make a flick, and to complicate things, fan filmmakers are always drawn like moths to the flame toward the most visually ornate subjects—sci-fi, comic book heroes, and the like. It's a natural attraction, however, because those are the genres of dreamers, and a fan with a camera in his hand is already dreaming big if he's contemplating a fan movie. If amateur auteurs were realistic about their movies, they wouldn't try to re-create a galaxy far, far away or a British boarding school full of magic kids. They'd make a fan film that was something easy, something simple, something that could be achieved with the stuff they really have around them. They'd make *Ordinary People II*.

That, of course, hasn't happened. Instead, the DIY look of early fan flicks has been shown the door, and the unwritten rule now is that you have to start at the top of your game. It may be that high-end efforts like *Star Wars: Revelations* have created an aesthetic arms race, or that first-timers have become too shy to share their first filmic steps in a world where anything placed on the Internet now follows you for eternity. Whatever the case may be, the punk rock–like "shoot it, show it, shove off" attitude of a classic like James Monegan's 2005 short *A Message from Batman* is now the exception rather than the rule. The three-minute flick is simply one long take of Monegan in a wetsuit and a Batman mask, jowly beard be damned, lecturing youngsters on making the right decisions: "I haven't always been a superhero; one time, I was a kid, too, and I made some tough choices. . . . I decided that the only way to really avenge my parents was to dress up as a giant bat and attack criminals. [*Pause.*] I'm still kinda working that one out."

The charms of such low-key fare only go so far, however, so in recent times the fan film world has increasingly subscribed to the Hollywood principle that bigger is better, aiming for that glossy slickness with an evangelist's conviction. It's not a bad thing per se, but it does change the game. Now, some fan flicks, like *Revelations*, come fully loaded with extensive effects, huge budgets, aggressive publicity, and professional help on both sides of the camera; in such cases, the end product—and it *is* a product—often isn't so much an homage as it is a Mini-Me. These elaborate imitations of "the real thing" readily wear the time, money, and effort put into them as badges of honor—and nowhere is that mind-set more evident than in the average $40,000 episode of *Star Trek: New Voyages*. Yes, "episode." They dropped that kind of cash more than once.

When the original *Star Trek* was cancelled in 1969 after three seasons, it left the U.S.S. *Enterprise*'s fabled five-year mission in limbo. Seeking to correct that slight, *New Voyages*—later rechristened *Star Trek: Phase II*, though we'll use the original name here—began building a fourth season in 2004, averaging one

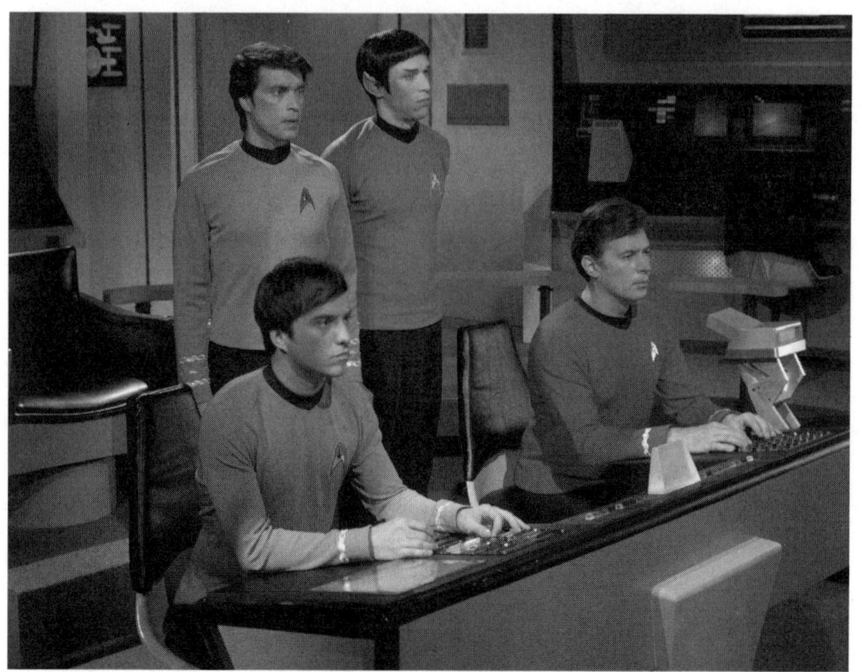

James Cawley (standing left, as Captain Kirk) built the U.S.S. *Enterprise* bridge set for his fan film series, *Star Trek: New Voyages*, using the original blueprints at a cost of $100,000.
(Courtesy of Jeff Hayes/Cawley Entertainment Co)

episode a year. The shows were near perfect re-creations of the real thing, and with good reason. The costumes? Cut from the original 1960s patterns. The scripts? Sometimes scribed by pros, including *Trek* writers D. C. Fontana and David Gerrold. The special effects? The handiwork of more *Trek* vets. The complete 360-degree bridge of the *Enterprise*? Built from the original blueprints for a cool $100,000.

In fact, the only tip-off that *New Voyages* episodes haven't been buried in a film vault for decades is the cast, because the familiar faces of Leonard Nimoy, DeForest Kelly, and William Shatner are nowhere to be found. Instead, multiple people have portrayed Mr. Spock, including a video store clerk; Bones McCoy is, in reality, a urologist from Oregon; and Captain Kirk is played by a professional Elvis impersonator. You can't make this stuff up.

The linchpin behind this massive effort is executive producer James Cawley, who plays the captain when he's not the King. Having built a formidable rep reenacting Elvis over the course of two decades, Cawley funds most of the show himself, producing it in a shuttered Chevy dealership in the tiny resort village of Port Henry, New York. "The Chamber of Commerce loves us," says Cawley. "It's a small town and we bring in upwards of 235 people for two weeks whenever we shoot. Restaurants and hotels get business, we've had a lot of national exposure for what we've done, plus Paramount gets a kick out of what we're doing, too."

Ah, yes—Paramount. The studio's view of fan films has changed dramatically since it fired off cease-and-desist letters like phasers in the eighties and nineties. While the company hasn't stated an official position, *New Voyages'* former executive producer and director, Jack Marshall, obtained a basic verbal agreement with the franchise's lawyer that the fan series could be produced if three stipulations were met: that no profits were made; that it wasn't shown at festivals or conventions where admission was charged for the film or the event itself; and that it was only available as a free download, not as a reward for a "donation." As Marshall once noted, "They are not giving us permission to do the show, but rather turning a blind eye to it as long as we stick to the rules."

That laissez-faire attitude probably worked well for both Cawley's crew and the studio itself. The early part of this decade found the official franchise in a state of red alert; after 10 editions, the Trek movies had turned into box-office bombs, while the fourth spin-off series, *Enterprise,* crashed and burned after four seasons. With no new *Trek* on TV to feed their habit for the first time in 18 years, fans stumbled across *New Voyages* on the Internet and turned it into a hit. Cawley is convinced it paved the way for the real franchise's relaunch via director J. J. Abrams's 2009 *Star Trek* feature film. "You can't look at a fan film that gets 30 million downloads as a lark," explains Cawley. "It must say to someone in marketing, 'Wow, maybe Captain Kirk *is* touchable.' Until we recast Kirk, it was taboo—nobody would think of it, nobody wanted to do it."

Dropping himself into the role wasn't an overnight process, either. When he started imitating Elvis in the late eighties, Cawley supplemented his income by taking on freelance piecework for William Ware Theiss, the costume designer on the original series and *The Next Generation*. When Theiss passed on due to complications from AIDS in 1992, he left behind some surprises for the young fan. "I ended up with the blueprints for the original sixties sets and the wardrobe," says Cawley. "Once I had that, I realized, 'Wow, I've really got the keys to the palace.'"

Over the next 10 years Cawley slowly pieced together the sets, and as they grew bigger they moved from an empty storefront to a rented space above the chamber of commerce to the cavernous, bat-infested Chevy dealership. Meanwhile, he continued to make friends with various *Trek* pros, including Doug Drexler, a sci-fi memorabilia store owner from the seventies who went on to win an Oscar for make-up on *Dick Tracy* in the nineties before becoming a visual effects pro for *Star Trek: Voyager* and *Enterprise*. "He said, 'James, if you ever get this crazy idea off the ground, I will do your effects'—and he did," Cawley recalls. "His enthusiasm got the attention of those around him, and they contacted me, too."

Even with their help, though, the first attempt was rough—the sets and costumes were perfect, but the acting was less than stellar (that first episode has since been pulled from the series website). Fans were encouraging but critical, unloading their best barbs on a surprising target: Cawley's hair. "People were saying, 'Oh my God, he has Elvis hair!'" he recalls. "If it didn't look that way, then I wouldn't have had the money to make the show. They didn't know I was performing as him five times a day, driving home an hour, showering, eating, throwing on a *Star Trek* costume and filming until 2 AM. I did that every day for a week until I was one of the living dead."

From that rocky start, the episodes improved—a fact that kept *New Voyages* going through a dark period in late 2005 when Marshall left the production. He had been instrumental in getting the show off the ground, encouraging the future Captain Kirk to stop building sets and start using them, then rounding up actors, providing a camera, and directing the first two episodes. When Marshall left after a falling out ("We were like oil and water," says Cawley), that could have easily have cut the *Enterprise*'s five-year mission short yet again.

Instead, two episodes followed that propelled the series even further: George Takei and Walter Koenig—"Sulu" and "Chekov"

Many professionals have become involved in *Star Trek: New Voyages*, the fan film series led by James Cawley (right); the episode "World Enough and Time" featured original series castmember George Takei (left) as his character, Sulu, and was directed and cowritten by Marc Scott Zicree (center), screenwriter for numerous official Trek series.
(Courtesy of Jeff Hayes/Cawley Entertainment Co.)

from the original series—agreed to appear as older versions of their characters in back-to-back shows. (It may have helped that they got paid for their work, as were all *New Voyages* cast and crew that belonged to the various actors', directors', and writers guilds.) Koenig found himself following in his son Andrew's fan film footsteps, as the younger actor had played the Joker in *Batman: Dead End*; he explained on NPR the Trek project's appeal: "For the first time, we've discovered who Chekov was—that he had an inner life and that he was a character that could evolve. He wasn't simply an expository character saying, you know, 'Warp factor 4.'" Meanwhile, Takei was game to try his hand at a fan film again, 20 years after the ill-fated *Yorktown II: A Time to Heal*, and was proud of the resulting episode, telling the Associated Press, "It's classic drama, and it's rip-snorting good." He wasn't the only one who thought so—the episode was eventually nominated for a "Best Dramatic Presentation, Short Form" Hugo Award (sci-fi fandom's equivalent to an Oscar).

But while Hollywood started coming to Port Henry, *New Voyages* members began migrating west to Tinseltown, leaving Cawley and the crew far behind. Marshall and Jeff Quinn—the video clerk turned Mr. Spock—joined the visual effects crew on the SciFi Channel remake of *Battlestar Galactica,* while three cast members had auditions with J. J. Abrams for the new Star Trek film.

"Doors have been opened that would not have been, had they not participated," says Cawley, "but the ultimate goal has always been to have fun. That said, I have never been shy about the fact that I'd love the studio to license [fan films]—there's a lot of money to be made if they're done properly." With 30 million downloads to his series' credit, that's definitely true, but at the same time, how many other fan filmmakers could rustle up all those resources to ensure their production was "done properly"? Certainly, few would be willing to drop $100,000 on a bridge set, as evidenced by the fact that numerous other unofficial Trek productions have shot on it, including *Star Trek: Of Gods and Men,* a movie starring nearly every Trek series regular who does more convention appearances than acting.

Licensing is certainly an interesting idea, but it takes such efforts out of the realm of fan production, making them more akin to independent contractors. Would a studio license out its intellectual property if the money was right? Could a franchise survive an avalanche of subdirect-to-DVD product if people were asked to pay for it? Perhaps, but if money is involved, then they're pro productions, regardless of how qualified the cast and crew may or may not be. Professional work is measured on a very different scale by studios and viewers (not to mention unions), so if someone holding the purse strings is saying no, they likely have their reasons, whether it's that the franchise is too valuable, or that even top-shelf amateur work just isn't pro enough.

Or, it could be that the best financial move is to keep a high-profile amateur production at arm's length. After all, it's free publicity that adds value and interest to a brand without costing a cent. A "brand ambassador" like *New Voyages* got 30 million people to watch new episodes when none were being officially produced, restimulating interest in a franchise that had been left to go fallow. If the amateur effort proved to be a gentle reminder to viewers—"Hey, remember how you used to like *Trek?*"—the fans' next move to rekindle their own interest would probably make Paramount a few bucks, whether it involved buying a DVD set, toys, or something else. For doing nothing, that's a great return on investment.

• • •

New Voyages and other high-end projects truly seem to point the way toward the future of fan films—and their tentative relationships with copyright holders—due to a variety of factors:

Absence Makes the Heart Grow Fonder. Fan films have always been emblematic of this cliché, because the longer a franchise has been laid in the ground and forgotten, the more likely a fan film about it is going to pop up. That happened with *Star Wars* during the 16-year gap between *Return of the Jedi* and *The Phantom Menace*, as fans began producing their own visual media in the absence of official material. The same effect was even more pronounced, however, with the shutting down of the Star Trek franchise in 2005. In the wake of that move, fans discovered a number of Trek fan series besides *New Voyages*, including *Hidden Frontier*, *Intrepid*, and *Starship Exeter*, among others.

The Canary in the Coal Mine. Fan films and whatever popularity they achieve can be seen as focus groups on the health of a franchise. Case in point: All those *Star Trek* fan series mentioned above were in production *before* the franchise was put on ice in 2005. With over 700 hours of official Star Trek available between all the TV series and movies, why would fans start making their own shows when arguably there was nothing left to explore?

"There's a lot left to explore," counters Cawley. "When people say that, they don't understand the nature of the show—and unfortunately, a lot of later series like *Voyager* and *Enterprise* didn't understand it, either. They fell back on what they thought worked, and their audience abandoned them; watch 10 minutes of *Voyager*—and less of *Enterprise*—and then there's 40 minutes of technical mumbo-jumbo about how to get out of it. That's not what Star Trek is about. It's about people, where we're going and who we are, and once you get it back into that kind of storytelling, you have stories again. If we run out of stories about people, my God, then there's no human race."

The original 1960s TV series was respected for (clumsily) exploring social issues, whether taking on racism in "Let That Be Your Last Battlefield" or, surprisingly, adopting an allegorical pro-Vietnam stance in "A Private Little War." Launched in 2000, the startlingly prolific *Hidden Frontier* series returned to that ideology and spent seven years tackling a variety of issues, from terrorism to post-traumatic stress. Far and away, its most notable move, however, was to boldly go where no Star Trek had gone before with the introduction of openly gay characters, exploring their lives and relationships as much as any other individuals on the show. *New Voyages*, too, eventually produced an episode dealing with homosexuality and an AIDS-like virus, based on a David Gerrold script that had been turned down years earlier by *The Next Generation*.

"Fan-created production is borne out of a mixture of fascination and frustration," explains MIT's Henry Jenkins. "If fans were not deeply invested in *Star Trek*, for example, then they wouldn't continue to want to engage with the material at that level [i.e., making fan films]. On the other hand, if the episodes that already existed already satisfied them, then there would be no need to continue to extend it. . . . All of this points to the idea that there's something that fans are gravitating toward that's really interesting to them, but that the end result is something that didn't fully satisfy. That's an inevitable consequence of a world where mass media is produced for a mass audience—and then retrofitted to the desires of individual niche consumers."

That concept might be able to be reverse engineered—that is, if one looks at fan films made by hardcore fans (Jenkins's "individual niche consumers"), it's possible that the flicks could provide clues as to why a franchise is succeeding or failing. In the case of Star Trek, these hardcore aficionados were attempting to revive an aspect—social commentary—that they felt was missing; meanwhile, later episodes of the last official series, *Enterprise*, attempted to win over hardcore fans by addressing continuity issues such as why the appearance of Klingons changed between the original series and the later franchise revivals. While that approach was an interesting concept, it wasn't what fans truly desired—plus, it served to further seal off the series from casual fans and complete newbies to *Star Trek*, helping hasten the demise of *Enterprise*.

A Toe in the Water. While a fan film can provide insight into a franchise's health, it may also be indicative of when one is ready to rise from the dead. While major studios have already encouraged fans to make movies based on certain aging franchises, it's just as plausible that they'd use a fan film to test whether it's time to revive one.

To take an example from the music world, Guns N' Roses' first release was a fake live EP, *Live ?!*@ Like a Suicide*; recorded in the studio, it was released by the major label Geffen Records under the guise of an equally fake indie label, Uzi Suicide Records. The benefit of the EP was twofold: to test reaction to the band outside its home turf of Los Angeles, and to give the group a patina of indie credibility, so that its official major label debut, *Appetite For Destruction*, would appear to have stemmed organically from the presumed "success" of *Suicide*.

A faux fan film, then, would be a cost-effective way to try out a feature film or TV remake, for instance, as it would cost, at worst, thousands of dollars as opposed to the millions required to cast and shoot a feature or TV pilot. Additionally, the pseudo-indie effort would raise public awareness at the hardcore fan level while providing the same "because fans demanded it" fake credibility that Guns N' Roses benefited from in its early stages.

Occasionally, this scenario has played itself out even as the copyright holders were adamantly against it. For instance, in 2008, a fan production based on the *Max Payne* video game series was forced to shutter by Fox Studios, which owned the motion picture rights to the property, while the previous year, a fan film based on the long-running G.I. Joe toy line and 1980s cartoon series was shut down by the toy's copyright owner, Hasbro. Since the studios had the "real" feature films in development, it's quite plausible that they didn't want any thunder stolen by the amateur efforts. (Ironically, Hasbro manufactures another line of dolls that have been used in countless fan films: Star Wars action figures.)

Advertisement Advisement. That Guns N' Roses EP had a third purpose: it worked as an advertisement, whetting

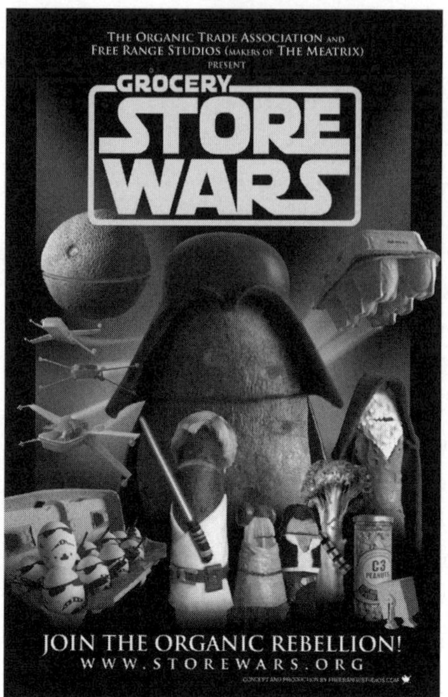

The amateur aesthetics of fan films are increasingly being adopted for advertising and marketing, as seen in *Grocery Store Wars*, a viral video created by the Organic Trade Association to promote organic food choices.
(Courtesy of the Organic Trade Association)

appetites for, uh, *Appetite*. In many ways, fan films are simply ads for the franchises they're set in—and don't think Madison Avenue hasn't noticed. As Kevin Roberts, CEO worldwide of Saatchi & Saatchi, has blogged, "The wisdom of empathy tells us that if we immerse ourselves in the passions of consumers, we will be in the right space to come up with creative products and brands that win their hearts. If you believe this, as I do, one place to pay close attention to is fan films [that] map ideas, personalities and aspirations with serious powers of attraction."

The ad industry has already appropriated the look and style of fan films on numerous occasions, such as short films created with Lego bricks by London-based animation house Spite Your Face Productions. The company's flicks, which include officially commissioned Star Wars, Spider-Man, and Monty Python "bricksploitation" shorts, have been used for viral marketing efforts as well as DVD extras.

Likewise, the U.S.-based Organic Trade Association commissioned San Francisco production house Free Range Studios to create pseudoamateurish efforts like *Grocery Store Wars,* used to promote organic food choices. A $75,000 short starring Cuke Skywalker, Tofu-D2, Chewbroccoli, and Obi-Wan Cannoli, the flick was shot at two grocery stores over the course of a week, from 10 PM to 7 AM every night. "We needed a few cucumbers to play Cuke," remembers director Louis Fox, "and Ham Solo was pretty slimy by the end of the shoot. We tried to keep him in the fridge, but he got really rank and we couldn't wait to throw him out."

Grocery Store Wars and its sister flick, *The Meatrix,* have been seen by over 20 million people combined, and much like Spite Your Face Productions' flicks, have been so successful yet amateuresque that many viewers mistakenly think they're fan efforts instead of corporate-sponsored endeavors.

Mini-Me's Mini-Media. Fan films aren't made to serve the copyright holders, of course; they're there for the fans first and foremost. That, in turn, has seen the rise of a miniature media industry based around fan films, taking people behind the scenes on other fans' filmmaking efforts. Much as the amateur flicks imitate TV series and movies, this similarly amateur media microcosm, which ranges from print to websites to YouTube videos, takes its cues from the real-life magazines and nightly shows that follow every aspect of Hollywood.

Much like the fan films they cover, the quality among these entities varies, and most of them are short-lived. For instance, U.S. Army Major David Noble founded *Fan Films Quarterly,* an extensive zine that often ran as high as 76 pages, before it had to be put on hiatus while he served a tour of duty in Iraq. "We attempted to [emulate] all the cool aspects of magazines we loved to read like *Wizard, Entertainment Weekly, People, Premiere,* and others," he explains. "We took some ideas straight from their pages in terms of layout, content themes, and methods of presentation, but we tailored the product to our own subject." Similarly, *New Voyages/Phase II* produces its own downloadable fanzine that often looks as slick as a licensed Star Trek magazine.

Fan productions can wind up in strange places once they're released on the Internet, as U.S. Army Major David Noble, founder of *Fan Films Quarterly*, discovered while serving in Iraq. Seen with two Nepalese security guards, Noble purchased a bootleg of the fan film *Return of the Ghostbusters*, which was being sold as *Ghostbusters III* in a local Baghdad video store.
(Courtesy of David Noble)

Other fan film entertainment media include websites offering fan film news and interviews, as well as review podcasts. Much as the mainstream media has taken note of fan films through countless news articles, TV reports and even feature films like 2008's *Be Kind Rewind, Son of Rambow,* and *Fanboys* (the latter of which started out as an unfinished fan film until Hollywood bought the script), it seems inevitable that coverage of fan productions will progressively be taken more seriously and commoditized by the corporate world, whether through entertainment destination websites, how-to magazines, or, gee, this book.

The Future Is Now. When a major studio has sunk millions of dollars into a new entertainment property, it's desperate to build the kind of fervid fan base that will eventually want to make fan films based on that property. Once the show or movie is a hit, the studio can follow the example of *Battlestar Galactica, Red Dwarf, Star Wars,* and even *Dungeons & Dragons,* all of which have encouraged fan flicks with contests; some of them have gone so far as to create websites that provide a smattering of official footage and sounds for fan production use. The result is goodwill among fans, added mindshare in the heads of amateur filmmakers as they spend hours thinking about the franchise, and plenty of free publicity as the short films traverse the Internet to be seen by millions.

The thing is, the examples above are all long-standing franchises that don't need the publicity, but why should studios wait for a property to become a hit before tapping that level of fan enthusiasm?

Instead, it's easy to envision that a studio will soon aggressively encourage fan filmmaking as part of its efforts to launch a brand-new property. If fan movies are a grassroots movement, then it would be simple enough to pour Miracle Grow on it by including a fan filmmaking toolkit DVD as a video box-set extra. Studios could get an even earlier jump-start by creating a toolkit area on the show's website as an ongoing, developing feature, not just a temporary platform for a one-off contest. Such a move would essentially say, "Hey, here's a bunch of great visual effects shots and cool sounds, plus some freeware video editing software. Go crazy with it and make sure you spread your fan film based on our show all over the Internet."

Job Placement. Companies across all forms of media are watching fan films with an increasing intensity—not for copyright violations, but for tomorrow's talent pool. Many of the next generation of media makers will likely have a fan film or two under their belts, making directors like Eli Roth—the creator of the Hostel movies who remade *Texas Chainsaw Massacre* in his basement at age 16—the rule rather than the exception. As seen in earlier chapters, the fan film milieu is starting to be treated like a baseball farm league for Hollywood and other media forms, taking a page (so to speak) from the Japanese manga comic book industry. There, it's already a common practice for writers and artists of *dojinshi* comics—amateur comic book equivalents of a fan film, except they're illegally sold for money—to be snapped up by publishers to go pro. In a move akin to that, U.S. fan filmmaker Zeb Wells was recruited in 2002 to write Spider-Man comic books for Marvel after making two goofy superhero shorts for a contest sponsored by *Wizard* magazine.

Fair Use of "Fair Use." There are plenty of entertainment companies whose reaction to efforts like fan productivity is to petition the government for more stringent laws concerning fair use. They're tired of watching people brazenly use their images, songs, characters, and movie clips—the very stuff that fan films are based on—without getting permission or paying royalties. Fair use doctrine is a fragile thing, because it's merely a good idea, not a right, so it's a malleable concept that's open to interpretation—and abuse. To attack fair use, however, might be a shortsighted move; *Fair Use in the U.S. Economy*, a 2007 study by the Computer & Communications Industry Association, suggests that "industries benefiting from fair use and other limitations and exceptions make a large and growing contribution to the US economy. The fair use economy in 2006 accounted for $4.5 trillion in revenues and $2.2 billion in value added, roughly 16.2 percent of US GDP. It employed more than 17 million people and supported a payroll of $1.2 trillion. It generated $194 billion in exports and rapid productivity growth." Fan films, though a drop in the bucket, contributed to those numbers.

Regardless of whether fair use laws get changed, they won't make a difference without an effort to educate the masses. In 2007, two professors at American University and the Washington College of Law surveyed their students, only to discover that 87 percent uploaded copyrighted material to sites like YouTube or Facebook without getting permission from copyright holders, and 76 percent thought that this was OK because it was covered by fair use—although none of them could accurately define the fair use doctrine. You can't get people to stop breaking the law—or even work within it—unless they know what the law is in the first place.

Anything Worth Doing Is Worth Doing Well. All signs point to user-generated content—and, thus, fan films—continuing to rise for the foreseeable future. UK think tank The Future Laboratory predicted that by 2012, a quarter of the entertainment consumed worldwide "will have been created, edited and shared within [people's] peer circle rather than coming out of traditional media groups."

If fan films are going to be seen by more people than ever before, then it wouldn't hurt to explore why some are more successful—and that's already happening at Five Towns College in Dix Hills, New York, about an hour outside New York City. There, one can take a Comics to Film class, where students each shoot their own fan flicks, as well as a fan film done as a group; classwide projects

Professor Dan Galiardi (back row, in glasses) teaches a Comics to Film class at Five Towns College in Dix Hills, New York, where students make fan films for assignments. For *Iron Fist: The Dragon Unleashed*, the cast included professional actor/martial artist Albert Lamont (back row, shirtless).
(Courtesy of Dan Galiardi)

have included Marvel Comics heroes Black Panther and Iron Fist.

The first production proved difficult—the Black Panther got food poisoning on the first day of shooting and a groin injury on the second day—so for the class's *Iron Fist* effort, adjunct professor Dan Galiardi brought in a professional martial artist to play the title role. For Albert Lamont, it was an opportunity to add to his acting résumé. ("Fighting and acting are the same in that you have to be in the moment," he says, "but there's less bruises in acting.") For Galiardi, who was a camera assistant on 1995's *Batman Forever*, the class provided a chance to educate while fulfilling a personal goal: "I wanted to see *Iron Fist* come out well as a great example for the course, but I also wanted to see the character come to life. I love comic books and fan films, so I want to inspire more people to make them, whether they're in the class or watching the film later on YouTube."

For those who find the physical production of a fan film too similar to something resembling work, there's also the academic study of fan films. Professor Daryl Frazetti at Lake Tahoe Community College in California teaches an Anthropology of Star Trek course both at the school and online, covering different aspects, including Trek-related fan films. "I think people are interested in keeping Trek alive through these kinds of creative efforts because they've been so deeply affected by *Star Trek* creator Gene Roddenberry's message of acceptance," he says. "When you put the early series' value system into a fan film, you're showing fans more of the Star Trek ideology than the official series have in recent times."

They're hardly the only academics studying fan films, though; a variety of educators have been exploring the realms of fan fiction and fan cinema for some time, and some of the most noted scholars became involved in an entity from the fan creativity world: the Organization for Transformative Works (OTW).

In its own words, the OTW is

> a nonprofit organization established by fans to serve the interests of fans by providing access to and preserving the history of fanworks and fan culture in its myriad forms. . . . OTW was created to work toward a future in which all fannish works are recognized as legal and transformative, and accepted as legitimate creative activity. Our mission is to be proactive and innovative in protecting and defending our work from commercial exploitation and legal challenge, and to preserve our fannish economy, values, and way of life by protecting and nurturing our fellow fans, our work, our commentary, our history, and our identity, while providing the broadest possible access to fannish activity for all fans.

While no one can be certain what the future will bring for fan films—and, to take a larger view, fan works in general—clearly there's a concern that they be able to continue and flourish while coexisting with official products. While an entity like OTW can come into existence to help promote and protect fan efforts, the fact that people with the most educated views on creative fan hobbies feel it's necessary is notable; the organization's arrival may well portend difficult times to come for all fan-created efforts.

• • •

While fan films are more popular than ever before and are increasingly becoming part of mainstream media, they are also in a state of flux, expanding to include a greater range of film genres as well. While fan films may be a subgroup of fan fiction, these days, they're better defined as part of "fan cinema"—a newer term that can include nonfiction fan films, vidding, dubs and other moving image-related formats.

For instance, there are "fan edits," where fans re-edit feature films, often to remove what they perceive to be dead weight. Most famously, there are numerous versions of *The Phantom Menace* that hack out the dreaded Jar-Jar Binks, but flicks that have gone under the knife are as varied as *Star Trek V*, Tom Hanks' *Cast Away* (removing the "character" of Wilson The Ball), and even rote chick flicks like *Love Actually* and *13 Going on 30*.

Another growing area has been fan documentaries, and ironically many of these productions eventually "go pro," finding legal and proper release. Arguably, they follow in the footsteps of Jason Wishnow's clever *Tatooine or Bust*, a 12-minute short following fans across the United States as they waited for the 1997 Star Wars special edition rereleases. In its wake, a plethora of feature-length fan documentaries were released to coincide with the prequels. Sporting names like *Star Woids, Star Wait,* and *A Galaxy Far, Far Away,* they all followed fans waiting on lines for months to see the various prequels debut; unfortunately, the only thing more boring than standing on a line is *watching* people stand on a line.

Exhibiting even more cross-pollination within fan cinema, fans have started making documentaries based on the fan edit concept—case in point, *Deleted Magic,* an ingenious effort that shows how the original *Star Wars* was made. Editor Garrett Gilchrist cobbled together an alternate cut of the film—built entirely from deleted scenes, alternate takes, and backstage footage, all culled from "making of" TV specials, DVD extras, and the like—and then augmented it with pop-up "fun facts." The surprising result is that his bootleg production is likely the best documentary ever on the first *Star Wars* film.

In all these cases, the concept of what a fan film can be is expanding, but to determine where fan films are going in the future, one has to look at what the films have arisen from: not the franchises but the fans themselves.

Fandom of anything—from sci-fi to sports to birding—is, in many ways, a form of nostalgia (yes, even if it's for a TV show—or bird—you saw ten minutes ago). If most fan films are about sci-fi and fantasy, and many fans first discover those genres as preteens, then it's fair to suggest that the emotional heart of making a fan film—the drive, if you will—has something to do with reclaiming one's childhood. Kids play with dolls (or" action figures," if you prefer) or playact with each other in order to experiment with how adults interact on a simplistic level; they play at being a hero, modeling behavior and coping skills without the associated risks that come with being shot at, flying, and other stunts. Any adult who likes superheroes, for example, likely spent far more hours as a child making up valiant stories on the fly during playtime than he or she did watching the characters on TV or in the movies. As a result, that adult's most familiar experience with a favorite superhero might not be as a complacent viewer but as the author of the hero's adventures.

Making a fan film, then, can be a return to that authorial position—an opportunity to reclaim that sense of ownership and authorship, putting the filmmaker back in touch with one of the reasons that a franchise appealed to him in the first place. As a kid, the franchise may well have provided the chance to use one's own creativity, making the characters and the universe they inhabited a truly proprietary creation, customized to each young fan's tastes, so the chance to explore that world all over again as an adult—and play with grown-up toys such as video cameras in the process—can wind up being just as inviting as playing superheroes may have been back in childhood.

Of course, throwing on a mask and a cape, running around the backyard, and declaring to the world loudly that you're Batman is socially acceptable if you're eight; tack on 20 years and you'll get locked up for psychiatric observation—unless you have a video camera on and are making a fan film (then there's only a 50/50 chance).

Make no mistake—that doesn't mean making a fan flick is a regressive act. For many it's a stepping stone to reawakening their creativity, opening up the door to a whole side of themselves that may not have seen the light of day in some time. Kids are encouraged to be creative—then they grow up a bit and society recommends that they cut it out, fall in line, get it together, act their age, and make some money. Ironically, the money part is what causes many people to start making fan films—because without disposable income, how would they buy the equipment?

If their creativity picks up where it was left off, they're certainly likely to become reinterested in superheroes, space epics, or what have you. Nothing creates nostalgia for the simplicity of childhood more than a nine to five grind, and that basic emotion can be a heady opiate. Svetlana Boym, author of *The Future of Nostalgia*, has defined it as "longing for a home that no longer exists or perhaps has never existed." Certainly people yearn for places like Hogwarts, Tatooine, or Metropolis without ever having set foot in those fictional settings, but they also miss the fact that childhood allowed them to enjoy the respective franchises without having to label them as "guilty pleasures." It's disingenuous for adults to have to adopt such a pose, particularly when for many of them as kids, enjoying a guilty pleasure was more of a survival mechanism.

For example, Cris Macht, who codirected the fan documentary *The Force Among Us* with his sister Cortney, points out, "If you look at family life around when *Star Wars* first came out, a lot of us in Generation X were coming from broken homes, divorces, and single parents. That movie was a positive thing in the lives of a lot of kids, and they used it as a tool to get through hard times. I think that's why so many people feel such a deep, personal connection to it even now as adults."

With that in mind, it's no coincidence that when Macht's age group brought fan films into the mainstream in the late nineties, it did so in the form of Star Wars productions. Most of Generation X was in its twenties at that point—the age when childhood is declared over once and for all. Millions of slackers were ripe for the onset of nostalgia for a kid's existence.

Younger suburban generations have been raised differently, however. Ultraregimented after-school agendas of sports and classes have replaced unstructured playtime in many areas, so once today's kids reach a nostalgic age they're likely to be fond of something else other than drawing straws to see which kid has to play the bad guy—because they never had the chance to experience that. Instead, with multiple age groups now raised on video games, machinima—the fan cinema genre where video games are used to tell a story—seems primed to take the place of traditional fan films. If Gen X fan filmmakers can be seen as making fan flicks in order to relive the days when they played in the backyard with action figures, machinima fans will likely be doing that with the video games they've played.

Because of shifts like this, the days of the fan film as we know it—as it's been illustrated throughout this book—are probably numbered. Fan creativity will still be around, and fan fiction will be as plentiful as ever, but fan cinema—including fan films—will change to reflect the most popular media forms of the day. We're already seeing that shift as the popularity of 40-minute fan films gives way to 40-second fan shorts on YouTube. Where entertainment goes, fan media follows, and not merely in form but in content as well.

Entertainment—that is to say, pop culture—is always about the momentary buzz, the brief escape from the now. Fan films, then, are the faint echo of that buzz; they aren't designed to hold up over time, but are instead gut reactions to current popular media—and if a blockbuster movie can make $150 million yet be out of theaters in less than two months, even the best fan creations that spring up around it are going to be temporary as well.

When viewed without acknowledging a larger societal context, fan media that is particularly of its time—like 1969's *Bambi Meets Godzilla*, for instance—experiences a relevancy half-life; it may continue on through the years, but its significance decreases the farther away it gets from the original point of impact.

Watching *Bambi Meets Godzilla* today, it is hard to fathom the short's impact, because we don't see it under the same conditions as its early fans did—at 1 AM on a Saturday night in a crammed, college-town movie theater full of students probably high as hell, who didn't have advertisers selling them subversion and pseudo-individuality on every corner as they do today. The shock and effect of a short like *Bambi Meets Godzilla* ripped reality (already in a tenuous grasp under those circumstances) a brand-new one—and yet we can't truly appreciate that today, even though it was enough to propel the short to a cult status that continues to this day.

Context is a key ingredient for understanding why fan films are made and what their ultimate effect on fandom is, if any. You can never go back to the first time you encountered a franchise and re-experience to the same degree how it affected you. As a result, for some fans, the only way to get close to that experience is to find out how the original was made and then make their own version—to re-create it in the new context of now. Certainly, that's what Hollywood does with its endless stream of sequels, remakes, and knockoffs. Maybe, for a fan whose enthusiasm as been tapped-out, that's the only way to make G.I. Joe or Star Wars feel fresh again.

But if you're reaching that far to keep something relevant, regardless of whether you're a fan or a studio development executive, maybe it's time to let it go. If sci-fi traditionally portends the future, why cling to franchises that are decades old? Just because a genre franchise has been around forever doesn't mean it can remain relevant forever, nor that it can be updated. Flash Gordon has been brought back plenty of times but never truly successfully. The same thing goes for the Lone Ranger and his fictional descendant, the Green Hornet, yet they're cherished characters to a certain age group that grew up with them.

Most franchises are supported by casual fans; people like a TV show or movie, enjoy it and either become hardcore fans or move on. If a franchise can no longer sustain the number of casual fans necessary to continue as a going concern, studios should let it die—and let it die for good. Dead franchises should be bequeathed to the fans like a rich old fogie's estate being turned into public park lands. Let the plebeians—the diehards—run around, play with it, and enjoy it. When a franchise has created 700 hours' worth of material—700 stories!—the only people who really need to explore it any further are its most ardent fans; let them make fan films, fan fiction, and the like—and let the rest of the world move on.

Few studios heed that call, however; it's all too apt that franchises are called "properties" because they always wind up getting overdeveloped until the original splendor has been obliterated. Arguably the worst thing that ever happened to the Star Wars franchise was more Star Wars. When the original trilogy concluded, there were only 6 hours and 19 minutes worth of movies to watch. Because of that, there was plenty left unexplored in that "universe"; it was a wonderful, tantalizing unknown. Once you add a prequel trilogy, TV shows, and "expanded universe" books and comics ad nauseam, inevitably new information about laws, customs, and history adds a patina of detail, but it also makes the window looking into the unknown that much smaller.

And yet the unknown is attracts people to any movie or TV series in the first place, regardless of whether it's *2001: A Space Odyssey* or *Sex in the City*—because folks want to watch something that they haven't seen before. Take away the unknown and the sense of escape, and all you have left is the known—the antithesis of escape.

People have always needed to vacate their lives for a while; it's part of why we dream. But we can dream without Hollywood's help—we all have creativity in us, whether it's lying there dormant or being used every second of the day. Fan creations—whether they're fan fiction, films, or crocheted potholders with the Hulk's face on them—all may be derived from mass entertainment, but they use it more as a springboard for jumping headlong into the pool of one's own ingenuity.

If fan films are proof of anything, then, it's that society's expectations—cultural, interpersonal, and sometimes even legal—can't stop regular people from getting in touch with the artist within and using the materials of the world around them to create something new. Sometimes those materials are a set of watercolors that will be used to paint a pastoral landscape, and other times, it's a camera watching kids who think they're in an Our Gang movie. It's just a different paradigm, and whether the result is brilliant or wretched is completely beside the point. A fan film may be, as noted in chapter 1, the cinematic equivalent of a two-year-old drawing on a wall, but so what? Making one's own movie is a step, an action, an experience—and having an experience means you're living your life instead of passively watching someone else's on a screen.

Bibliography

Abbott, Myles. Interview by author. E-mail. April 22, 1999.

Ackerman, David. *Women and Digital Lifestyles Report*. Toronto: Solutions Research Group, 2008.

"Adobe Premiere 5.0 Now Shipping." Adobe.Com; web.archive.org/web/19980703085508/www1.adobe.com/aboutadobe/publicrelations/HTML/9805/980518.prm5.html (accessed November 18, 2007).

Age of Disconnect Anxiety. Toronto: Solutions Research Group, 2008.

Allen, Jeff. "Trooper Clerks." Trooper Clerks; http://www.trooperclerks.com (accessed November 20, 2007).

———. Interview by author. E-mail. January 21, 1999.

"Alpha Dog Productions." Alpha Dog Productions; http://www.alphadogproductions.net (accessed September 15, 2007).

"Amateur Fiction Filmmaking as a Family Bond." Northeast Historic Film: A Moving Image Archive Specializing in Northern New England; http://www.oldfilm.org/nhfWeb/ed/05Symp/05Symp_Barstow.htm (accessed July 2, 2007).

"An American Animator in Canada." *Words & Pictures*. Portland, OR: KBOO-FM, October 31, 2006.

"Andy Warhol 1964." Andy Warhol: Warholstars; http://www.warholstars.org/chron/1964.html#batman (accessed November 1, 2007).

"Andrew Koenig." Internet Movie Database (IMDB); http://www.imdb.com/name/nm0462809 (accessed December 9, 2007).

Ante, Spencer. "Hollywood at Hyperspeed." Wired News; http://www.wired.com/wired/archive/6.06/newmedia.html?pg=7 (accessed November 21, 2005).

"Apple's iMovie Software Brings Digital Video Editing to Consumers and Classrooms." Apple.Com; web.archive.org/web/19991128234124/http://www.apple.com/pr/library/1999/oct/05imovie.html (accessed November 18, 2007).

Arnett, Bryant. Interview by author. Phone. New York, March 26, 1998.

"Average Home Has More TVs Than People." USAToday.com; http://www.usatoday.com/life/television/news/2006-09-21-homes-tv_x.htm (accessed February 20, 2008).

Bacon-Smith, Camille. *Enterprising Women: Television Fandom and the Creation of Popular Myth*. Publication of the American Folklore Society. Philadelphia: University of Pennsylvania Press, 1992.

"Bambi Meets Godzilla (1969)." Internet Movie Database (IMDB); http://www.imdb.com/title/tt0064064 (accessed May 19, 2007).

"Bambi Meets Godzilla @ EOFFTV." The Encyclopedia of Fantastic Film and Television. http://www.eofftv.com/b/bam/bambi_meets_godzilla_main.htm (accessed May 19, 2007).

"Bambi Meets Godzilla." British Film Institute Film & TV Database; http://ftvdb.bfi.org.uk/sift/title/142823 (accessed May 20, 2007).

Barnes, Brooks. "Direct-to-DVD Releases Shed Their Loser Label." *NYTimes.com via Yahoo! Finance,*; http://biz.yahoo.com/nytimes/080128/1194741363753.html?.v=8 (accessed January 28, 2008).

Barstow, Robbins, Jr. Interview by author. Phone. January 31, 2006.

———. "The Robbins Barstow 20th Century Family Home Movie Collection." *Barstow Family 2005 Christmas Newsletter*, December 2005.

Barthes, Roland. *Image, Music, Text*. Edited by Stephen Heath. London: Fontana, 1977.

Basinger, Stuart. Interview by author. Phone. September 25, 2007.

———. "Moonraker '78: Behind-the-Scenes of a Classic James Bond Fan Film." Dr. Shatterhand's Botanical Garden; http://shatterhand007.com/Moonraker78/Moonraker78.html (accessed September 24, 2007).

Bat in the Sun Productions; www.batinthesun.com (accessed December 17, 2007).

Baumgarten, Martin W. "Eight Millimeter Film History: A Short History of Small Gauge Movie Films." 8mm Film Stock; http://www.8mmfilmstock.com/history.html (accessed October 12, 2007).

Beck, Jerry. *50 Greatest Cartoons as Selected by 1000*. Nashville: Turner, 1980.

Benfer, Amy. "Just Don't Tell Mom We Burned Up the Basement." *Metro*, July 6, 2007.

Bertges, Jim. "Sandy Collora: Art & Passion." *Modeler's Resource*, October 1, 1999.

Binninger, Art. "Art Binninger's Star Trix: Of Clay and Cardboard"; http://spritzer93436.tripod.com (accessed December 27, 2007).

———. Interview by author. E-mail. December 27, 2007.

Bird, Cameron. "Raiders of Spielberg's 'Ark.'" *Newsday*, July 4, 2007.

"Blasovits Family Tree." DonaldFGlut.com; http://www.donaldfglut.com/SavedSites/btree.htm (accessed May 22, 2007).

Bohus, Ted A. "Hugh Hefner." *SPFX* 8 (July 2000).

Borland, John. "Homegrown Star Wars, with big-screen magic intact." CNet News.www.news.com/Homegrown-Star-Wars%2C-with-big-screen-magic-intact/2100-1026_3-5678819.html (accessed February 13, 2007).

Botwin, Michelle. "Force Is with 'Star Wars' Fan Site." *Chicago Sun-Times*, December 5, 2000.

———. "Imitation Is Silliest Form of Flattery." *Los Angeles Times*, April 24, 1999.

Brady, Frank. *Hefner*. New York: Macmillan, 1974.

Brady, Terrence. "Comics2Film: Dan Poole Interview." Comics2Film; http://www.comics2film.com/DanPoole.shtml (accessed September 9, 2007).

Burfitt, Kevin. Interview by author. E-mail. April 22, 1999.

———. "StarLego—Torps Productions." The Torps. http://www.torps.com/starlego.html (accessed January 25, 2008).

Busam, Joe. Interview by author. E-mail. June 1, 2007.

Busse, Kristina, Francesca Coppa, and Karen Hellekson. *Fan Fiction and Fan Communities in the Age of the Internet*. Jefferson, NC: McFarland, 2006.

Button, Joseph. "Screensaver—Interview with Sandy Collora." Silverbulletcomics.com; http://www.silverbulletcomics.com/news/story.php?a=5667 (accessed December 17, 2007).

Calhoun, Bob. "Hardware Wars: The Movie, the Legend, the Household Appliances—Salon." Salon Directory; http://dir.salon.com/story/ent/movies/feature/2002/05/21/hardware_wars/index.html (accessed May 28, 2007).

"California Dreaming." *Airbrush Action*, October 1, 1995.

Campbell, Jane. "Cartoon Festival Is a Big Draw." *Independent*, October 17, 2005; http://findarticles.com/p/articles/mi_qn4158/is_20051017/ai_n15710692 (accessed May 20, 2007).

Campos, Eric. "Batman: Dead End." Film Threat; http://www.filmthreat.

com/index.php?section=reviews&Id=4789 (accessed December 17, 2007).

———. "Review: The Real Spider-Man: The Making of the Green Goblin's Last Stand." Film Threat; http://www.filmthreat.com/index.php?section=reviews&Id=2540 (accessed September 9, 2007).

Cardozo, Bruce. Interview by author. E-mail. March 30, 2008.

———. "Spider-Man Movie." *Foom*, winter 1974.

———. Interview by author. Phone. May 31, 2007.

———. Interview by author. Phone. June 14, 2007.

Cawley, James. Interview by author. Phone. New York, February 5, 2008.

"Cinemagic." Monster Magazines: The First Decade—Fanzines; http://www.geocities.com/unifan2001/Cinemagic.html (accessed October 3, 2007).

"Charlotte Fullerton." Enigmacon X Info; http://www.enigmacon.org/content/view/151/33 (accessed November 21, 2005).

"Clark Bartram—America's Most Trusted Fitness Professional." Bodybuilding.com; http://www.bodybuilding.com/fun/clark.htm (accessed December 17, 2007).

Cohen, Karl. "Module 2 Lecture." Webshiva home; http://www.webshiva.com/Spring_2005_History_Animation/lectures/module_2.html (accessed May 19, 2007).

Collora, Sandy. Interview by author. E-mail. May 14, 2007.

———. Interview by author. E-mail. February 14, 2008.

"Comic-Con 2003: Sandy Collora Interview, Director of Batman: Dead End." iFilm.Com; www.ifilm.com/video/2474411 (accessed December 3, 2007).

Cooke, Bill. "Spooks-A-Talkin'! Video Maverick Mike Vraney on the Making of his *Spook Show Spectacular* DVD." *Video Watchdog*, March 2002.

Cooper, A. David. "Rise of the Real Batman." MacDirectory Magazine; http://www.macdirectory.com/newmd/mac/pages/NTRVU/RealBatman/index.html (accessed December 17, 2007).

Coppa, Francesca. "In Media Res Blog Archive: Celebrating Kandy Fong: Founder of Fannish Music Video." MediaCommons; http://mediacommons.futureofthebook.org/videos/2007/11/19/celebrating-kandy-fong-founder-of-fannish-music-video/ (accessed March 11, 2008).

Cordell, Kasey. "Pueblo Artist Deals in Lore Cards." Pueblo Chieftain Online; http://www.pueblochieftain.com/metro/1092722400/7/sea+%22world+comics%22+%22hardware+wars%22&hl=en&ct=clnk&cd=3&gl=us&client=firefox-a (accessed May 28, 2007).

Cosentino, John. "Paragon's Paragon." *Cinemagic*, spring 1976.

Cowings, Dawn. Interview by author. E-mail. May 2, 2007.

Cox, Dan, and Benedict Carver. "Tatty Tapes Tout Tyros (Filmmakers Break into Hollywood with Short Videos)." *Variety*, December 7, 1998.

Culbreath, Myrna, and Sondra Marshak. *Star Trek: The New Voyages*. New York: Bantam Books, 1976.

———. *Star Trek: The New Voyages 2*. New York: Bantam Books, 1977.

"D. Ray Craig." D. Ray Craig; http://usersites.horrorfind.com/home/horror/moviemaker/draycraig.html (accessed May 22, 2007).

Davidson, Sean. "Web Slinger." Sean Davidson; http://www.sean-davidson.com/articles/web_slinger.html (accessed September 9, 2007).

Davies, Dave. "From Fun to Fame: A Videomaker's *Star Wars* Spoof Has Become an Internet Hit." *Camcorder*, July 1998.

Dean, Katie. "May the Farce Be with Them." Wired News; http://www.wired.com/culture/lifestyle/news/2002/04/51939 (accessed January 26, 2008).

"DIY Filmmakers: *The Star Wars* Creators Troy Durrett and Lance Robson." Film Threat. http://www.filmthreat.com/index.php?section=interviews&Id=42 (accessed November 19, 2007).

"Don Dohler, Times-Herald Editor and Filmmaker, Dead at 60." Times Herald Online. http://www.timesheraldnews.com/2006/12/08/don-dohler-times-herald-editor-and-filmmaker-dead-at-60 (accessed October 3, 2007).

Doughrity, Joe. "In the Scope: Sandy Collora." PopCultureShock; http://popcultureshock.com/features.php?id=1074 (accessed February 23, 2006).

Duxbury, Warren. Interview by author. E-mail. March 5, 1999.

Eggerton, John. "Study: Students Don't Understand Copyright Rules." Broadcasting and Cable; http://www.broadcastingcable.com/article/CA6432259.html (accessed April 12, 2007).

Estes, Marilyn. "Troops Script Supervisor Journal." *Troops Bootleg* (DVD-ROM Extra) 1 (1998): 1.

Evangelista, Benny. "Lights, Sabers, Action! *Star Wars* Fan Films Out of This World Thanks to Cheaper, Powerful Technology." *San Francisco Chronicle*, May 9, 2005.

Evans, Sam. "Zeb Wells: Tangled Zeb." Comics Bulletin; http://www.comicsbulletin.com/features/103438653075245.htm (accessed March 11, 2008).

"FanFiction.Net-Books." FanFiction.Net; www.fanfiction.net/book (accessed February 8, 2008).

Farr, Toryn. "What's Wrong with This Picture? An Interview With Kevin Rubio." Echo Station; http://www.echostation.com/interview/kevin_rubio.htm (accessed December 1, 2005).

Felux, Shane. Interview by author. Phone. New York, February 8, 2005.

Ferrington, Adam J. "A Borrowed Plot." Columbia Chronicle; http://www.columbiachronicle.com/paper/arts.php?id=1459 (accessed September 4, 2007).

Fleming, Michael. "*Batman* Captures Director Nolan." Variety.Com; http://www.variety.com/index.asp?layout=story&articleid=VR1117879566&categoryid=13&cs=1 (accessed December 17, 2008).

Ford, Luke. "The Erotic Horror of Don Glut." Luke Ford; http://www.lukeford.net/profiles/profiles/don_glut.htm (accessed May 22, 2007).

Fosselius, Ernie. Interview by author. Phone. June 21, 2007.

Fox, Louis. Interview by author. Phone. June 30, 2005.

Frazetti, Daryl. Interview by author. Phone. November 12, 2007.

Freedman, Jeffrey M. "Screenwriting, Writing Contests." Script Magazine; http://www.scriptmag.com/earticles/earticle.php?404 (accessed May 28, 2007).

Freedman, Mark. "Marv Newland's International Rocketship: A West Coast original." *Take One*, June 22, 1997.

Freer, Ian. "Steven Spielberg on the Lessons and Legacy of Indy." *Empire*, October 2006.

Fullerton, Charlotte. Interview by author. Phone. March 26, 1998.

Galiardi, Dan. Interview by author. Dix Hills, NY, November 2, 2007.

Gasking, Lincoln. Interview by author. E-mail. March 16, 1999.

"George Lucas in Love." G4 TV; http://www.g4tv.com/techtvvault/features/18189/George_Lucas_in_Love.html (accessed October 26, 2007).

"George Takei Does Internet *Star Trek*." CBS News; http://www.cbsnews.com/stories/2006/09/25/ap/entertainment/mainD8KBU6P00.shtml (accessed September 25, 2006).

Gerrold, David. *The World of Star Trek*. New York: Ballantine Books, 1979.

Glut, Don. *Jurassic Classics: A Collection of Saurian Essays and Mesozoic Musings*. Jefferson: McFarland & Company, 2001.

———. Interview by author. E-mail. May 16, 2007.

———. Interview by author. Phone. December 9, 2005.

Gordon, Andrew. "ET as Fairy Tale." *Nursery Realms: Children in the Worlds of Science Fiction, Fantasy, and Horror*. Proceedings of the J. Lloyd Eaton Conference on Science Fiction & Fantasy Literature. Athens: University of Georgia Press, 1993.

Gore, Chris. "DIY Filmmakers: Kevin Rubio's *Troops*." Film Threat. http://www.filmthreat.com/index.php?section=interviews&Id=76 (accessed January 25, 2008).

———. "Interview with Michael Wiese." Michael Wiese Productions & Books; http://mwp.com/about_us/interview.php4 (accessed May 29, 2007).

———. "The Real Spider-Man: Dan Poole Interview." Film Threat; http://www.filmthreat.com/index.php?section=interviews&Id=105 (accessed September 9, 2007).

Grandjean, Pat. "Tarzan Lives." *Connecticut*, December 2007.

Grocery Store Wars press release. Greenfield, MA: Organic Trade Association, 2005.

Halter, Ed. "A Jones for Indiana." Village Voice; http://www.villagevoice.com/nyclife/0727,halter,77128,15.html (accessed October 2, 2007).

Harmon, Amy. "'Star Wars' Fan Films Come Tumbling Back to Earth." New York Times; http://query.nytimes.com/gst/fullpage.html?res=9D0DE6DA1F3FF93BA15757C0A9649C8B63&scp=18&sq=&st=nyt (accessed November 30, 2005).

Head, Steve. "The Making of *George Lucas in Love*: An Interview with Creators." TheForce.Net; http://www.theforce.net/jedicouncil/interview/glil.asp (accessed November 20, 2007).

Hefner, Hugh M., and Bill Zehme. *Hef's Little Black Book*. New York: Harper Entertainment, 2004.

Henderson, Jan Alan. "Monster Rumble." *FilmFax*, February–March 1999.

Hepola, Sarah. "*Lost Ark*, Resurrected: Three Kids on a Seven-Year Shoot Produce One Heck of an Homage." Austin Chronicle; http://www.austinchronicle.com/gyrobase/Issue/story?oid=oid%3A161565 (accessed September 5, 2007).

Hilberman, Jessica. "Monsters, Inc.: The Making of Sandy Collora." Wired News; http://www.wired.com/wired/archive/12.02/play_pr.html (accessed December 17, 2007).

Hills, Matthew. *Fan Cultures*. Sussex Studies in Culture and Communication. New York: Routledge, 2002.

Howard, Fred. Interview by author. Phone. March 26, 1998.

Hudgens, John. "Dragon*Con Biography: John Hudgens." Welcome to Dragon*Con! http://www.dragoncon.org/people/hudgenj.html (accessed October 23, 2007).

———. Interview by author. E-mail. February 27, 1999.

Jenkins, Henry. *Convergence Culture: Where Old and New Media Collide*. New York: New York University Press, 2006.

———. Interview by author. Phone. March 3, 2008.

Jimenez, John. "George Lucas in Love." *Video Store Magazine*, January 14, 2001.

Johnston, Rick. "World's Favourite . . . But Not Warners."" Comic Book Resources. http://www.comicbookresources.com/columns/index.cgi?column=litg&article=1929 (accessed December 16, 2007).

Jones, Sara Gwenllian, Xavier Mendik, and Steven Jay Schneider. *Underground U.S.A.: Filmmaking beyond the Hollywood Canon*. New York: Wallflower Press, 2002.

Katz, Louis. Interview by author. E-mail. December 23, 1998.

Kaufman, Alan. *Jew Boy: A Memoir*. New York: Fromm, 2000.

Kim, Liz. "A New Generation Discovers Making Movies with Super 8." Columbia News Service; http://jscms.jrn.columbia.edu/cns/2006-11-28/kim-super8filmmakers (accessed October 2, 2007).

Kimball, Marc. Interview by author. E-mail. New York, May 1, 2008.

———. "Superman Trailer Download Today." Postforum—Digital Post Production Resources. http://www.postforum.com/forums/read.php?f=38&i=210&t=210 (accessed December 10, 2007).

King, Brad. "May the Shorts Be with You." Wired News; http://www.wired.com/entertainment/music/news/2002/05/52231 (accessed May 28, 2007).

Kjb. "IGN: Spotlight on Fan Films." IGN Movies; http://movies.ign.com/articles/543/543203p1.html (accessed January 25, 2008).

Knowles, Harry. "Raiders of the Lost Ark Shot-for-Shot Teenage Remake Review." Ain't It Cool News. http://www.aintitcool.com/node/15348 (accessed September 4, 2007).

Knowles, Jay. "Father Geek Has a Talk with Batman: Dead End Director Sandy Collora. . . ." Ain't It Cool News; http://www.aintitcool.com/node/15721 (accessed December 17, 2007).

Lamont, Albert. Interview by author. Dix Hills, NY, November 2, 2007.

Lasica, J. D. *Darknet: Hollywood's War against the Digital Generation*. New York: Wiley, 2005.

Lemire, Christy. "Women Directors Shine; Numbers Still Low." USAToday.com; http://www.usatoday.com/life/movies/2007-08-01-1773314053_x.htm (accessed August 1, 2007).

Lenburg, Jeff. *Who's Who in Animated Cartoons: An International Guide to Film and Television's Award-Winning and Legendary Animators*. New York: Applause Books, 2006.

Levitz, Paul. Interview by author. New York, April 18, 2008.

Levy, David. *Your Career in Animation: How to Survive and Thrive*. New York: Allworth Press, 2006.

Levy, Frederick. *Short Films 101: How to Make a Short and Launch Your Filmmaking Career*. Chicago: Perigee Trade, 2004.

Levy, Piet. "Talk about Adventure: A 'Lost Ark' Is Discovered." *Chicago Tribune*, May 29, 2002; http://metromix.chicagotribune.com/movies/mmx-0505290449may29,0,2002495.story?coll=mmx-movies_heds (accessed February 5, 2007).

Lewisohn, Mark. "*Monty Python's Flying Circus*." BBC—Comedy Guide; http://www.bbc.co.uk/comedy/guide/articles/m/montypythonsflyi_1299002137.shtml (accessed May 19, 2007).

Lichtenberg, Jacqueline, Sondra Marshak, and Joan Winston. *Star Trek Lives: Personal Notes and Anecdotes*. New York: Bantam Books, 1975.

Linzmayer, Owen. *Apple Confidential 2.0: The Definitive History of the World's Most Colorful Company*. San Francisco: No Starch Press, 2004.

"Little Stabs at Happiness." Frieze Magazine; http://www.frieze.com/issue/article/little_stabs_at_happiness (accessed November 1, 2007).

"Live Like a Suicide, 1986." Bebo.com; http://www.bebo.com/MusicAlbum.jsp?MusicAlbumId=3301071947&MemberId=1956661140 (accessed March 31, 2008).

Long, Jason. Interview by author. E-mail. February 6, 2007.

Lyman, Rick. "An Internet Star Is Born." *New York Times*, June 12, 2000.

Lynch, Richard. "1960s Fan History Outline, Chapter 6." Jophan.Org; http://www.jophan.org/1960s/chapter6.htm (accessed October 3, 2007).

Macht, Chris. Interview by author. Phone. May 10, 2007.

Mamet, David. *Bambi vs. Godzilla: On the Nature, Purpose, and Practice of the Movie Business*. New York: Pantheon, 2007.

Markham, Curt. Interview by author. E-mail. April 14, 1999.

Markman, Kris M. "Star Trek, Fan Film, and the Internet: Possibilities and Constraints of Fan-Based Vernacular Cultures." All Academic Inc.; http://www.allacademic.com/meta/p14905_index.html (accessed October 29, 2007).

Marples, Gareth. "The History of Camcorders—The Smaller the Better." The History of . . . ; http://www.thehistoryof.net/the-history-of-camcorders.html (accessed September 4, 2007).

Marriott, F., and S. Marriott. "Home Movies: The Family Historian's Perspective." Marriott World; http://www.marriottworld.com/articles/film_history.htm (accessed October 11, 2007).

Martin, Bob. "John Carpenter." *Fangoria*, October 1980.

Martin, Maurice. "Film: Tobey Maguire Got the Big Bucks, but Dan Poole Got to Spider-Man First." Baltimore City Paper; http://www.citypaper.com/film/story.asp?id=4600 (accessed September 9, 2007).

Mather, Evan. "Evanmather.com." Evanmather.com; http://www.evanmather.com (accessed October 23, 2007).

———. Interview by author. E-mail. March 17, 1998.

McGuire, Marc. "Fans at the Helm." *Albany Times Union*, February 12, 2006.

Mcweeny, Drew. "Is Sandy Collora Going to Direct *Shazam*?" Ain't It Cool News; http://www.aintitcool.com/node/16520 (accessed December 17, 2007).

———. "Wait a Minute . . . There." Ain't It Cool News; http://www.aintitcool.com/node/15693 (accessed December 17, 2007).

Meddis, Sam Vincent. "Tech Extra: Tickle Your Funny Bone or Tickle Elvis." *USA Today*, May 19, 1999.

Melnick, Monte A., and Frank Meyer. *On the Road with the Ramones*. London: Sanctuary, 2003.

Mirapaul, Matthew. "Making Movies, the Do-It-Yourself Way, on the Web." New York Times; http://www.nytimes.com/library/tech/99/01/cyber/artsatlarge/21artsatlarge.html (accessed October 23, 2007).

Morris, Clint. "Star Wars: The Dark Redemption: Interview." Web Wombat; http://www.webwombat.com.au/entertainment/movies/darkr_int.htm (accessed May 17, 2007).

Moshier, Christopher. "Green Goblin's Last Stand Creator Dan Poole." Comic Book Bin; http://www.comicbookbin.com/fanfilmfolliesinterview_danpoole.html (accessed September 9, 2007).

Moskowitz, Sam. *The Immortal Storm: A History of Science Fiction Fandom*. Westport, CT: Hyperion Press, 1988.

Nelson, Peggy. "Portrait of the Artist as a Young Indiana Jones." OtherZine; http://www.othercinema.com/otherzine/index.php?issueid=1&article_id=4 (accessed January 26, 2008).

———. "Round Table Roundabout." OtherZine 7; http://www.othercinema.com/otherzine/index.php?issueid=1&article_id=6 (accessed January 26, 2008).

"New Findings Based on Gender Stereotypes." Geena Davis Institute on Gender in Media; www.thegeenadavisinstitute.org/downloads/2_1_08GDIGMRelease.pdf (accessed February 8, 2008).

Nobel, David. "From the Editor's Desk." *Fan Films Quarterly*, spring 2007.

"Nokia Predicts 25% of Entertainment by 2012 Will Be Created and Consumed within Peer Communities." WebWire; http://www.webwire.com/

ViewPressRel.asp?aId=54227 (accessed December 7, 2007).

"Not That Starr War." *Newsweek*, September 28, 1998.

Notarile, Chris. Interview by author. E-mail. April 13, 2007.

Nowak, Peter. "*Star Wars* on a Shoestring." New Zealand Herald; http://www.nzherald.co.nz/section/story.cfm?c_id=5&objectid=10122816 (accessed February 13, 2008).

Noxon, Christopher. "Fan Fare." Christopher Noxon; http://www.christophernoxon.com/inside_sub_fanfare.html (accessed December 8, 2005).

Nussbaum, Joe. Interview by author. E-mail. November 2, 2007.

Ono, Kent A., and John M. Sloop. "The Critique of Vernacular Discourse." *Communication Monographs* 62 (1995).

"Organization for Transformative Works." Organization for Transformative Works; http://www.transformativeworks.org (accessed March 30, 2008).

"Over $1 Million Worth of Hollywood Memorabilia Sold at Profiles in History's Auction on December 10, 2004." BNET.com; http://findarticles.com/p/articles/mi_m0EIN/is_2004_Dec_11/ai_n8564369 (accessed December 6, 2007).

Perez, Valerie. Interview by author. E-mail. November 20, 2007.

Perkins, Stephen. "Approaching the '80s Zine Scene: Science Fiction Fanzines." The Book of Zines; http://zinebook.com/resource/perkins/perkins2.html (accessed September 30, 2007).

Perry, Steve. *Shadows of the Empire*. New York: Spectra, 1997.

Phillips, David R. "LFL and Internet Copyright Issues." Echo Station; http://www.echostation.com/features/lfl_wookiee.htm (accessed February 4, 2008).

Poole, Dan. Interview by author. Phone. September 9, 2007.

Pyne, Erin. Interview by author. E-mail. April 11, 2007.

"Pyramid Media." Pyramid Media; http://www.pyramidmedia.com/index.html (accessed May 28, 2007).

Ramone, Tommy. Interview by author. Phone. June 22, 2007.

Ramschissel, Kurt. Interview by author. E-mail. March 17, 1998.

Reid, Glenn. "iMovie 08 Doesn't Cut It." GlennReid.com; http://blog.glennreid.com/ (accessed November 19, 2007).

"Remake of the Lost Ark." *Empire*, October 2006.

"Rest and Retaliation." *Star Trek: New Voyages Communications eNewsletter*, January 22, 2008.

Richards, Andrea. Interview by author. E-mail. February 11, 2008.

Rinzler, J.W. *The Making of Star Wars: The Definitive Story behind the Original*

Film. New York: Del Rey, 2007.

Roberts, Kevin. "KR Connect: Fan Films." KR Connect; http://krconnect.blogspot.com/2007/07/fan-films.html (accessed January 12, 2008).

Robischon, Noah. "George Lucas in Love." *Entertainment Weekly*, December 17, 1999.

Robson, Lance. Interview by author. E-mail. November 26, 2007.

Rogers, Thomas, and Andrew Szamosszegi. *Fair Use in the U.S. Economy: 2007 Economic Contribution of Industries Relying on Fair Use*. Washington, D.C.: Computer & Communications Industry Association, 2007.

Rossignol, Joyce. "Robbins Barstow Follows His Bliss with His Camcorder and Community Television." *Wethersfield Life*, December 1997.

Roth, Eli. Interview by author. E-mail. September 21, 0007.

Rubio, Kevin. Interview by author. E-mail. May 20, 2007.

———. Interview by author. Phone. March 26, 1998.

Russo, James. "The World of Super 8 Film." Home Toys—The Home Technology Information Source; http://www.hometoys.com/htinews/dec05/articles/russo/super8.htm (accessed August 31, 2007).

Sandza, Richard W. "Herald Editor Don Dohler Dies at 60." Times Herald Online; http://www.timesheraldnews.com/2006/12/08/times-herald-editor-don-dohler-dies-at-60 (accessed October 2, 2007).

"Sandy Collora Biography." Collora Studios; http://www.collorastudios.com/sandymain.htm (accessed December 3, 2007).

Sansweet, Stephen J., and Peter Vilmur. *The Star Wars Vault: Thirty Years of Treasures from the Lucasfilm Archives*. New York: Harper Entertainment, 2007.

Schoenke, Aaron. Interview by author. Phone. December 27, 2007.

"Scott Mathews Extended Biography." Scott Mathews: Multi-Platinum Award Winning Music Producer and Songwriter; http://www.scott-mathews.com/biography.html (accessed July 2, 2007).

Scott, Michael. "Cinemagic." GeoCities; http://www.geocities.com/unifan2001/Cinemagic.html (accessed October 3, 2007).

Seibold, Chris. "This Day in Apple History: July 24, 2000: Steve Jobs Predicts iMovie will be bigger than Desktop Publishing." Apple Matters; http://www.applematters.com/index.php/section/history/july-24-2000-steve-jobs-predicts-imovie-will-be-bigger-than-desktop-publish (accessed November 18, 2007).

———. "This Day in Apple History: June 29, 1998: Glenn Reid Tastes the Apple." Apple Matters; http://www.applematters.com/index.php/section/history/june-29-1998-glenn-reid-tastes-the-apple/ (accessed January 25, 2008).

Sellers, Dennis. "Macsimum News Interviews Creator of iPhoto, iMovie, Bubbler." Macsimum News; http://www.macsimumnews.com/index.php/archive/macsimum_news_interviews_creator_of_iphoto_imovie_bubbler/ (accessed January 25, 2008).

Serjeant, Jill. "Spoof Short of Lucas Is a Runaway Hit on the Web." *Chicago Tribune*, May 20, 2000.

Shafer, Anthony. Interview by author. E-mail. February 6, 2007.

Shapiro, Mark. "History of Camcorders." Internet Video Magazine; http://www.internetvideomag.com/Articles-2006/112706_historyofcamcorders.htm (accessed September 4, 2007).

Silverman, Jason. "A Wretched Hive of Fan Films." Wired News; http://www.wired.com/entertainment/music/news/2004/07/64067 (accessed January 7, 2008).

———. "Gallery: The Making of Raiders of the Lost Ark: The Adaptation." Wired News; http://www.wired.com/entertainment/hollywood/multimedia/2007/05/gallery_raiders?slide=1&slideView=5 (accessed September 4, 2007).

———. "Ultimate *Indy* Flick: Fanboys Remake Raiders of the Lost Ark." Wired News; http://www.wired.com/print/entertainment/hollywood/news/2007/05/diy_raiders (accessed September 4, 2007).

Simpson, M. J. "Forrest J Ackerman interview." MJSimpson.co.uk; http://www.mjsimpson.co.uk/interviews/forrestjackerman.html (accessed June 18, 2007).

Smith, Kevin. Interview by author. March 6, 1999.

"Spider-Man: From Beyond the Grave—A Rockomic!—The Webspinners." Movie Grooves; http://www.moviegrooves.com/shop/spidermanlp.htm (accessed February 21, 2008).

"Star Trek Fan Films Live Long and Prosper." *Weekend Edition Saturday*, NPR. New York: WNYC, July 22, 2006.

"Star Wars Fan Movie Challenge." AtomFilms; http://www.atomfilms.com/2007/starwars/challenge/infoguide.jsp#award (accessed January 26, 2008).

Stokes, Trey. Interview by author. Phone. January 13, 2008.

———. "The Pink Five Production Blog." Pink Five Production Blog; http://rop5.blogspot.com/ (accessed January 26, 2008).

Streible, Dan. Interview by author. Phone. New York, November 2, 2007.

———. "Itinerant Filmmakers and Amateur Casts: A Homemade 'Our Gang.'" *Film History* 15, no. 2 (2003).

Strompolos, Chris. Interview by audience Q&A. Anthology Film Archives, New York, November 16, 2007.

———. Interview by author. Phone. July 23, 2007.

"Sulu's Solo Trek." *Starlog*, June 1987.

Sutherland, Matt. "The Tao of Stacey—Return of Pink Five Documentary." YouTube.Com; youtube.com/watch?v=pjJiuP8toFE (accessed January 12, 2008).

Swanson, Dwight, and Caroline Frick. "In Search of the Kidnappers Foils." Melton Barker and the Kidnappers Foil; http://www.meltonbarker.com (accessed November 28, 2007).

Szczulkun, Stefan. "Exploding Cinema 1992–1999: Culture and Democracy," RCA, 2002; http://www.stefan-szczelkun.org.uk/phd206.htm (accessed October 11, 2007).

Templeton, David. "Web Master: The 'Real' Spider-Man Has His Say." Metroactive; http://www.metroactive.com/papers/sonoma/05.23.02/talk-pix-0221.html (accessed September 9, 2007).

Tepper, Fred. Interview by author. E-mail. January 12, 1999.

"The Amazing Spider-Man: A Rockomic: From beyond the Grave" (Buddah, KSS-117, 1972)." Scar Stuff; http://scarstuff.blogspot.com/2006/01/amazing-spider-man-rockomic-from.html (accessed February 21, 2008).

"The Future of Nostalgia." *The Connection*, NPR. Boston: WBUR, December 28, 2001.

"The Orlando Harry Potter Club." *Life Story Movie Magic*, April 2007.

Thompson, Clive. "May the Force Be with You, and You, and You . . ." Slate Magazine; http://slate.msn.com/id/2117760 (accessed February 10, 2008).

Thompson, Dave. *Black and White and Blue: Adult Cinema from the Victorian Age to the VCR*. Toronto: ECW Press, 2007.

Thompson, David. "Slash Cinema." Mute Beta; www.metamute.org/en/node/6322 (accessed December 3, 2007).

"Times-Herald Editor and Filmmaker, Dead at 60." Times Herald Online; http://www.timesheraldnews.com/2006/12/08/don-dohler-times-herald-editor-and-filmmaker-dead-at-60 (accessed October 3, 2007).

"Titanic (1997)—Box Office/Business." Internet Movie Database (IMDB); http://www.imdb.com/title/tt0120338/business (accessed November 20, 2007).

Torres, Sasha. *Camp: Queer Aesthetics and the Performing Subject—A Reader.* Triangulations: Lesbian/Gay/Queer Theater/Drama/Performance. Ann Arbor: University of Michigan Press, 1999.

"*Troops* (1998)—Trivia." Internet Movie Database (IMDB); http://www.imdb.com/title/tt0153301/trivia (accessed December 2, 2005).

Tushnet, Rebecca, Jonathan Gray, Cornel Sandvoss, and C. Lee Harrington.

Fandom: Identities and Communities in a Mediated World. New York: New York University Press, 2007.

Tsutsui, William M. *Godzilla on My Mind: Fifty Years of the King of Monsters*. New York: Palgrave Macmillan, 2004.

Verevis, Constantine. "Andy Warhol." Senses of Cinema; http://www.sensesofcinema.com/contents/directors/02/warhol.html (accessed November 1, 2007).

"Untamed Cinema—Home of John Fiorella and Award Winning Grayson." Untamed Cinema; http://www.untamedcinema.com/ (accessed December 17, 2007).

Van Hise, James. *Trek: The Printed Adventures*. San Francisco: Pioneer, 1993.

Wallace, Amy. "Can Studios Tame the Net?" *Los Angeles Times*, May 16, 1999.

Ward, Matthew. "Matthew Ward." Online Home of Matthew Ward; http://www.studioward.com (accessed October 30, 2007).

———. Interview by author. E-mail. December 4, 1998.

"Warner Bros. Addresses Fan Films." Superhero Hype.Com;. http://www.superherohype.com/index.php?id=1885 (accessed December 10, 2007).

Watson, James. Interview by author. New York, February 23, 2007.

Weiner, Steve. *100 Graphic Novels for Public Libraries*. Milwaukee, WI: Kitchen Sink Press, 1996.

"Weird NJ Stories, Jungle Habitat." Weird NJ; http://www.weirdnj.com/stories/_abandoned05.asp (accessed June 22, 2007).

Wells, Tish. "A Star Wars Fan Film Is Born." McClatchy Washington Bureau; http://www.mcclatchydc.com/staff/tish_wells/story/11255.html (accessed February 13, 2008).

Wen, Howard. "Want to Make Your Own Star Wars Movie? We Did." Guardian. http://film.guardian.co.uk/cybercinema/storynonav/0,,402055,00.html (accessed May 15, 2007).

West, Bob. Interview by author. E-mail. March 12, 1999.

Whitaker, Tom. "Web Watching." *Total Film*, July 1999.

Whybank, Mike. "An Indie Indy." *Now Playing*, Winter 2006.

Wiese, Michael. "The Farce Is Back!." *Videography*, May 1997.

———. Interview by author. E-mail. March 26, 1998.

———. Interview by author. E-mail. May 23, 2007.

———. Interview by author. E-mail. May 29, 2007.

Windolf, Jim. "Raiders of the Lost Backyard." *Vanity Fair*, February 2004.

"Windows Movie Maker 2.0 Review." WindowsMovieMakers.NET; http://www.windowsmoviemakers.net/Articles/WMM2Review.aspx (accessed

November 18, 2007).

Wolfman, Marv. Interview by author. E-mail. June 19, 2007.

Wolk, Douglas. "Electromedia: Starry Eyes." *CMJ New Music Monthly*, August 1999.

Wolk, Josh, and Albert Kim. "Troop Dreams." *Entertainment Weekly*, March 20, 1998.

"Women Online: Taking a New Look." eMarketer; http://www.emarketer.com/Report.aspx?emarketer_2000388&src=report1_head_info_newsltr (accessed April 9, 2007).

"World War II Honoree." Frank C. Glut; http://www.wwiiregistry.org/search/plaq.asp?HonoreeID=37205 (accessed May 22, 2007).

Worley, Rob M. "Hero Fan Films Absent at This Year's Comic-Con." Comics2Film.com; www.comics2film.com/StoryFrame.php?f_id=8019&f_sec=16 (accessed September 23, 2005).

Yockel, Michael. "Don Dohler Bio1." Don Dohler's Home Page; http://www.dondohler.com/dondohlerbio1.html (accessed October 20, 2007).

Young, Justin R. "FFX Interviews Marc Kimball." Fanfilmxchange.com; www.fanfilmxchange.com/ffx/interviews/i00011.htm (accessed April 3, 2002).

Younis, Steven. "Exclusive Sandy Collora Interview." Superman Homepage; http://www.supermanhomepage.com/movies/movies.php?topic=interview-sandy-collora (accessed December 3, 2007).

Zahn, Timothy. Interview by author. Phone. New York, January 22, 2008.

———. *Star Wars: Allegiance*. New York: Del Rey, 2007.

Zala, Eric. Interview by author. July 5, 2007.

———. Interview by author. Phone. July 20, 2007.

Zimmermann, Patricia Rodden. *Reel Families: A Social History of Amateur Film*. Arts and Politics of the Everyday. Bloomington: Indiana University Press, 1995.

DVD Releses

Andy Warhol: A Documentary Film. DVD. Directed by Ric Burns. 2005; Los Angeles: PBS Paramount.

George Lucas in Love. DVD. Directed by Joe Nussbaum. 1999; Los Angeles: Red Hill.

Hardware Wars—The Original Edition. DVD. Directed by Ernie Fosselius. 2002; Studio City, CA: Michael Wiese.

Hearts of Darkness—A Filmmaker's Apocalypse. DVD. Directed by Eleanor Coppola. 1991; Hollywood: Paramount.

Homage to H. Lee Waters: Orphanistas Attend Orphans 4. Theater viewing. Directed by Bill Brand. 2006; Columbia, SC: University of South Carolina.

Hugh Hefner: American Playboy. DVD. Directed by Kevin Burns. 2003; Hollywood: Image Entertainment.

I Was a Teenage Moviemaker—Don Glut's Amateur Movies. DVD. Directed by Donald F. Glut. 2006; Los Angeles: Cinema Epoch.

Monster Kid Home Movies. DVD. Various directors. 2005; Cincinnati, Ohio: PPS Group.

Monsters Crash the Pajama Party (Spook Show Spectacular). DVD. Directed by Unknown Director. 2001; Hollywood: Image Entertainment.

The Phandom Menace. DVD. Directed by Craig E. Tonkin. 2002; Oaks, PA: Eclectic DVD Distribution.

The Real Spider-Man: The Making of the Green Goblin's Last Stand. DVD. Directed by Dan Poole. 2002; Baltimore: Alpha Dog Productions.

The Sci-Fi Boys. DVD. Directed by Paul Davids. 2006; Washington, D.C.: Universal Studios.

The Work of Director Sandy Collora Promo DVD. DVD. Directed by Sandy Collora. 2003; Los Angeles: Collora Studios.

World's Finest Promo DVD. DVD. Directed by Sandy Collora. 2004; Los Angeles: Collora Studios.

Index